PRAISE FOR *THE KEY TO INCLUSION*

The book is packed with rational and practical guidance, examples and case studies. It challenges the thinking around DEI and demonstrates not only the obvious of putting inclusion at the core of organizational purpose and strategy, but argues one step further – thinking of inclusion as the strategy. Perhaps we do that and all the rest we are after comes as a result. The book delivers new and refreshing ideas, bringing in nicely the Industry 4.0 and future of work perspectives, to provide the reader with a plethora of ideas and practical tools to unlock talent and teams potential. A fantastic read and highly recommended for people who are in a position to look after other people – all of us.
Traian Ivanov, Multinational Professional Services Firm

This is a must read practical guide for anyone in business today. Not only does this book include practical tools and methodologies to cultivate and embed an inclusive culture at work, but it also challenges our own mindset and unconscious biases to promote self-awareness, enabling better decision making.
Rumi Das, Multinational Professional Services Firm

Essential to leaders, academics, D&I experts, and strategists across sectors and disciplines, *The Key to Inclusion* is a truly comprehensive and applied work that can act both as a support for individual and team growth, as well as a catalyst for tangible change in all forms of organizations. Accessible, robust, researched, grounded and compassionate, the team have spanned the full range of individual, social and systemic factors in this complex topic.
Jonathan Stott, Chartered Psychologist and Founder, honne Partners

The Key to Inclusion democratizes D&I for leaders at all career stages, reflecting modern challenges and rapidly evolving environments, with abundant actionable insights to make a significant positive difference from tomorrow.
Masanobu Kurihara, Global Consulting Firm

The Key to Inclusion takes an holistic approach in this insightful and practical guide, helping the reader understand what individuals, teams and organizations can do to move towards a more inclusive workplace and foster a sense of belonging at work. Each of us has a responsibility to take action now.
Fiona Pargeter, Business Psychologist and D&I Leader

The Key to Inclusion is a great read for anyone looking to create true inclusion by changing their personal and organizational behaviours. The book tackles key topics such as hybrid working, polarisation and the future of inclusion, bringing together experiences and examples from a number of expert voices.
David Fairs, Executive Director for Regulatory Policy, Analysis and Advice, The Pensions Regulator

This book is a must read for those wanting to make significant impact in how their organization think about and implement inclusion initiatives.
Sharad Mohan Mishra, President, Group Strategy, TVS

The Key to Inclusion is a handbook for those seeking to release the benefits and overcome the challenges associated with DEI. Stephen and the contributors' innate understanding of the interconnected topics is undeniable. This book demystifies seemingly complex subjects, empowering the reader to conceive programmes and initiatives that alter attitudes and biases, creating a pathway for racial equity and fairness to flow. Social justice just gained a new weapon and I highly recommend anyone championing DEI to arm themselves with a copy.
Darren Miller, Co-Founder, The Black Business Institute

The Key to Inclusion

A practical guide to diversity, equity and belonging for you, your team and your organization

Edited by Stephen Frost

KoganPage

Publisher's note

Every possible effort has been made to ensure that the information contained in this book is accurate at the time of going to press, and the publishers and authors cannot accept responsibility for any errors or omissions, however caused. No responsibility for loss or damage occasioned to any person acting, or refraining from action, as a result of the material in this publication can be accepted by the editor, the publisher or the author.

First published in Great Britain and the United States in 2022 by Kogan Page Limited

2nd Floor, 45 Gee Street	8 W 38th Street, Suite 902	4737/23 Ansari Road
London	New York, NY 10018	Daryaganj
EC1V 3RS	USA	New Delhi 110002
United Kingdom		India
www.koganpage.com		

Kogan Page books are printed on paper from sustainable forests.

ISBNs

Hardback	978 1 3986 0620 3
Paperback	978 1 3986 0613 5
Ebook	978 1 3986 0621 0

British Library Cataloguing-in-Publication Data

A CIP record for this book is available from the British Library.

Library of Congress Control Number

2022016327

Typeset by Integra Software Services, Pondicherry
Print production managed by Jellyfish
Printed and bound by CPI Group (UK) Ltd, Croydon CR0 4YY

For Mum, Em and Tim

CONTENTS

LIST OF FIGURES AND TABLES

ABOUT THE CONTRIBUTORS

RAAFI-KARIM ALIDINA

Raafi-Karim Alidina is a Consulting Manager and the Data and Product lead at *Included*, where he has worked with clients all over the world, including the leadership of several Fortune500 and FTSE100 companies. His key areas of expertise lie in the statistics and measurement of diversity and inclusion, and behavioural economics of inclusion in organizations.

IRFAAN ARIF

Irfaan Arif is a diversity and inclusion specialist with a grounding in psychology and behavioural science. He runs his own consultancy, Develop Minds Ltd. His work involves using behavioural science principles and tools to embed inclusion into organizational design, decisions and behaviours to maximize psychological safety and increase individual and collective performance.

ELANI BUCHAN

Elani Buchan has over 10 years' experience working and investing in start-ups. Her expertise is in scaling companies after finding product market fit and building diverse, equitable and inclusive cultures where purpose and profit co-exist.

NICK BASANNAVAR

Nick Basannavar is an inclusion consultant, leadership adviser, historian and author who serves as Head of Consulting at *Included*. He is the author of *Trailing Abuse* (Palgrave Macmillan, 2021) and is an Honorary Fellow at Birkbeck, University of London.

YASMINE CHINWALA

Yasmine Chinwala is a partner at capital markets think tank New Financial and leads its diversity and culture programme. Yasmine has been a driving force behind the strategic development of the HM Treasury Women in Finance Charter since its inception, work for which she was awarded an OBE in 2020.

HELEN CORBISHLEY

Helen Corbishley is a diversity and inclusion consultant, gender advocate and champion for inclusion and change. Described by those who know her as diligent, loyal, jocular, pragmatic, Northern, a committed coffee drinker, long distance runner and 'dog mum'.

LYDIA CRONIN

Lydia Cronin is Marketing Manager at *Included* and has previously worked in publishing, events, and digital start-up organizations. She holds a Diploma in Professional Marketing and is an Associate of the Chartered Institute of Marketing (CIM). She is also a diversity and inclusion advocate.

SINEAD DALY

Sinead Daly is a leader who's passionate about helping fast-growth tech companies balance purpose, not just profit. As Director of Culture, Experience and Impact, Sinead takes a leading role on areas that make a positive impact on people, communities and the planet.

STEPHEN FROST

Stephen Frost is a leadership, communications and inclusion expert. He worked with clients worldwide to embed inclusion in their decision making as CEO and Founder of *Included*. He was formerly Head of Diversity and Inclusion for the London Organizing Committee of the Olympic Games and Paralympic Games (LOCOG) 2007–2012, and is currently a Visiting Fellow with the Women and Public Policy Program at Harvard Kennedy School. He is also Vice President (Diversity) of the Chartered Institute of Personnel and Development.

KARL GEORGE

Karl George is a thought leader, author and internationally established consultant in governance. He is a partner and Head of Governance at the leading professional services firm RSM and creator of The tgf Governance Code, the RACE equality code and the effective board member programmes, working with boards and senior executives in the private, public and voluntary sectors.

DEIRDRE GOLDEN

Deirdre Golden has been in the vanguard of diversity and inclusion for over 20 years. Guiding organizations through the transition from diversity 101 to embracing inclusion as a business imperative and intrinsic motivator of employee engagement in the global environment.

ROB NEIL OBE

Rob Neil was born in Paddington, the son of Jamaican parents. He is a former civil servant. After a 38 year career during which he qualified as a trainer via the Civil Service College, Rob realized his dream of starting his own consultancy, Krystal Alliance (KA). When he's not chilling out with family and friends, Rob shares his discretionary time between KA as the director, RELATE as a Trustee, The Reach Society as Director of Social Media, *Included* as a consultant and QPR FC as a long-suffering supporter.

ANJANI PATEL

Anjani Patel works in collaboration with broadcasters and the wider industry to drive inclusion across the content production sector in film and television. She also offers advice and guidance to the UK's independent production companies on developing their strategies and approaches to inclusion. Anjani is the creator of the Pact Inclusion tool, a bespoke online resource for embedding inclusion across production process both on and off screen. Prior to this, Anjani worked as a producer and director across factual genres in television.

PRIYA RADIA

Priya Radia joined *Included* in 2021 as Associate Consultant and supports delivery of day-to-day client work. Prior to this, she spent three years in financial services before joining a management consultancy to develop as a business analyst in technology consulting.

ACKNOWLEDGEMENTS

RAAFI-KARIM ALIDINA

First, thank you to our editor, Steve. His support and mentorship have always been valuable, especially encouraging me to write more. I'd also like to thank my colleagues and clients from whom I am constantly learning. From our differences in style and background I have come to develop more informed and nuanced perspectives and I can't wait for that to continue. Finally – and most of all – thank you to my family for their constant support. In particular, I want to thank my partner, Zuzanna, for always pushing me to do better, helping me think more deeply and keeping me smiling.

IRFAAN ARIF

A big thanks to Stephen Frost for inviting me to be part of this book. I really enjoyed the opportunity and look forward to writing more in the future as a result! A personal thanks to my partner Zarmeena and three kids Zakariyya, Mariam and Ibraheem for supporting me throughout (the kids generally supporting me by pulling me away from the computer for regular breaks).

NICK BASANNAVAR

I would like to thank the many people who contributed to this book either directly (via helpful interviews or exchanges) or indirectly (where their work has been an influence on my thinking). This list includes, but is not limited to, Raafi-Karim Alidina, Lydia Cronin, Marianne Fraiture, Stephen Frost, John Graham-Cumming, Lynda Gratton, Jason Hickel, Gethin Hine, Traian Ivanov, Masanobu Kurihara, Baroness Doreen Lawrence, Rebekah Martin, Claudia Nigeon, Priya Radia, my robot vacuum cleaner Robert, Jonathan Stott, Louise Townsend, Catherine Wallwork and Jun Yamaguchi (RIP). My biggest thanks, as always, go to Yuko.

ELANI BUCHAN

I'd like to thank the co-founders of Valla, Danae Shell and Dr Kate Ho for the dedication they bring not to just creating an inclusive and equitable business, but a more just world. To Jessica Graves, for always challenging me and getting me to think more expansively, and to Paul Buchan who has always supported me through the good and also the challenging times of working in the startup ecosystem.

YASMINE CHINWALA

With thanks to New Financial's member firms for their support and contributions to the research and to Jenny Barrow, William Wright and the team at New Financial.

HELEN CORBISHLEY

Thanks to Steve and all at *Included*, Mum, Dad, Clare, Maarten, 'The Ladies', Lord Trevor the Wonderdog and Emma Varsanyi at Reebok for their wise words, support, contributions and their belief in inclusion and in me. It's been a blast!

LYDIA CRONIN

With thanks to Stephen Frost, Rob Neil, Rebekah Martin, Jennifer Hursit, Imani Dunbar and Cathy Taylor. A personal thank you to my family, the Kogan Page circle, Ana, Emma, Sam, Summer and 'The Four'.

SINEAD DALY

A shout out to Niamh Kelly for her words of wisdom and Tope Medupin for her keen eye and thoughtful feedback.

STEPHEN FROST

I would like to thank all my fellow authors, from whom I have learnt so much over the years. It's genuinely a team effort. I'd like to thank the entire *Included* team, the Kogan Page team and everyone else involved who has seen the value in what we are trying to do – our clients, partners, stakeholders and colleagues far and wide. I'd particularly like to thank those individuals who have believed in us from the early days, even when it wasn't the *topic du jour* DEI is now. As ever, in this work, we are standing on the shoulders of giants.

KARL GEORGE MBE

I would like to acknowledge the organizations that I have worked with over the last few decades in developing my corporate governance frameworks and, more recently, those that have made brave commitments as a part of their journey in tackling race inequality.

DEIRDRE GOLDEN

My thanks to the following people who have shared conversations with me and provided thoughtful insights and feedback: Stephen Frost, Pauline Miller, Barbara Pryce, Maria Angelica Perez, Jill Rothwell, Lt. Michael Golden RN, Mary Walsh, Sinead Daly, Lydia Cronin.

ROB NEIL OBE

I would like to thank the entire team at *Included* for their encouragement, support and inspiration. I would also like to thank Jennifer Izekor, CEO at Above Difference, for doing diversity differently and for showing me the beauty of cultural intelligence (CQ). I would like to thank David Livermore for his leadership and pioneering work with CQ, including the legacy of an expanding global network. Finally, I'd like to thank both Ritika Wadhwa and Emily Dorschler for their additional and fresh offering in this field which is now available across the UK via CQC UK.

ANJANI PATEL

Edel Brosnan – Pact project manager and freelance drama writer
Bryony Arnold – Producer
Grainne McGuiness – Producer and Co-owner of Paper Owl Film
Minnie Ayres – CEO Triforce network and productions
Mel Walden – Freelance Casting executive
Addie Orfila – Production manager and trainer
John McVay – CEO Pact

PRIYA RADIA

Thank you to Stephen Frost and Nick Basannavar for this opportunity. A personal thank you to Raafi, the Included team, Aniqa, my family and my friends for all your support.

Introduction

STEPHEN FROST

This is a book about how to solve the seemingly intractable challenges that get in the way of workplace inclusion, however nebulous that might at first appear to be.

It is focused on the 'how' rather than the 'why'. The 'why' is covered extensively in my earlier books, *The Inclusion Imperative*, *Inclusive Talent Management* (with Danny Kalman) and *Building an Inclusive Organization* (with Raafi Alidina, who also writes in this book). That's not to say we won't touch on it here, but this is primarily a book for people who want to get things done.

Inclusion is only nebulous in the abstract. Inclusion is also very real. Ask anyone whether they have been excluded and most people can reply easily and quickly: left off the invite list for a wedding or a team retreat; passed over for promotion; never made the first team in school sport; the offsite was inaccessible; people didn't respond to your intervention in a team meeting, just leaving a long, awkward silence… We often understand inclusion best by the counterfactual – exclusion. This is in the Foucault tradition of the fact we rarely understand what things are, only what they are not.

Inclusion relates to diversity. This also makes it very real. Diversity is simply the different people that inhabit our world, our workplaces, our communities, our families. Inclusion is whether we include them or not. The oft-quoted Verna Myers adage, 'Diversity is being invited to the dance, inclusion is being asked to dance'[1] is relevant here. In this book, we will go beyond inclusion to belonging. We'll also cover equity, which is defined as 'people getting what they need to succeed'. It is distinct from equality, which is everyone being treated the same, irrespective of need. We'll explore these terms and more, where this whole discourse has come from and where it is going.

Context for the book

This book came about in the context of the COVID-19 global pandemic, the catalytic success of the Black Lives Matter (BLM) movement and ongoing and accelerating technological, social, political and economic change. Having worked on diversity, equity and inclusion (DEI) issues for over 20 years, I have, in the past, felt like a lobbyist. I don't deny I'm an activist, but I'm also a professional consultant. Only in recent years has the perceived lobbying turned into recognized consulting, as all organizations confront the reality of ever more diverse workforces. It's not a question of *should* we include, so much as *how* we include different people in order to get work done.

The move from 'equal opportunities' to 'diversity' and now to 'inclusion and belonging' is not a linear event. And it's not equally paced. The tempo has accelerated substantially in the last few years. What has happened in terms of boardroom awareness, employee activism, social media discourse and subsequent political catch up is nothing less than an inclusion revolution.

Let me give more evidence to stem any potential accusations of hyperbole. Consider HR director priorities as recent as 2018, where DEI didn't make the top five at all.[2] Now, DEI is up there as number one priority with mental health and wellbeing.[3] Consider CEO priorities. As recent as 2018 it was growth and some aspects of workforce productivity.[4] Now, 'proving commitment to DEI' is right up there as a C-suite priority.[5] Consider board agendas. Again, DEI has moved from interesting occasional topic to standing agenda item and a core part of good corporate governance.

The number of employee networks or employee resource groups (ERGs) has exploded, both in terms of number and scope. Whereas most organizations would have had none, or a few, focused on gender and perhaps parents and carers, there are now the full scope from LGBTQ+ to bi allies, mental health and different religions and cultural associations. This is not just an Anglo-Saxon cultural trend, it's now global. Governments of right and left, as well as CEOs of all kinds of industries, are having to respond to growing media pressure and employee activism.

In one sense, it's beyond time. Mental health concerns have always existed, albeit there's a new concern for the added pressures that isolation, stress, technology and social change bring. LGBTQ+ people have always existed, it's just there's now a lot more awareness and consideration for them. Employee wellbeing has always mattered, it just wasn't always prioritized by bosses who weren't subject to online judgement in quite the same way as they are now. In one sense, analogous to climate change, there's a revolution under-way and we are bearing witness to profound change in how people are responding to some of the biggest challenges in our lifetimes.

Just as we need to include biodiversity to meet our environmental challenges, we need to include human diversity to meet our social, political, economic and workplace challenges. We hope this book can act as your guide to play your part in the inclusion revolution.

The authors

Imani Dunbar, Head of Equity Strategy for LinkedIn, challenged me about the diversity of authors in publishing. I've learnt a lot from Imani and agreed with her that publishing has a diversity challenge. Rather than simply empa-thize, I decided to do something about it. I have the good fortune to be surrounded by a diverse, talented team. We put out a call for co-authors and have assembled some of the best DEI consultants I have ever had the privi-lege to work with.

In the pages that follow, you'll meet Included employees, contractors, clients and partners. All of them are experts in what they do. We don't agree on everything. As you'll see, we touch on real issues of concern from trans rights to tensions in psychological safety versus feedback culture. In one sense, we are nothing more than a microcosm of society writ large. However, it's the methods of our work and the outcomes we seek that unite us. We genuinely want people to deal with the challenges they face (outlined below). We do want to turn fear into allyship, to make sure that use of language does not get in the way of education and behavioural change. Above all else, we want to stop shutting down conversation and avoiding the work at a time when we have much to do.

Silver bullets

Good people desperately want DEI answers. People want to move from 'why' to 'how'. However, this well-intentioned desire often backfires in the form of superficial actions. Smart people, expert at their day jobs, demand quick results and think they can apply their existing smarts to another field instantly. In fact, this jumping to actions, while laudable, frequently results in trite actions that simply would not be tolerated in any other field.

An accountant would not tolerate their DEI level of proficiency in their own subject. The same goes for a lawyer, a medic or a banker. Yet we persist in superficial actions in the absence of anything more substantial.

In previous books, I have outlined the theory of change, 'understand, lead, deliver', and the simple fact that in order to avoid trite actions and develop often profound behaviour changes (which is inclusion) we need to understand first and take personal responsibility second. In doing so, we can then focus on the following five seemingly intractable problems that we want to tackle in this book.

1 STRESS

Overall, people are more stressed in their work now than at any time before. This seems somewhat ironic given that we are surrounded by tools that are supposed to make our jobs easier. In fact, what were designs to help us, have simply ended up accelerating the work so that we do more of it. And while the amount of input has increased, our cognitive load has not, and so the gap between what we are expected to do and what we are able to do has increased exponentially. We'll start off with a look at cognitive load and stress as the often-ignored foundation of an inclusive culture.

2 POLARIZATION

Our societies seem to be more polarized than ever. This links to the above point on stress. When people are 'full up' they have less room for empathy or considering the needs or perspectives of others, especially those who are different from them. We'll look at how we can, in our own way, in our own teams, and in our own organizations, build community across divides to provide practical ways of tackling polarization before it goes too far and the divide seems too great to bridge.

3 WALKING ON EGGSHELLS

The term 'cancel culture' has evolved to describe the un-platforming or de-listing of people whose views we consider offensive. While this is unhelpful to debate, free speech and critical thinking, it must not be confused with 'call out' culture, or simply accountability, where we can legitimately highlight discriminatory practice that might otherwise go unchecked. We'll explore how to walk the line between excluding people and avoiding collusion with bad practice.

4 DIVERSE REPRESENTATION

In many ways, this is the most foundational challenge of all: the lack of diversity at senior levels in almost all aspects of society. We will look at ways to accelerate the attraction, recruitment, promotion and retention of diverse talent in its widest sense. Often the focus on diversity ignores the need to focus on inclusion, which is the sustainable answer to diverse representation.

5 GETTING WORK DONE

Finally, we need to tackle head-on the remaining supposition that 'doing diversity' is a trade-off with the day job. This false dichotomy belies the fact that many people don't understand what inclusion is, why it's important and how to behave differently. Properly executed, not only is inclusion the antithesis of a trade-off, it's a useful ingredient in productivity and growth.

So, this book is for you, the time-poor, savvy, yet weary professional who wants to be inclusive but doesn't want to lower standards, engage in trite soundbites or waste time. You want some rigorous logic, some professional and personal stimulation and a bucket load of practical advice.

We'll start with you. We'll explore your own cognitive diversity, your biases and the landscape you must now navigate. We'll then move on to your team, as inclusion is primarily exercised in teams and they are the primary source of your happiness (and frustration). We'll then go wider to your organization and introduce the concept of system change. We'll finish with a nod to wider society – how does inclusion play out in the world at large?

The new path

Work, of course, is a privilege. And it's an amazing time to be in work. At this moment in history, we really do stand at a crossroads for inclusion.

On the one hand is a concerning path towards polarization. We see it in terms of women exiting the workforce in their millions, returning to the stereotype of primary care giver and unpaid domestic worker, while predominantly men maintain a professional career. We see it in terms of political extremism and the seeming inability to have civil discourse, especially behind the faux armour of social media handles. We see it in terms of the unbundling of 'diversity' such as the trans v gender debate and previous allies becoming enemies in a supposed hierarchy of rights.

However, there is another path. Acknowledging the many challenges that exist, a more hopeful and civil route forward lies in the smashing of hierarchy and unproductive convention and protocol that existed pre pandemic – often for no good reason. There are changes to where people work, when they work, how they work – which unlocks the potential for people to maximize their individual productivity in a new way, unfettered by the law of averages and in so doing catapult their organization's performance and contribution to the world. We saw it in the empowerment of millions of disabled people who for the first time ever faced an approaching-level playing field where technology is king and the workplace is virtual. We see it in the plethora of information allowing us to challenge our views, form new connections and build new communities.

This book takes the second path. It will guide you in solving the seemingly intractable problems that get in the way of inclusion. It will also guide you on a hopeful journey about how you can behave in a more inclusive manner, benefitting you personally, professionally, your team, your organization and the wider world.

References

1   Cho, J H (2016) Diversity is being invited to the party; inclusion is being asked to dance, Verna Myers tells Cleveland Bar *Cleveland.com* www.cleveland.com/ business/2016/05/diversity_is_being_invited_to.html (archived at https://perma. cc/C8TX-CQUV)

2   Davis, J (2018) Special from #SHRM2018: Top 5 Priorities for an HR Department of One *HR Daily Advisor* hrdailyadvisor.blr.com/2018/06/18/ special-shrm2018-top-5-priorities-hr-department-one/ (archived at https:// perma.cc/B2ZC-9EEX)

3   Mayer, K (2021) HRExecutive, 'Massive shift' in HR leaders' top 5 priorities for 2021 hrexecutive.com/massive-shift-in-hr-leaders-top-5-priorities-for-2021/ (archived at https://perma.cc/8QVV-APKA)

4   Gartner (2018) Gartner Survey Reveals That CEO Priorities Are Shifting to Embrace Digital Business www.gartner.com/en/newsroom/press-releases/2018-05-01-gartner-survey-reveals-that-ceo-priorities-are-shifting-to-embrace-digital-business (archived at https://perma.cc/C82Q-RYJW)

5   Deloitte (2022) Winter 2022 Fortune/Deloitte CEO Survey www2.deloitte.com/ us/en/pages/chief-executive-officer/articles/ceo-survey.html (archived at https:// perma.cc/DL37-KD46)

PART ONE

Unlocking you

Introduction

STEPHEN FROST

We start with you. It was Anita Roddick who said, 'if you believe you are too small to have an impact, try going to bed with a mosquito in the room'.[1] You have more power, more influence and cast a bigger shadow than you perhaps realize. If we can engage you, whatever your race, creed, colour, gender or any other aspect of diversity, we are already winning. This matters because, from the outset, we need to make it clear that you are the key to inclusion. This is not about somebody else, someone 'more diverse', 'more qualified' or in a particular role. That's because inclusion depends on leadership and you can't outsource that.

There are a few terms you need to know. 'Diversity' we've already covered: the mix of different people. In the UK there are 'protected characteristics' – age, disability, gender reassignment, marriage and civil partnership, pregnancy and maternity, race, religion or belief, sex and sexual orientation. These are replicated similarly in many other countries. Recently, we have also seen increasing emphasis on cognitive diversity and socio-economic status. Beyond all of these characteristics there are more still, spanning from introversion/extraversion to flexible working arrangements. Diversity is infinite.

The reason many aspects of the human being are protected is because of the potential for systemic discrimination. It's not a coincidence that there is a paucity of Black or female talent at the top of many organizations. And just because 'cognitive diversity' is of obvious interest to the quality of Boardroom discussion, or scientific decision-making, does not mean it can be focused on to the detriment of race or disability. Also be aware of intersectionality. This is where multiple identities co-exist and people can be the subject of multiple or intersecting patterns of discrimination. For example, we found that Black women were often the most excluded in organizations, more than White women and more than Black men.

Inclusion we have already touched on – including the above said diversity. Belonging is going further. If inclusion is a choice, belonging is a feeling. An organization and its leaders might choose to be inclusive, but it's whether employees feel like they belong that really unlocks discretionary effort and money-can't-buy attachment. Think of it as analogous to communication. It's not what you say, it's what's heard. Good communication is not simply transmitting, it's what people understand, and then go on to do.

Equity and equality are also important, and sometimes confused. Equality is everyone treated the same. This runs deep. It's one of the three foundational principles of the French Republic. However, when people are inherently different (see above) if we treat them 'the same' we end up with unequal results. Enter 'equity' stage left, where we treat people according to what they need. Not everyone needs the same. This can be illustrated with reference to Black Lives Matter. Clearly all lives matter, but when one group is consistently and systemically disadvantaged then we can focus on that group to try and make a difference.

A rule I've found useful in my work over the years is the Platinum rule. Using that tradition of counterfactuals again, I can explain the Golden Rule, which is 'treat others as you would wish to be treated'. This is how I was brought up. However, to be inclusive, we should try and adapt to others, instead of expecting them to adapt to us. In this case, adopt the Platinum rule – adapting yourself to them, rather than expecting them to adapt to you.

This adaptation process lies at the heart of inclusive leadership. And it's not just about being nice. Every management report, self-help book, World Economic Forum report published points to the kind of skills we need to develop or acquire to succeed in the modern age. Right up there is agility and adaptation. We need to lean into discomfort, not run away from it. Otherwise, we risk succeeding only within existing parameters and our existing echo chambers, within which there is no real growth potential and no insurance policy from external shocks and risks that are multiplying.

So, to navigate this world, and to start with ourselves, we need to reflect on how people learn best. In the past it was didactic learning, or acquiring knowledge

FIGURE 0.1   An example learning curve

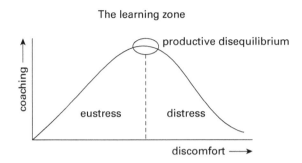

in a relatively simple almost lecture style process. Now it is experiential learning, acquiring knowledge through immersion in a complex, multi variable environment and testing our responses in real time. Through experiencing different environments, people and cultures we learn about ourselves, as well as about others. The more we do it, the more we can iterate, the more it will sink in. We need to be allowed to make mistakes, from which we learn a lot, and this makes the whole experience unique and personal to us. When it's experiential, personal and memorable it becomes sustainable and scalable.

The final point I'd make is about the learning zone. If we are too comfortable, even entertained, there's not much learning going on. We are bottom left of the learning curve in Figure 0.1. If we are too uncomfortable, even distressed, we shut down and there's also not much learning going on. To succeed and grow as a leader we need to lean into a productive disequilibrium, the top of the bell curve, where we get comfortable with being uncomfortable. This is the optimum learning zone, at the edge of our comfort zone, not in distress but at the peak of eustress. If you can maintain this mindset as you read on, you'll get the most out of the book.

Reference

1   Elmer-Dewitt, P (1993) Anita Roddick: Anita The Agitator. TIME. content.time. com/time/subscriber/article/0,33009,977524-3,00.html (archived at https:// perma.cc/4227-F88K)

01

Cognitive load

STEPHEN FROST AND DEIRDRE GOLDEN

The World Health Organization (WHO) identified long working hours, over extended periods of time, as 'the risk factor with the largest occupational disease burden', tied to strokes and heart disease.[1] Work related stress, fatigue and information overload impacts physical, mental and emotional health. It can cause burn out, and in some situations result in work-related suicide. In Japan, this has its own name, Karoshi. The pressures created by work overload can impact decision making and have a detrimental effect in any job.

There is added impact when making life and death decisions, such as in medicine or the airline industry. Here, human error has been a factor in a number of disasters, involving significant loss of life. This is the potential impact of heavy cognitive load.

What is cognitive load?

Everyday life and work creates cognitive load. When well managed, we experience good stress, or 'eustress'. We get excited, even though the task might be challenging. But when too much is being asked of us, cognitive load can cause distress and negatively affect our decision-making, ability and wellbeing.

The concept of Cognitive Load[2] was developed by John Sweller, an Education Psychologist, in the 1980s, out of a study of problem solving. It relates to the amount of information that working memory can hold at any one time. It has never really been applied to DEI until now.

There are three different types of cognitive load:

- **Intrinsic load (short-term or working memory):** The mental effort required to learn something new. It's the initial effort our brain has to make, to compute information.

- **Extraneous load:** The manner in which information is presented to the learner. For example, good instruction can reduce extraneous cognitive load, by making complex concepts easily digestible.
- **Germane load (long-term memory):** The work required to transfer information from short-term to long-term memory. Once something is in your long-term memory, you can recall it in short-term memory, allowing habits to form and concepts to be internalized.

Cognitive load enables us to understand the limitations of working memory. When dealing with new information, the working memory is very limited. It can only deal with somewhere between two to four elements of information at a time, and hold information for around 20 seconds.

How can we function with such a limitation on learning? Fortunately, our long-term memory has 'no known limits of capacity, and no known limits of duration'.[3] Long-term memory information can easily be recalled into working memory, and build the capacity of short-term memory. The challenge when educating is to move new information from working memory, into the long-term memory, where it becomes embedded. One-off training sessions don't do this. If we want to become more inclusive, it requires a different approach.

Why understanding cognitive load is important

Cognitive load has an important role in the employee experience. For example, when organizations go through major change, such as introducing new technology, business processes, or downsizing, they can add significantly to cognitive load and induce stress or anxiety.

Understanding the impact of high cognitive load is essential for engaging people to do things differently, and sustain the amended behaviour over time. For DEI work to succeed, we need to recognize people's cognitive load, and adapt accordingly.

Cognitive load is a barrier to inclusion

Cognitive load is the silent blocker of DEI work. While racism and misogyny are recognized as established barriers to inclusion, cognitive load hasn't been fully appreciated yet. And yet, not only is cognitive load a challenge in itself, it's also a barrier to tackling racism and misogyny. People may be too busy thinking about other things to recognize discrimination or lack of inclusion.

The amount of information in our midst is roughly doubling every two years.[4] The amount of data we are expected to process, in order to do our jobs, is increasing exponentially, while our cognitive capacity is not.

The human brain can only deal with so much information at any one time, pushing lots of information into the brain will not result in the retention of the information, some of it will be lost in the process.[5]

We hopelessly work harder, longer hours, and try various techniques. But we rarely consider diversity – which is free and in infinite supply – to be our saviour. If we could see different perspectives as calibrating the decisions we are accountable for, diversity could help reduce, or at least ameliorate, cognitive load.

The interplay between cognitive load and diversity is only recently being fully appreciated. Lockdowns and forced disruption to established social contact, has promoted mental health to the top of DEI considerations alongside race and gender.

How does cognitive load block diversity?

We know from research that many diversity trainings don't work and are even less likely to work if people are stressed.[6] They will be in 'fear and flight' mode, not amenable to being challenged and stretched. They may view diversity as simply 'unnecessary work' that is disposable, as the working memory is full.[7]

In line management, we know that inclusive leadership is about adaptation to other people, rather than expecting them to adapt to you. Adaptation is far less likely from people with a high cognitive load. They are also less able to change their behavior as adaptation requires thought, reflection and effort.

In recruitment, one of the key KPIs is time to hire. Time is often the enemy of diversity. Stressed recruiters and under pressure hiring managers are less likely to take a perceived risk on diversity than are calm, thoughtful interviewers.

In promotion, affinity bias and confirmation bias are key obstacles to objective selection, based on ability and merit. These biases are compounded and amplified by people who are stressed with a high cognitive load. They simply lack the space to adapt.

A high cognitive load is not an excuse for bias or any kind of racism or discrimination. But, it's important to recognize it in order to tackle the load, and to facilitate and enable work on tackling racism and sexism.

Managing cognitive load

The first step in managing cognitive load is to recognize it, and understand how it is affecting you or your colleagues. This seems simple enough, but cognitive load is often masked in talk about multi-tasking. We have become used to managing a variety of things at one time. The effort is keeping everything spinning at once, but with one slip up, everything can come crashing down. The weight of expectation to continue to do this with minimal help is heavy.

Likewise, how often have you heard the refrain, 'you must be more resilient'? The problem is seen as being with the individual and their perceived inability to cope. In many walks of life, it is easier to default to using labels to describe a problem rather than taking the time to understand what is going on.

Understanding cognitive load, and its role in how we learn, enables us to better manage how we introduce topics, ideas, and practices without overloading. This is hugely beneficial for DEI training.

The COVID-19 global pandemic and the impact of lockdowns placed enormous pressure on people and the consequences are still being worked through. We remain in a working era of change and discombobulation that has left people even more stressed due to isolation, family pressures and having to learn new ways of working. Therefore, without addressing cognitive load, we may find many diversity efforts are in vain. How we work with people is just as important as what work we do.

Heavy cognitive load is the enemy of free thinking and creativity because it clogs up the mind with other things that may not be relevant to the decisions we need to make. If you are living and working in firefighting mode it is difficult to find the space or time to step away.

Start talking

The next step is for leaders, managers, and supervisors to talk about cognitive load to help their employees understand what it means and its impact.

We are living in a time when mental health is a key priority for organizations, not least because of the impact of the COVID-19 lockdowns. Understanding cognitive load and how it affects employees' mental health if it is too heavy should become a staple to any mental health discussions.

In raising awareness of cognitive load, and in taking it seriously, leaders need to be prepared to make adjustments to workload if necessary, without defaulting to inducements to multi task more effectively, or urging employees to become more resilient.

Encourage self-reflection

An additional step is for leaders to encourage people to carve out thinking and reflection time. Embedding it into their work schedule, by making it a calendar entry, just like any other meeting, and encouraging employees to be open and visible about taking thinking time, and better still, to role model this behaviour to others.

Steve regularly undertakes walking meetings with colleagues and clients, a chance to get away from the desk, get some fresh air and a change of perspective. It might be a gym session, reading time or whatever else is needed to disrupt and challenge potential stymied thought.

Understanding the role of cognitive load in relation to how education, learning and training takes place is key to getting important information or messaging absorbed. In addition to the traditional methods of embedding D&I (diversity and inclusion) into the organization, encourage time to read, talk, and be mentored to aid the learning process in the most personalized and psychologically safe way possible.

Embed inclusion into your work

Frame inclusion as a method that helps solve problems, rather than another separate activity on the 'to do' list. This activates the business case in a real and targeted manner. Rather than diarize another meeting, reflect on how you can run the existing meeting in a more inclusive manner. Look for proof points and concrete examples of how being more inclusive will help manage cognitive load, rather than increase it.

Examining data analytics is a critical lever for organizations to understand their business and people systems better. Measuring cognitive load on business performance may be the new frontier of people analytics.[8]

Cognitive load is one of the many factors in the work environment, but recognizing how it can affect people's mental health will be a significant and often overlooked contribution to organization inclusion efforts.

How can you manage the impact of cognitive load on employees?

When DEI is seen as an intrinsic part of the business, it does not add to cognitive load. Where it is not, it will be seen in terms of a potential drain on resources rather than as a lever to achieving the organization's mission.

Managing cognitive load should be a lens when considering how to roll out D&I training, managing the amount of information people can absorb to ensure they retain it in their long-term memory. It may mean undertaking shorter and more frequent training sessions rather than taking a sheep-dip approach.

Allocate an email free day or half day e.g. Friday afternoon when emails are held until the next working day, to provide time for free thinking. Naturally a contingency needs to be put in place to ensure urgent emails are dealt with, but this need only involve those directly responsible.

Weekend working should be discouraged, and holidays should be taken without interruption. In Japan, as a response to the issue of work-related suicide (Karosi) the Government introduced regulations to enforce holidays and limit overtime working.

Delegate tasks effectively by identifying who is best skilled or placed to receive the task and discussing this with the individual so you are not just passing the load onto someone else.

Micro-managing only adds to cognitive load, not just to your own but to someone else who you may be prevented from getting on with their job. This is a particularly tricky thing to see in yourself, but getting feedback from your colleagues or team, may help this process.

Impact of high cognitive load

Many of us shrug off high cognitive load because we don't recognize it, or we assume we are just stressed as part of working life. However, the impact of high cognitive load should not be underestimated. It can seriously and adversely impact you as an individual, your team, your organization, and has potentially serious ramification for the decisions you are accountable for. It can impact those closest to us, whom we love and are dependent on for the basic human needs of love, kindness and compassion.

On 28 February 2012, Steve was commuting home from his job as Head of Diversity and Inclusion at the London 2012 Olympics and Paralympics. It was the final phase before the Games started in July and he was working extremely long hours, responsible for thousands of staff and dealing with a strained relationship. About 7pm, Steve received a call on the mobile from his Mother letting him know his Father had suddenly died.

Sometimes it takes a crisis to make you stop and recognize what you are currently experiencing. The ideal is that we recognize the buildup to crisis before it occurs. The harsh reality was that Steve had very little left in the tank to process the life changing news his Mother delivered down the telephone at 7pm on that dark February evening. Not only that, but he had to suspend his own needs to focus on his Mum and Sister. As anyone who has experienced profound loss will appreciate, the dark irony is that, on top of all this, you then have to organize an event in the midst of your own grief.

At his lowest point, Steve had a boss who was supportive and another boss who became part of the problem. The supportive one told him to take time off, take all the time needed. He understood Steve had caring responsibilities and, even though his job was mission critical at the Games, death puts things in perspective. The unsupportive boss called Steve a couple of hours before the funeral wanting some work. This might have been partly due to their own high cognitive load, and not stopping to think about the impact of their actions.

Steve went into maintenance mode for the remainder of the Games and then grieved when the Games were over, taking a few months off to travel. This management of cognitive load, with support from friends and colleagues, was essential to not only survive, but ultimately thrive. So many of us exist in maintenance mode, and don't truly get to control our cognitive load.

CASE STUDIES

The good news is, it is possible to manage cognitive load. It starts with recognition, and we can learn from practices in other sectors that involve critical decision making, such as in the aviation industry.

A pilot flying a passenger aircraft requires intense concentration and mastery of information in fast moving situations. Managing cognitive load is a critical factor in the safe functioning of the aviation industry. These environments rely on consistent high mental performance and attention to detail. Despite many safety and computer generated tools, it is human error that has been documented as a primary contributor in more than 70 per cent of commercial aircraft accidents.[9]

Critical to learning from previous errors is not to immediately apportion blame. In aviation this is referred to as a 'Just Culture'. James Reason described a 'Just Culture' as an atmosphere of trust in which people are encouraged, and even rewarded, for providing essential safety-related information, but in which they are also clear about where the line must be drawn between acceptable and unacceptable behaviour'. On the basis of this, people may be more inclined to identify potential problems before they occur.

Other important mechanisms to control and mitigate potential risks include putting in place structures to manage the in-flow of critical information and how it is assessed for impact.

Referred to as 'situational assessment' it has three levels:

1 Perceiving the situation (equivalent to recognizing what is happening at the time).

2 Understanding the situation (understanding fully what is happening).

3 Projecting the situation (equivalent to being able to project ahead to predict what is likely to happen next).

Each stage is reliant on the one below it.

The airline industry is still imperfect, like every other sector. However, a recognition of the impact of cognitive load, combined with practical steps to manage it, has resulted in sustained improvements in safety performance over the years.

A pharmaceutical company in rapid growth

A pharmaceutical client of *Included* was in an exciting growth phase. Under the direction of a new CEO, they were growing at 20 per cent a year and expanding globally, at a rapid pace. They had a whole suite of superior products under their belt and were beating the competition, and a growing market, from which they were increasing their market share.

However, whenever we spoke to the CEO, HR Director and Head of Talent, they were visibly stressed. At first, they would cover, and pretend everything was fine. However, as we got to know them, it became clear they were suffering from extraordinarily high cognitive load. They began to share, and would openly admit they were stressed, saying as much in our regular meetings.

When stress gets to an acute level, highly capable people become frozen. We were not even dealing with the issues we were contracted to tackle anymore. It became far more fundamental than that. We discussed the fact that while the company's situation was incredibly exciting, they would not be able to actively and usefully participate or contribute if they carried on as they were. Ironically, the high cognitive load they were experiencing (that they attributed to the growth pressures) was now at risk of limiting the growth goal.

We met the CEO and had a challenging meeting to discuss ways in which the key people could decrease their cognitive load with immediate effect. That was not only essential for them, but especially for their teams around them. One of the solutions we came up with was greater trust, to empower people to control their own diaries (resting and exercising when they needed to) as well as delegate decisions (meaning that there were fewer bottle necks). While the growth is still 20 per cent and the trajectory is ambitious, they feel they have more contingency in reserve than previously.

A central bank

A central Bank *Included* worked with contained some exceptionally talented people. They were all deeply committed to public service and the mission of the Bank, to maintain monetary stability. However, we knew from surveying the staff there was suboptimal psychological safety, at all levels. This meant a lack of sufficient contribution to decision making. This went to the heart of the Bank's mission as they needed the maximum contribution possible, to calibrate decisions they made, given the consequences to the wider economy.

When we investigated the results, we discovered that there was no overt racism or other discriminatory practice. But what there was, in abundance, was high cognitive load leading to a lack of empathy. Examples included a junior economist summoned to present to a senior meeting who had prepared a 20-page deck overnight but was then asked to skip to slide seven, throwing them off their stride. A one-to-one with a senior economist where they had failed to realize the other employee was distressed and ploughed on with the interrogation of data, oblivious to the discomfort of the other person in the room. Clumsy language being used. Falling asleep in meetings.

None of these things seemed a key threat in and of themselves, but the cumulative effect added up to low psychological safety, harming the Bank's key mission. And the cause was high cognitive load. Too many brilliant minds were cluttered, and lacked space to process and empathize.

This demonstrates that no matter how brilliant people are, none of us is brilliant enough to be impervious to cognitive load. The Bank had some of the world's best economists and mathematicians, but as they were processing too much without a break or adequate support, they became dysfunctional. Now, the organization is focused on mental health and awareness of cognitive load as a priority, led from the top.

Dr Bawa-Garba

In 2011, Dr Bawa-Garba, a National Health Service (NHS) trainee pediatrician, returned to work from maternity leave. Any woman returning to work from maternity leave will appreciate the pressure that entails. In Dr Bawa-Garba's case, she returned to a new hospital and received no induction. She then proceeded to work a 13 hour shift without a break.

During the course of the 13 hour shift, a number of significant issues developed. The IT system, used to review test results, was temperamental. There were insufficient staff. The on-call consultant was not on-site until the afternoon, and the other registrar due on duty was attending a training day, with no cover provided in their absence. Doctor Bawa-Garba, who was responsible for a young child's care, made critical decisions relating to his care which was later held to contribute to the child's death.

The Trust's internal investigation concluded no single root cause could be identified, and multiple actions were recommended in order to minimize risk to future patients. However, over the course of the next seven years, a series of criminal convictions and professional sanctions followed for Dr Bawa-Garba and another nurse involved in the child's care. The doctor was convicted of manslaughter and suspended from the General Medical Council register for a year, prior to being struck off the register.

While we must never forget the tragedy at the centre of this case, concerns have been raised by doctors about what some perceive to be scapegoating of a doctor for systemic failures beyond their control. Considering the doctor worked 13 hours without a break in a high-pressure environment, one can reasonably assume this influenced her ability to think and respond clearly. Unfortunately, this case is an example of a blame culture that is the opposite to the 'Just Culture' in the aviation industry. How can lessons be learnt if identifying issues results in condemnation?

As these examples from pharmaceuticals, banking and medicine demonstrate, excessive cognitive load is not only miserable for us as individual professionals, it can have grave consequences for those around us. If we become aware of our cognitive load, take steps to pre-emptively manage it and even over time reduce or control it, we can not only help ourselves and our teams, we can become part of the solution to greater inclusion in our midst.

Key takeaways

1 Cognitive load is the amount of information that working memory can hold at any one time. Information can be transferred from working memory into long-term memory in order to retain it and be able to call it back easily when it is needed.

2 Inclusive leadership is about adaptation to other people, rather than expecting them to adapt to you. Adaptation is far less likely from people with a high cognitive load.

3 Recognizing cognitive load, offering clear instruction, and making complex concepts simple and easily digestible can all ameliorate cognitive load.

Further reading

Birnbaum, J (2018) What a Load of ...Cognition! The Crucial Importance of Cognitive Load in Training. Training Industry trainingindustry.com/articles/content-development/what-a-load-of-cognition-the-crucial-importance-of-cognitive-load-in-training/ (archived at https://perma.cc/24V3-944Z)

CAA (2016) Flight Crew Human Factors Handbook, CAP 737. Civil Aviation Authority, London

Cohen, D (2018) The inside story of a six-year-old boy's death. And the trainee doctor who took the blame. BBC News www.bbc.co.uk/news/resources/idt-sh/the_struck_off_doctor# (archived at https://perma.cc/K9V4-75HJ)

Daniel, C O (2019) Effects of Organizational Change on Employee Job Performance. Asian Journal of Business and Management www.researchgate.net/publication/337777934_Effect_of_Organizational_Change_on_Employee_Job_Performance (archived at https://perma.cc/5X4N-739S)

Federal Aviation Administration (FAA)/Aviation Supplies and Academics (ASA) (2017) FAR/AIM 2017: Federal Aviation Regulations / Aeronautical Information Manual (FAR/AIM series) Aviation Supplies and Academics, Newcastle www.forbes.com/sites/forbesbusinessdevelopmentcouncil/2020/06/30/why-cognitive-load-could-be-the-most-important-employee-experience-metric-in-the-next-10-years/ (archived at https://perma.cc/UCH3-EG4R)

Hempsons (2018) A summary of the Dr Bawa-Garba case – and what this may mean for trusts www.hempsons.co.uk/news-articles/summary-dr-bawa-garba-case-may-mean-trusts/ (archived at https://perma.cc/23TK-Y67C)

Kenny, D J (2013) Written in blood, AOPA www.aopa.org/training-and-safety/
    air-safety-institute/accident-analysis/featured-accidents/written-in-blood
    (archived at https://perma.cc/6ALT-LV7V)]
Reason, J (1997) Managing the Risks of Organizational Accidents. The University
    of Michigan Press, Lansing
Risa (2021) Death by Overwork: All About Karoshi, The True Japan thetruejapan.
    com/all-about-karoshi/ (archived at https://perma.cc/RL8D-KL8R)
Royal Courts of Justice (2018) Bawa-Garba v GMC Final Judgement www.
    judiciary.uk/wp-content/uploads/2018/08/bawa-garba-v-gmc-final-judgment.pdf
    (archived at https://perma.cc/PR8Y-UYGU)
Sweller, J (2021) The eLearning Coach Podcast: What you need to know about
    cognitive Load (2019) [Podcast] 23 April theelearningcoach.com/podcasts/55/
    (archived at https://perma.cc/AJH5-6SWX)

References

1 World Health Organization, International Labour Organization (2021) Long
    working hours increasing deaths from heart disease and stroke: WHO, ILO www.
    who.int/news/item/17-05-2021-long-working-hours-increasing-deaths-from-
    heart-disease-and-stroke-who-ilo (archived at https://perma.cc/2ZJZ-BGAM)

2 Frost, S (2021) The biggest unrecognized barrier to inclusion is cognitive load,
    Forbes www.forbes.com/sites/sfrost/2021/05/11/the-biggest-unrecognised-
    barrier-to-inclusion-is-cognitive-load/ (archived at https://perma.cc/3RTY-8XPL)

3,5,7 Sweller, J (1988) Cognitive Load During Problem Solving: Effects on
    Learning Cognitive Science 12 (2): 257–285

4 Tardi, C (2021) Moore's Law, Investopedia www.investopedia.com/terms/m/
    mooreslaw.asp (archived at https://perma.cc/8VM2-2W3P)

6 Dobbin, F, Kalev (2016) Why Diversity Programs Fail. Harvard Business Review
    hbr.org/2016/07/why-diversity-programs-fail (archived at https://perma.cc/
    3JQG-5VW9)

8 Freed, J (2020) Why Cognitive Load could be the most important employee
    experience metric in the next ten years, Forbes

9 Graeber, C (2016) Human Factors, Aero Boeing www.boeing.com/commercial/
    aeromagazine/aero_08/human_textonly.html (archived at https://perma.cc/
    ZH4K-BPH4)

02

Mindset

IRFAAN ARIF

'I am an invisible man. No, I am not a spook like those who haunted Edgar Allan Poe; nor am I one of your Hollywood-movie ectoplasms. I am a man of substance, of flesh and bone, fiber and liquids – and I might even be said to possess a mind. I am invisible, understand, simply because people refuse to see me. Like the bodiless heads you see sometimes in circus sideshows, it is as though I have been surrounded by mirrors of hard, distorting glass. When they approach me they see only my surroundings, themselves, or figments of their imagination – indeed, everything and anything except me.

The invisibility to which I refer occurs because of a peculiar disposition of the eyes of those with whom I come in contact. A matter of the construction of their inner eyes, those eyes with which they look through their physical eyes upon reality.'

RALPH ELLISON, 1952, THE INVISIBLE MAN

Ralph Ellison's novel is about a Black man in the in the U.S. during the pre-Civil Rights era, where Black Americans lived in absence of basic human rights. He describes an experience where he accidentally bumps into a white man, who then insults him. The white man refuses to apologize, and so our protagonist resorts to violence before realizing that the white man had not really *seen* him. Instead, the white man was one of many 'sleepwalkers' who had seen the protagonist as a caricature, a lesser human and someone that only existed in the lower echelons of society.

The idea of invisibility struck a chord with me. Growing up in Sheffield, England, through the eighties and nineties, I regularly experienced insults and violence because of race. I still remember walking home from school one afternoon, alone, across a large playing field, headphones wrapped over my head linked to my chunky Sony Walkman, playing a new 'Naughty by Nature' cassette I had borrowed from a friend. I walked rhythmically, miming the lyrics to the song. Moments later, I'm curled up on the floor trying to cover my face, head and stomach, from a barrage of punches and kicks arriving from all angles.

My headphones and Walkman were on the floor smashed, my clothes covered in mud and my body bruised. I had just been jumped by two fellow school boys, a couple of years senior to me, who had earlier taunted me about my 'dirty brown skin'. This was not my first experience of being attacked but it did act as a catalyst to me taking part in violent retaliations.

One particularly vivid memory included me, as a 14-year-old boy, standing outside a school in Rotherham (South Yorkshire, UK) I was with my friends. They were all like me, 14-year-old British Pakistani boys. And we were carrying some kind of weapon. One of my friends had earlier passed me a machete. We were on the lookout for two 'white boys' that had, in the previous week, hospitalized one of our friends because he was a 'Paki'.[i] As these things often go, an eye for eye is the default response.

Deep down, I didn't want to hurt anyone – I was following my group. I was also angry because of my own experiences. I am however, grateful to my younger self, for deciding at the last minute to drop the machete and leave. A few others left with me. Luckily, the ones who remained couldn't find the boys they were after. Things could have been very different.

Change your mindset

The notion of invisibility sticks. The purpose of racism (or any other ism) is ultimately to take away individuality and dignity, to demonize and dehumanize those that are deemed lesser in some way. Ellison alludes that these 'sleepwalkers' are likely to repeat the same mistakes or be complicit in the lack of change. Ellison begins his book with *I* but ends with *you*. He urges readers to change the way they see the world – to change their mindsets

The death of George Floyd in 2020, and the allegations of institutional racism at Yorkshire Cricket Club in 2021, suggest that ideas and beliefs (about race, gender or other protected characteristics) from our history linger, on like a deep stubborn stain. Ideas, like racism for example,[ii] are woven through the fabric of our society, transmitted through our institutions and left hibernating in our minds waiting to be triggered by a face, a news story, or a negative experience. They influence our mindset, which collectively can have a powerful impact on the culture and performance of an organization and who succeeds or fails. Truly *seeing* each other as individuals requires us to really look past the camouflage we assign to groups where invisibility is not a superpower, but a curse. By the end of this chapter, we will also move from *I* to *you*.

Mindset, behaviours, and bias

We can't change the way our brain works. However, the roadmaps and ideas that populate it can be altered through understanding, awareness and developing an open and inclusive mindset. This can help you embrace difference in profound, rather than superficial, ways.

Consider the Black Lives Matter movement (BLM). Organizations large and small began posting messages in support of BLM and began labelling their efforts as part of wider anti-racism efforts. Training on the subject increased significantly as more organizations came under pressure to follow this 'social movement'. However, corporate statements and training were often seen as lacking real empathy (although Nike and Ben & Jerry's were seen as bold in their approach as they were more explicit about their role in racism).[1]

There were also arguments against the BLM movement, namely, those that preferred the term 'All Lives Matter'. Organizations themselves reported less confidence in tackling race issues (compared to gender for example). Most people would probably agree that there is more fairness today than there has ever been, and that racism (and other isms) is the problem of a *few bad apples*.

Herein lies the crux of the problem and why many D&I initiatives fail to make lasting or meaningful change. Most people understand racism or sexism etc. as 'interpersonal' issues. That Person A does or says something offensive to Person B and therefore Person A must be the problem. That anyone else must, by default, be inclusive. A lack of understanding of 'systemic' or 'institutional' biases may lead us to taking it personally and withdrawing from the conversation.

Recent interventions in D&I have turned to 'mindsets' and the influence they have on behaviour as a catalyst or inhibitor of inclusion. Mindset has been conceptualized in many ways from being characterized as cognitive filters that direct our decision making, to linking mindset with core beliefs about how we see those around us and ourselves.[2]

This chapter will provide readers with an understanding of how mindsets, bias and behaviours are shaped. We'll learn how they operate within societal or ideological echo chambers formed by historical events, designed to differentiate and oppress. We'll explore how these echo chambers contribute to bias and behaviours, favouring some more than others. Inclusion and growth mindsets will be discussed as key to challenging the innate attraction to 'sameness' and implicit biases.

Socialization and social cognition

Most of us have heard of the 'nature vs nurture' debate. Proponents of the *nature* argument propose that the DNA and genotype we are born with determines our personality traits and ultimately who we are. The *nurture* advocates argue that we are essentially born with a 'blank slate' and that we acquire different attributes through learning experiences and interactions with the world around us.[3]

It is a controversial debate because it led to the field of eugenics (a term coined by Frances Galton). Eugenics suggested that negative traits could be bred out of the human species by discouraging reproduction by those considered inferior. It laid the groundwork for forced sterilization laws in the U.S. and Nazi 'racial hygiene' programs and the Holocaust. Although eugenics still exists in some corners of the academic world, it has largely been discredited as a field, but the nature vs nurture debate still influences our thinking on how we perceive and judge people.[4]

Alongside our genetic makeup, as shown by studies on twins,[5] it's our social environments that determine how we develop and see our world. Socialization refers to this process, of how we acquire culture or subculture and how these cultural norms, behavioural patterns, language, symbols and collective traits shape who we become.

We develop norms, values, language and behaviour through family, along with other psychological and social traits associated with gender, race or class. For example, representations of race are historical and stem from ideas of superiority and inferiority. Racial categories have their roots in colonization and the transatlantic slave trade where Europeans constructed their identity as 'white' superiors compared to less developed darker-skinned 'others'.[6]

We can see the impact of this in the stories we see around us in society. For example, in the UK, we can hear negative stories of Black kids as criminals and gang members or lazy. We form a societal map of what is good or bad, normal or abnormal, intelligent, superior and inferior.

How we think about and react to others is known as social cognition. We might view being ignored in a meeting as accidental and overlook it, or see it as others having some form of prejudice towards us. We notice behaviours of others and tend to fit new information into our worldviews in systematic ways.[7] Understanding and interpreting these thought processes can help us become more aware of possible prejudice or bias.

Incorporating what we see and feel into our existing psyche (e.g. an interviewee reminds you of someone you like and so you feel good about this person), is linked to cognitive consistency.[8] The process of acquiring information is related to attribution processes.

Attribution theory

Fiske and Taylor (1991) propose that we're quite lazy thinkers and often look for quick, efficient and effortless ways of making sense of situations. They coined the term 'cognitive misers' to describe our reluctance to expend cognitive energy, instead using shortcuts to interact and understand our world.

Imagine you meet someone for the first time as they walk into an interview room. Your brain takes a quick snapshot of this person and acquires information about their appearance and facial features. Let's say the interview candidate has a frown on their face and they seem a little cold when they meet you. Your first thought might be that this person is unfriendly and so you begin developing a feeling about whether this person will fit into your organization. Based on this information we sort and categorize this person into our existing psyche (e.g. who is a good fit and who isn't). We might experience this as a positive or negative feeling or intuition about someone's capabilities.

The attributions we make can be seen as either internally located – the cause of bad behaviour for example, is linked to a colleague's personality or traits, or externally located – where the bad behaviour of a colleague maybe a result of a difficult experience at home.[9]

Attributional biases

The fundamental attribution error (FAE) is a bias which leads us to 'underestimate the impact of the situation and overestimate [the impact of] the individual's traits or attitudes' Myers (2012) when trying to explain behaviour, performance or success of another person. By not considering situational factors, people develop direct associations between someone's trait's (e.g. personality) to specific observable outcomes (e.g. performance).

Closely related to the FAE is the actor-observer bias, a cognitive bias that refers to the tendency of people to attribute internal or dispositional causes to other people's behaviour (as with the FAE) but situational attributions for their own.[10] For example:

> 'Referring to an error in her work the manager told his colleagues that she's
> so careless – while referring to his own mistake as an accident caused by stress
> at home.'

Taking the fundamental attribution error one step further, Pettigrew (1979) described the ultimate attribution error (UAE) as a bias that is linked to intergroup contexts and refers to people's tendency to make attributions which are consistent with their prejudices. It refers to the idea that if out-group members (people different to you and your networks) behave badly or perform poorly at work, we attribute this behaviour to their disposition (bad person or not talented) but if they show positive behaviours, we attribute these behaviours to external factors (they were supported in their success).

Ingroups are social groups towards which we feel loyalty and respect, usually due to being part of that group. This creates an ingroup bias. Ingroups can be related to race, religion etc or even a football team. Similarly, outgroups are social groups that we do not identify with and we're generally more negative towards them. Consequently, according to the just-world hypothesis, people get what they deserve and deserve what they get (Learner, 1980). Those who hold just-world beliefs are more likely to blame immigrants for local problems or even victims of sexual assault or robbery of causing their misfortune. The problem with this kind of attribution is that the world isn't just; people are affected by unfair circumstances.[11]

What can you do?

1 Reflect on a time you thought a colleague was incompetent. Did you consider and try to understand situational factors that might have affected this person's work?

2 Challenge attribution error by balancing out a negative perspective with positive ones. You can do this by showing gratitude – write down a list of three to five positive qualities the person also holds. This helps to widen the lens through which you see the individual.

3 Embrace your vulnerabilities – practice self-awareness by reflecting on your own behaviour regularly – remembering that your own achievements or failures have much to do with situational factors as well your character or personality. It is the same for others.

Cognitive consistency

While attribution is important, what follows is the need for consistency. Our brains are wired to make our lives as easy and comfortable as possible. For example, cognitive dissonance theory[12] refers to the experiencing discomfort when two ideas or views about a person are inconsistent. In order to reduce this discomfort, we change our attitudes or behaviour to be more consistent with our actions. An example, of this might be a Black member of staff making a complaint to a HR manager about racism. This might contradict the HR manager's belief that racism exists in the organization or that the person whom the complaint was made against could be racist, and so to ease the dissonance, the HR manager might explain away the possibility of racism or cite the lack of evidence.

The HR manager might employ confirmation bias to ease the dissonance experienced. Confirmation bias is the tendency to seek out information that is consistent with what we believe and expect, ignoring or dismissing any information that might be inconsistent. Furthermore, the need to be consistent can lead others to behave in ways that are consistent with our beliefs. This is known as the self-fulfilling prophecy. For example, if a direct report continually doubts her ability to perform at her job, she might inadvertently sabotage herself by putting less effort and time into it.[13]

What can you do?

1 **Embrace cognitive dissonance** – it is our brain's way of telling us that our beliefs, values, thoughts and ideas might be not always line up with our behaviour or other people's perceptions of us. By embracing dissonance, we open ourselves up to other perspectives and in turn are more likely to learn new things or grow as individuals.

2 **Be careful of confirmation bias** – sometimes to overcome dissonance we look for information to confirm what we might be feeling or our beliefs. Act as your very own devil's advocate.

Stereotypes

We're aware that people are different in many ways, but when we describe others, we tend to rely on generalizations to describe them.

In her TED talk in 2009,[14] Author Chimamanda Ngozi Adichie adopts the phrase 'single stories' to describe how we create simplistic and often false perceptions about individuals, groups and even countries and explains that:

> 'I've always felt that it is impossible to engage properly with a place or a person without engaging with all of the stories of that place and that person. The consequence of the single story is this: It robs people of dignity. It makes our recognition of our equal humanity difficult. It emphasizes how we are different rather than how we are similar...
>
> The single story creates stereotypes, and the problem with stereotypes is not that they are untrue, but that they are incomplete. They make one story become the only story.'

Stereotypes can be seen as fixed characteristics or traits attributed to social groups (Hinton, 2000). As part of the unconscious mind, stereotypes are essentially networks of associations within our semantic (knowledge) memory which are activated automatically when triggered.[15] So related concepts will have a stronger association than unrelated concepts e.g. in terms of gender, a surgeon may be more strongly linked to men as opposed to women.

What can you do?

1 **Accept that we all stereotype** – it is a natural part of how we navigate our world. However, accept that while they help us, they can also limit how we see others.

2 **Look for counter stereotypical examples** – consider who the role models are within your organization. How diverse are they? Diverse role models are one way of helping to challenge and break stereotypes.

3 **Call out stereotyping when you see it** – e.g. in meetings, are women regularly asked to take minutes even though that isn't their role? Consider how we ascribe gender roles in the workplace e.g. by inviting men to join us for after work drinks or dinners while assuming women will need to get home.

Unconscious bias

In the UK, self-report measures of prejudicial attitudes to different social groups have declined steadily[16] but inequalities still exist in all aspects of public services and life. One of the reasons given for these disparities is the presence of implicit bias, which consists of negative evaluations that have been observable through indirect measures designed to bypass conscious processes.[17]

Several mental processes operate implicitly or without conscious awareness or attentional focus. These processes include memory, perception, attitudes, stereotypes and many others.[18] Attitudes are often defined as an 'evaluative disposition – that is, the tendency to like or dislike, or to act favourably or unfavourably towards, someone or something' (ibid, pp 948). Implicit attitude is the attitude towards someone that is not in ones' conscious awareness and can differ from conscious attitude.

Unconscious biases are a product of implicit stereotypes and implicit attitudes. They can produce behaviour that is completely out of line with conscious and intentional attitudes and beliefs.[19]

Phelps et al (2018) used functional magnetic resonance imaging (fMRI) to understand the neural mechanisms involved in how Black and white social groups are evaluated. The focus of their research was the amygdala, a small part of the brain in the subcortical structure, that plays a role in emotional learning and evaluation (e.g. how we respond to danger). They found using Implicit Association Tests (IAT, a test to measure implicit biases)[iii] for white subjects who, they found had stronger associations with white=good compared to Black =good. Other results showed greater amygdala activation in seeing Black faces compared to white faces.

A recent study undertaken by RunRepeat,[20] a Danish research firm, looked at football commentary from 80 games in the Premier League, Serie A, La Liga and Ligue 1. They analysed over 2,000 statements and found that when praising 'lighter skin tone' players, commentators would refer to intelligence, work ethic and quality, compared to physical and athletic attributes when referring to 'darker skin tone' players.

Findings like this point back to how historical ideas of inferiority, superiority, physicality or intelligence can have on how we subconsciously perceive those from different groups.

What can you do?

1 **Acknowledge your own biases and assumptions** – Undertake an Implicit Association Test (IAT) which can help identify the strength of associations you might have between groups and behaviours or attributes. E.g. do you associate men with science and women with the arts.

2 **Diversify your in-groups** – reflect on your personal and professional networks. Who is in your circles of trust? How diverse are they? Surrounding yourself with as much difference possible is a great way to cover your blindspots, challenge false stereotypes and subsequently minimize the impact of unconscious bias.

Echo chambers and shifting mindsets

Bats use echolocation, sending sound waves from their mouth or nose, to determine where objects are. Bats are not blind, but they can find and navigate their environment in total darkness, by creating a picture of their world through sound. If you ever go into a large empty hallway with hard surface floors, you can shout and here the echoes of your voice come back to you.

What we read or consume is the same as what we share or put out into the world. Like an echo, information and beliefs come back to us creating what popular psychology calls an echo chamber.[21] Given our tendencies to associate with like-minded people we tend to also shroud ourselves in a limited and often narrow perspective of the world. Our beliefs about the world become our navigation system where our maps act as the filters that take us away from anything that might be contrary to what we believe.

Brexit provided a stark reminder that a radical division exists among people. Like in a science fiction film, different groups seem to exist within alternate realities, with facts and ideas that differ greatly. People create 'epistemic bubbles' by forming communities with like-minded people that rarely get the chance to see the views of those from opposite sides. Echo chambers develop when people from a group distrust anyone outside of their own community, something which is exclusionary by design.[22]

Unlike academic textbooks, which must go through a series of filters to check for quality, the internet has no such filter. Online echo chambers represent a sort of supercharged confirmation bias where challenge is avoided, and beliefs and views are sought and confirmed using selective evidence. We need to look outside of our echo chambers to see the world anew. Often this can require a change in mindset.

Consider the use and constant updating of technology. A new phone or television will come, and old ones will be thrown out, while some new products will never be accepted and be condemned to the history books (e.g. compare VHS to Betamax). However, unlike technology, ideas or ideologies (such as racism) stay long after they have been rejected.

Barry Schwartz, who coined the term 'Ideas Technology' discusses this in his TED Talk in 2014.[23]

> 'With things, if the technology sucks, it just vanishes, right? Bad technology disappears. With ideas—false ideas about human beings will not go away if people believe that they're true. Because if people believe that they're true, they create ways of living and institutions that are consistent with these very false ideas.'

Imagine you're consistently excluded from meetings, overlooked for promotions, given low scores in your annual reviews and generally not valued in the workplace. What will you believe at the end of the year? It is likely that by this point you will have internalized certain negative messages about your ability and worth. Now imagine, as a society we've received messages of superiority of white people and inferiority of Black people for centuries. What might be the impact on the mindsets of white people and Black people? What will be the internalized beliefs? The chances are there will be a fixed mindset about oneself and the other. These ideas will then be perpetuated across our personal and working lives.

A reflective and inclusive mindset is vital in steering deeply entrenched false ideas. Growth mindsets are one way to begin thinking how we might do this.

Fixed, growth and inclusive mindsets

Carol Dweck (2015) distinguishes between fixed and growth mindsets. She states that, 'In a fixed mindset, people believe their basic qualities, like their intelligence or talent, are fixed traits. They spend their time documenting their intelligence or talent instead of developing them. They also believe that talent alone creates success—without effort'. Whereas in a growth mindset 'people believe that their most basic abilities can be developed through dedication and hard work—brains and talent are just the starting point'. This view creates a love of learning and a resilience that is essential for great accomplishment' (Dweck, 2015).

In an organizational context, employees with a fixed mindset are more likely to struggle with change or adapting in the workplace. A belief that intelligence and talent is fixed, might lead to fear of failure and avoiding challenges. The fear of being seen as less smart might influence how they respond to critical feedback and how they interact in teams. Furthermore, those leading and managing teams might find it tricky if certain employees have a fixed mindset.

Fixed mindset people tend to locate the cause of behaviour and achievement internally, either for themselves or others. Whereas growth mindset people are more likely to question situational causes and be open to the circumstances that say act as barriers for outgroup members.[24]

Employees with a growth mindset tend to learn with more enthusiasm and accept that challenge and change are part of life. They are more likely to seek feedback and will view failures as opportunities with resilience a key part of their approach. Managing someone with a growth mindset may feel easier as the employee takes more ownership of their role and view the managers and leaders are partners in a collective goal.

Reverting back to the example of racial prejudices and stereotypes, we can agree that these are linked to a fixed mindset – that, racism is essentially a false idea about 'fixed' traits. This type of mindset and the unconscious biases that come with it can ultimately shape a company's culture. It can impact who gets hired, promoted, or even how we give constructive feedback. More importantly, a fixed mindset can lead to a workplace that excludes and creates a culture that values sameness rather than differences.

What we need is an inclusive mindset, that recognizes the fallacies we bring, including our irrational and judgmental tendencies. We need to be able to develop a belief that success and achievement are not linked to intelligence alone, but rather influenced by situation, experiences, and organizational culture. We need to use empathy and compassion as a core part of our approach while constantly reflecting on our own vulnerabilities and biases. We need to recognize that we are on a journey – both individual and collective – and that we all live in a world where differences act as triggers for exclusion and marginalization rather than unique aspects of who we are.

We are creatures of habit. We like to keep our environments under control as much as possible. We do this through navigating our world using short-cuts and creating habits of thought. Sometimes these habits become so strong that they can become fixed beliefs about people. In order to move away from these comfortable habits we sometimes need to move away from echo chambers and see things from another perspective. The more we see things from other viewpoints, question our assumptions and judgments about people, as well as exposing ourselves to as much difference as possible, the more we morph a fixed mindset into a growth and inclusive mindset.

'There is only one way to see things, until someone shows you how to look at them with different eyes'

Pablo Picasso

Key takeaways

1 **Begin with a little vulnerability** – accepting or acknowledging we might be biased is not always easy. As leaders we need to understand our motivations, history and privileges (the advantages society affords us for example, not having to worry or think about race or gender as a possible cause for discrimination). What does vulnerability look like for you? It could be having open conversations with your teams. Acknowledging your biases or giving others permission to call you out during meetings. Whatever it is, it can be the first step to recognizing what our mindset is, it's beliefs and values and how they might differ from others.

2 **Reflect on your mindset** – how do you see yourself and others? Do you view your abilities or beliefs as fixed or fluid? Do you recognize that situational factors will have an impact on the progression of some of your employees and colleagues? A growth mindset is necessary to stay motivated when approaching difficult diversity and inclusion challenges and setbacks.

3 **Be proactive** – Go beyond not discriminating, since this doesn't add anything new to the culture. See diversity, equity and inclusion as a purpose. Recognizing the invisible powers that limit and exclude people requires someone to take action to give voice, platform and model inclusive behaviours.

Further reading

Devine, P G (1998) Beyond the isolated social perceiver: Why inhibit stereotypes? In R S Wyer, Jr (Ed.), *Advances in social cognition: Vol. 11. Stereotype activation and inhibition* (pp. 69–81) Mahwah, N J: Erlbaum

Wegner, D M (1994) Ironic processes of mental control. *Psychological Review, 101,* 34–52

References

i   Paki is used as a racial slur, directed towards people of Pakistani descent mainly in British slang, and often used indiscriminately towards people of perceived South Asian descent in general

ii Racism at its core is an ideology (of superiority of white races in relation to others) that is absorbed by people in society, subsequently having an impact on language, behaviour, and overall inclusion

iii The test can be found on the Harvard University Website by searching for 'Harvard IAT'

1   Francis, Patricia (2021) Black Lives Matter: how the UK movement struggled to be heard in the 2010s

2   French, R P II (2016) The fuzziness of mindsets: Divergent conceptualizations and characterizations of mindset theory and praxis *International Journal of Organizational Analysis*, 24(4), 673–691

3   Tabery, J (2014) Nature vs nurture, April 29 eugenicsarchive.ca/discover/tree/535eed0d7095aa000000024 (archived at https://perma.cc/2J3U-Q7ZJ)

4   Norrgard, K (2008) Human testing, the eugenics movement, and IRBs *Nature Education* 1(1):170

5   Baker, C (2004) *Behavioral genetics: An introduction to how genes and environments interact through development to shape differences in mood, personality, and intelligence* [PDF] http://www.aaas.org/spp/bgenes/Intro.pdf (archived at https://perma.cc/6TWV-FUE7)

6   Salter, P S, Adams, G, and Perez, M J (2018) Racism in the structure of everyday worlds: A cultural-psychological perspective *Current Directions in Psychological Science*, 27, 150–155. doi:10.1177/0963721417724239 (archived at https://perma.cc/54G3-24DP)

7, 8, 13 Jones, J M, Dovidio, J F, and Vietze, D L (2014) *The psychology of diversity: Beyond prejudice and racism.* Wiley-Blackwell

9   Crisp, R J, and Turner, R N (2014) Essential Social Psychology: 3rd Edition SAGE Publications Ltd http://www.uk.sagepub.com/books/Book240655 (archived at https://perma.cc/XF6X-3333)

10   Malle, B F (2006) The actor-observer asymmetry in attribution: A (surprising) meta-analysis, *Psychological Bulletin, 132*(6), 895–919 doi.org/10.1037/0033-2909.132.6.895 (archived at https://perma.cc/M6DE-RKC4)

11   Van den Bos, K., and Maas, M (2009) On the psychology of the belief in a just world: Exploring experiential and rationalistic paths to victim blaming *Personality and Social Psychology Bulletin, 35,* 1567–1578

12   Festinger, L (1957) *A theory of cognitive dissonance* Stanford University Press

14   Adichie, C N (2009) The danger of a single story, TED www.youtube.com/watch?v=D9Ihs241zeg (archived at https://perma.cc/FEY7-G2QE)

15   Collins, A M, and Loftus, E F (1975) A spreading-activation theory of semantic processing, *Psychological Review, 82*(6), 407–428 doi.org/10.1037/0033-295X.82.6.407 (archived at https://perma.cc/KJ7X-GRZ5)

16   Biernat, M, and Crandall, C S (1999) Racial attitudes, In J P Robinson, P H Shaver, and L S Wrightman (Eds), *Measures of political attitudes* (pp. 291–412) San Diego: Academic Press

17, 19   Nosek, B A, Cunningham, W A, Banaji, M R, and Greenwald, A G (2000) Measuring implicit attitudes on the internet. Nashville, TN: Society for Personality and Social Psychology

18   Greenwald, A G, and Krieger, L. H (2006) Implicit Bias: Scientific Foundations. *California Law Review,* vol 94, issue 4

20   McLoughlin, D (2021) Racial Bias in Football Commentary (Study): The Pace and Power Effect, RunRepeat. runrepeat.com/racial-bias-study-soccer (archived at https://perma.cc/5X37-3Y6K)

21   Nguyen, C T (2020) 'Echo Chambers and Epistemic Bubbles.' Episteme 17 (2): 141–161. doi:10.1017/epi.2018.32 (archived at https://perma.cc/P465-WV5P)

22   Santos, B R G (2021) Echo Chambers, Ignorance and Domination, *Social Epistemology, 35:2,* 109–119, DOI:10.1080/02691728.2020.1839590

23   Schwartz, B (2014), The way we think about work is broken, TED www.ted.com/talks/barry_schwartz_the_way_we_think_about_work_is_broken/transcript?language=en#t-11625 (archived at https://perma.cc/7EKR-F6GN)

24   Fast, L A, Reimer, H M, and Funder, D C (2008) The social behavior and reputation of the attributionally complex *Journal of Research in Personality, 42* (1), 208–222

03

Building your cultural intelligence

ROB NEIL AND LYDIA CRONIN

Many of us have woken up. Following televised, racially-motivated murders, a life-threatening virus that penetrated national borders and permeated class structures, and state enforced lockdowns that arrested individual liberties, many of us have engaged in a reluctant and unexpected awakening. For all that our collective intelligence has delivered over the centuries, we are currently in a place we did not prescribe, could not have predicted and would never have proposed.

Many people are now listening to the experiences of others who are different from them. An increasing number are not just listening, but also hearing, ready to learn from others who were previously hidden in plain sight. Taking on the perspectives and stories of others that may have a lasting positive effect on diversity-related outcomes, by increasing individuals' internal motivation to respond without prejudice.[1] This chapter shares how many are now on a path to cultural change. They are embarking on a journey in cultural awareness, and doing more than ever before to truly understand, personally lead, and collectively deliver positive transformative change.

Where does cultural intelligence (CQ) come in?

CQ is the capability of an individual or group to adapt and operate effectively in a diverse range of national, ethnic, organizational, generational, and departmental cultural contexts. Developing our CQ improves how effectively we are able to work with, and relate to, people who are different from us. High CQ in leaders is positively correlated with organizational performance. It's a soft skill, about effective communication, crucial for leaders and managers working in cross-cultural contexts to be able to succeed in their roles.

How is CQ different from cultural competence, awareness and emotional intelligence?

Many of us will be familiar with the term 'cultural competence'. Cultural competence refers to knowing information about other cultures and their differences.

CQ goes beyond this. Instead of simply understanding information, CQ is your ability to use that information to adapt and function effectively in a range of culturally diverse contexts.[2] CQ is the ability to use all your senses to perceive how personalities you engage with are different from your culture, and the similarities that they may share with one another.[3] CQ can be measured and developed via an assessed quotient, similar to how we use IQ tests.

CQ is also different from emotional intelligence [EQ] because it moves beyond knowledge of self to focus on our capabilities to work more effectively with others across multicultural contexts. Where an emotionally intelligent person can read differences in others, a person with high levels of CQ can read the behaviours that would be true across groups and influenced by culture.[4] EQ focuses on the self, whereas CQ relates to working with others, and with systems that are culturally different.

Measuring CQ

CQ is measured in a similar manner to IQ, on the Cultural Intelligence Scale.[5] Across 20 items, four theoretical dimensions are addressed: Metacognitive, Cognitive, Motivational, and Behavioural.[6] It can be undertaken as a self-assessment, or compiled from observer scorings.

Why should you develop your CQ?

When you possess a high level of CQ, you automatically play a critical role bridging traditional divisions, and fear-filled knowledge gaps. With high CQ

TABLE 3.1 Theoretical dimensions of cultural intelligence

Dimension	Explanation
Metacognitive	A high scorer would question cultural assumptions, be consciously aware of others' cultural preferences, and be ready and able to change their own norms when interacting with others. (Brislin et al, 2006)
Cognitive	High Cognitive CQ involves understanding similarities and differences across cultures, and directing energy towards learning more. (Brislin et al, 2006)
Motivational	You direct your energy towards cross-cultural situations as this is something you are intrinsically interested in. (Deci and Ryan, 1985).
Behavioral	Exhibiting situationally appropriate verbal and non-verbal behaviours would indicate a high level of Behavioural CQ. (Gudykunst et al., 1988).

you will find yourself educating peers about different cultures, transferring essential knowledge between otherwise disparate groups, and helping to build interpersonal connections. Culturally intelligent employees also possess the potential to drive up innovation and creativity, due to their ability to integrate diverse resources. Additionally, job candidates who reflect mannerisms of recruiters from different cultural backgrounds to their own are more likely to be offered jobs.[7] A higher CQ increases your ability to perform in cross-cultural situations, better equipping you to manage more successfully in a globalized world of work (Kwantes and Glazer, 2017).

A person with high EQ (self-awareness, self-regulation, motivation, empathy and social skills), will grasp what makes us human and at the same time what makes each of us different from one another. However, EQ alone will not compel us to know more about those who are different, or indeed plan and act proactively in support of what is possible when we encourage, support and inspire that difference. A person with high CQ welcomes those differences across diverse teams and is driven to know more as an exciting feature of increased innovation, deeper shared empathy and even greater inclusion.

CQ helps you navigate your role in the organization

Organizations have distinctive cultures. Anyone who has joined a new organization, or even a new department, spends the first few weeks deciphering its cultural code, consciously and unconsciously. The increasing prevalence of hybrid and remote work means this deciphering stage is formed differently than those entering a new organization in the old world of work.

Within any organization there are nearly always sparring subcultures. This can take the form of HQ offices meeting the needs of operational staff, machine operatives alongside engineers and administrative staff supporting qualified experts such as lawyers and accountants. These exchanges often give rise to tensions rooted in difference as well as cultural hierarchies such as sales teams failing to talk to the engineers or HR losing patience with the internal legal team. Departments, divisions, professions and geographical regions each have a constellation of manners, meanings, histories and values, built up over time, that will sometimes confuse the interloper. It's during

FIGURE 3.1 Four key capabilities of CQ

Drive	The curiosity and motivation needed to work well with others. Having picked up this book, you likely have this curiosity already.
	You're more likely to be effective at working and relating with people who are different from you if you nurture your CQ drive by building on your curiosity, identifying your motivators.
	Our intrinsic motivators come from within ourselves, such as our values and beliefs. Extrinsic motivators come from external sources, such as financial reward, public praise or the avoidance of punishment. It's worth reflecting on which intrinsic and extrinsic motivations are most pertinent to you.
Knowledge	Understanding the kinds of differences that make one group distinct from another and may change how they experience and interact with the world of work. This supports your ability to relate to others and work successfully together.
Strategy	As with all elements of DEI work, it's important that CQ is embedded into how you and your organization approach work, rather than simply being an add-on.
	Using the CQ Knowledge that you have been nurturing, you can account for the cultural differences across your organization and markets and address these in your strategy. This can then be supported by prioritizing designing, planning and tracking a practical list of actions to help deliver the agreed outcomes from your strategy.
Action	Adapting your behaviour based on the three previous capabilities. This encompasses verbal and non-verbal communication and encouraging, supporting, and inspiring engagement from those around you.
	Being adaptable in your behaviours, while remaining authentic to yourself, gives you the best chance of being effective when working with a range of different people.

these moments in the journey that CQ can help and by prioritizing our attention to increasing our CQ we can embrace each of part of the journey as further learning.

CQ in practice

CQ is broken down into four key capabilities: drive, knowledge, strategy and action.[8] Working on each of these capabilities is central to improving your CQ.

Improving your CQ

Consider how the reaction and response to the Christchurch tragedy, by New Zealand's Prime Minister, Jacinda Ardern, impacted diverse communities. Her empathy for the Muslim community garnered international praise and, when asked why she reacted the way she did, she said it was 'intuitive' rather than 'deliberate').[9]

Some people are naturally predisposed to cultural intelligence, but, encouragingly, CQ can also be learnt. Improving our CQ helps us consciously identify our biases and implement effective strategies for managing them. If an organization collectively builds its CQ it can move from reacting unconsciously to taking more conscious, intentional actions aimed at progressive cultural change across the organization. To get beyond our own biases, we can invest our time and energy in developing our CQ and inspiring wider cultural transformation in our teams and organizations.

Here are three essential stages to help increase CQ and create a healthy environment for positive cultural change;

---

1 **Create a safe space.** The importance of psychological safety is often overlooked, but it's one of the most pivotal factors in making people feel included in an organization.

   If we are to facilitate healthy conversations around unconscious bias, we need to create environments where people feel they can share their real experiences without backlash or judgement. Without this fundamental provision, it will not be possible to get full disclosure, and open conversation will be compromised. We cannot achieve the key capability of CQ Knowledge without being able to engage in uncompromised dialogue that spaces with ensured psychological safety enable. We must have critical conversations, or we risk simply having shallow discourse or active avoidance, ultimately leading to people in our organizations feeling discouraged, frustrated and angry. See Chapter 4 for more information on safe spaces.

2 **Acknowledge fears.** Many of us have avoided challenging conversations in the past because of fear. This may have been because we were worried about saying the 'wrong' thing and the repercussions of this, or fear of appearing biased, or not wanting to come across uninformed when talking about a topic we know little about. All of these fears leave us feeling uncomfortable. As an alternative, increasing our CQ supports us in acknowledging our fears. We can instead turn our focus to normalizing these feelings of fear. Circling back to our CQ Drive and Knowledge key capabilities, we can commit to our own learning and actively build an atmosphere of trust. Those same fears need not hinder our capacity to understand, lead and deliver.

How do you acknowledge fears? After having created a 'safe space' where people feel able to share and speak openly, it is important to people to share their truth and remind everyone on the journey that even when fear subsides, they may still feel a level of discomfort. That's ok, that's because we're all still learning. By increasing the healthy, progressive challenge and support, in equal measure, we encourage advocacy and increase levels of engagement. Together we can all support the change we wish to see.

In *Included's* work with award-winning food producer Apetito we executed a reverse mentoring programme with their senior team, connecting them to colleagues across the organization's hierarchy.[10] The senior leadership team had entered the programme with a commitment to embed DEI into their work, in line with the CQ Drive capability. Starting with this drive, and creating a space for open conversation has meant leaders feel comfortable talking about it, sharing and being vulnerable across hierarchies, and it has contributed to their award-winning culture.

3 Name it. We often discuss unconscious bias in such broad and generic terms that we end up dancing around the real and sometimes toxic issues within our environments. It's important to be specific where possible to enable targeted interventions and to ensure we are all fully understanding the issue at hand. When named, we can confront these problems directly.

How can we name it? In order to achieve this, we can ask questions such as *What is the 'it' for your organization? What are the biases in your part of the organization? What does power look and feel like? Is it gender bias? Is it ageism? Is there a dominant culture and are different ethnicities disadvantaged?*

The specifics will vary based on a particular organization's work, and it's crucial to find what needs to be addressed in your organization. In *Included's* partnership with the charity Gatsby Africa[11]) we named the supposed tension between diverse educational backgrounds and the need for critical thinking. As a leading international development charity, operating in the complex contexts of East Africa, cultural intelligence is an essential element of work conducted.

Case studies

Let's look at three case studies that demonstrate different challenges, actions, and impacts from developing CQ.

CASE STUDY

When I Look In The Mirror: How Exploring Cultural Intelligence Helped Me Understand Myself[12]

Shahana Ramsden, Head of Diversity and Inclusion, NHS England and NHS Improvement

Self-awareness has been an essential aspect of my leadership journey. I have spent much of my career trying to understand how my leadership style fits in and what kind of leader I want to be – in a context where I am often the only non-white manager in the room. In my early career, I tried to adopt the leadership styles I witnessed around me, but when I tried to imitate the behaviours of people who didn't look like me, my interventions didn't land in the same way.

The first light bulb moment for me came when I explored the value related to hierarchy and status. I realized that my upbringing had taught me to respect authority and listen to my elders. I reflected on how this had influenced my approach to job interviews – remembering one unsuccessful job application process, where I was advised that there was just 'one point' on the interview scoring template between myself and the other candidate. The reason given was that the successful candidate had 'a certain ease and confidence' that I had not been able to demonstrate. I wonder whether a panel who had been trained in CQ® might have thought differently?

I realized that I might have misunderstood others who were very different from me due to the way they communicated. I reflected on how quickly I built relationships with colleagues who, like me, would openly share their emotions, personal stories, and family photos, and how it was harder for me to engage with people who were less expressive of their feelings and personal backgrounds.

I am conscious that in the complex field of DEI, there is a risk of over-simplifying lessons gained from CQ. On the one hand, not everyone from the same country or background will have the same cultural values, but on the other hand, understanding ourselves in a global context can be very powerful. CQ goes beyond simply understanding these differences to providing the skills to utilize them effectively.

30 years into my career, I reflect on those early days, looking in the mirror, trying to make sense of who I was, and whom I wanted to be. Now, through Cultural Intelligence training, I see the world from a different perspective and feel that when I look in the mirror, I have a better understanding of what I see.

CASE STUDY
Personal leadership: Finding your drive

Lea Paterson is a Board Adviser, writer, a fellow of the Chartered Institute of Personnel Development and former Chief People Officer at the Bank of England.

Challenge

I'd always prided myself as an inclusive leader, as someone who'd valued diversity and inclusion long before it was part of the corporate mainstream. As a long-standing champion of women's rights, the first senior employee in my company to work part-time, and a very active role in mentoring and coaching more junior women, I was proud of my track record on diversity. But that pride blinded me to the race privilege I enjoyed as white woman – a privilege that I did not, could not, recognize until an unexpected comment from a Black colleague made me pause.

I had never anticipated, going into a routine 'town hall' meeting of my company's gender Employee Resource Group, that I was going to hear something that would turn my career narrative on its head. I was chairing the meeting, and one of the last questions of the session was posed by a Black female colleague: 'I was wondering why the steering group of your gender network was all white, and how you see the network supporting ethnic minority women'. I looked around me to my immediate ERG team – they were all white, and, as embarrassed as I am to admit it, it had never even struck me that this was the case until that moment. My white privilege – Strike one.

Strikes two and three followed in quick order. One outcome of my colleague's intervention was that I agreed to sponsor a piece of work on the lived experience of ethnic minority women in our organization. Strike two came when I walked into a room to discuss that work and found I was one of only a handful of white women there. That made me feel uncomfortable, and I felt even more uncomfortable acknowledging my discomfort. Why did I feel like that? And what did it tell me about myself, my biases and my life experience?

Strike three came in the meeting itself. In discussion with a Black colleague, I found myself wondering out loud why I hadn't done more to actively support ethnic minority women. I explained that I was worried about inadvertently giving offence to ethnic minority colleagues, or misrepresenting the challenges at hand. 'Well if you don't mind me saying', my colleague replied, 'attitudes like yours are a big part of the problem.' Strike three. It was time to think differently about race, and how I could be an active anti-racist ally.

Action

A quick 'diversity check' of my immediate circles – social and professional – brought home quite how white they were. I did not grow up in an ethnically diverse area, nor did I live in one with my family. My social circles were pretty much all white. The picture at work was similar: my immediate professional contacts were about as ethnically un-diverse as you could get. The first step was to do something about that.

I made a mental note of the Black women that I had interacted with in the office in the recent past, and dropped them each a line. Would they have time for an informal one-to-one with me over coffee? When we met, I was upfront about the personal challenges I was facing – I wanted to do more to be an active ally and supporter, but wasn't sure where to start and was worried about making a mess of it. Would they minded if we had coffee every month or so – I wanted to listen to their experience and ask for their advice.

One of these early coffees started off another important change. 'As a Black woman,' one said to me 'I get tired of my white colleagues asking me to explain the problems of racism. You need to do the work yourself.' She was right, of course, and this led me to challenge myself to always have at least one book, podcast or article on the go that helped me improve my understanding. I began to diversify my social media contacts, looking to follow more diverse voices. Among other things, I started to plug the many gaps in my knowledge on slavery, and Britain's role in financing and facilitating it.

Impact

The momentum built from there. I began to have more confidence in talking actively about the challenges of race in the workplace. I realized how important it was to use my voice and influence to amplify those who would otherwise struggle to get heard. I began to appreciate that even relatively small actions – for example, commenting on and sharing internal blog posts by ethnic minority colleagues – could have big ripples. Perhaps the most important change happened in my head. In my regular review of our internal diversity statistics, for example, these stopped merely being numbers, and became people. Individuals. All with their own story to tell, and all with their own potential to be realized.

I've come to appreciate that just because I have a lack of privilege in one area – for example, a lack of gender privilege in a male-dominated workplace – that doesn't mean I don't benefit from privilege in another. And that I need to be a catalyst for positive change, including actively challenging the everyday racism that colleagues endure. Perhaps most important of all as a leader, I've learnt an important lesson in humility. About the critical need to seek out challenge to my world view, and to embrace enthusiastically the changes that this challenge brings.

Conclusion

Increasing CQ can help us be more inclusive. CQ is more than just being aware of differences between ourselves and others. It is about becoming an individual who can work with, and relate to, people across a variety of cultural contexts.

It is a set of skills that we can continuously improve and work on, and one that will continue to become even more valuable and critical as diversity grows and our working lives become more global and interconnected. Your drive [how you feel], your knowledge [what you know], your strategy [your plans], or your action [what you do], all four capabilities detailed earlier in this chapter, can be developed to improve our cultural intelligence.

Create time and space to reflect on both your successful as well as unsuccessful intercultural interactions. Make a note of what knowledge and skills you have used [or discovered where absent] during those interactions. Are there any clues you missed, did you misread any part of the interaction and how would you approach that exchange now? Specifically, was there any words, behaviour or actions you did not know how to interpret?

Finally, CQ is all about our capability to work effectively across a range of diverse cultural contexts. As we build our knowledge of others, we also minimize the application of bias. We learn to move from reacting unconsciously, to responding more consciously. By increasing our CQ we increase our inclusion and that's a journey in which we can all be included.

Key takeaways

1 **Yourself:** know and understand yourself. Think about your own 'in-group'; your friends and family. To whom do you reach out to and (possibly more important), to whom do you not reach out to (because you don't want to or it would make you feel uncomfortable)? Use this information to shape your motivations and build your ability to invite and work effectively with difference.

2 **Your leadership:** think about your leadership style. Are you expecting people to adapt to you, or are you willing to adapt to them? This attitude will have a great influence on your leadership and this introspection can help direct where your cultural intelligence improvements can be made.

3 **Your delivery:** Look at how you have previously delivered work and information. What have you done in the past? What have you done in the past to make this a better, more interesting place? Ideally, you let someone else share this while you take a back seat and listen to how they see what you've done. Opening this dialogue can help to increase your openness to richer learning and establish a progressive legacy which will inform your strategy going forward

Further reading

Ang, S, Ng, K, and Rockstuhl, T (2020) Cultural Intelligence. In R Sternberg (Ed), The Cambridge Handbook of Intelligence (Cambridge Handbooks in Psychology, pp. 820–845) Cambridge University Press, Cambridge

BITC, Inclusive Leadership: Culture change for business success (2020) www.bitc. org.uk/wp-content/uploads/2020/03/bitc-gender-report-inclusiveleadership-culturechange-march2020.pdf (archived at https://perma.cc/9R9U-FLBC)

Bluedorn, A C, Kalliath, T J, Strube, M J and Martin, G D (1999) Polychronicity and the Inventory of Polychronic Values (IPV): The development of an instrument to measure a fundamental dimension of organizational culture, Journal of Managerial Psychology, Vol. 14 No. 3/4, pp. 205–231 doi.org/ 10.1108/02683949910263747 (archived at https://perma.cc/Y7FK-2Y77)

Bourke, J and Dillon, B (2018) The diversity and inclusion revolution, Deloitte Review, Issue 22 www2.deloitte.com/content/dam/insights/us/articles/4209_ Diversity-and-inclusion-revolution/DI_Diversity-and-inclusion-revolution.pdf (archived at https://perma.cc/MG9Z-FRPC)

Brislin, R, Worthley, R, and MacNab, B (2006) Cultural intelligence: understanding behaviors that serve people's goals. Group Organ. Manag 31, 40–55

Caterine, G, Diletta G (2018) The Cultural Intelligence Scale (CQS): A Contribution to the Italian Validation. Frontiers in Psychology www.frontiersin.org/ article/10.3389/fpsyg.2018.01183 (archived at https://perma.cc/BA38-W53H)

Cultural Intelligence Centre (2021) Case Studies culturalq.com/case-studies-2/ (archived at https://perma.cc/6ZQH-CKSY)

Cultural Intelligence Centre (2021) Case Study Leadership culturalq.com/case-studies/case-study-leadership/ (archived at https://perma.cc/UP5V-MTQJ)

Cultural Intelligence Centre (2021) Case Study QUT culturalq.com/case-studies/ case-study-qut/ (archived at https://perma.cc/7YUA-93E7)

Deci, E L, and Ryan, R M (1985) Intrinsic Motivation and Self-Determination in Human Behavior. Plenum, New York

Gozzoli C, Gazzaroli D (2018) The Cultural Intelligence Scale (CQS): A Contribution to the Italian Validation, Frontiers in Psychology, 9. doi. org/10.3389/fpsyg.2018.01183 (archived at https://perma.cc/TA9W-NWTP)

Gudykunst, W B, Ting-Toomey, S, and Chua, E (1988) Culture and Interpersonal Communication. Sage, Newbury Park

Included, (2020) Impact Report 2020. www.included.com/wp-content/ uploads/2021/02/Included_Impact_Report_2020.pdf (archived at https://perma. cc/9HA5-2XR7)

Martin, S R (2016) Stories about Values and Valuable Stories: A Field Experiment of the Power of Narratives to Shape Newcomers' Actions, AMJ, 59, 1707–1724 doi.org/10.5465/amj.2014.0061 (archived at https://perma.cc/35TS-U9X6)

Mckinsey & Company (2020) Diversity wins: How inclusion matters www. mckinsey.com/featured-insights/diversity-and-inclusion/diversity-wins-how-inclusion-matters (archived at https://perma.cc/Y8WT-X4GN)

Ramsden, S (2019) When I Look in the Mirror: How exploring cultural intelligence helped me understand myself, Cultural Intelligence Centre.culturalq.com/blog/ how-exploring-cultural-intelligence-helped-me-understand-myself/ (archived at https://perma.cc/8GVZ-2L8J)

Sternberg, R J (2019) A theory of adaptive intelligence and its relation to general intelligence, Journal of Intelligence doi.org/10.3390/jintelligence7040023 (archived at https://perma.cc/78BS-NW7G)

References

1 Lindsey, A, King, E, Hebl, M et al (2015) The Impact of Method, Motivation, and Empathy on Diversity Training Effectiveness, J Bus Psychol 30, 605–617 doi.org/10.1007/s10869-014-9384-3 (archived at https://perma.cc/9AP4-73VJ)
2 Van Dyne, L, Ang, S, Koh, C (2008) Development and validation of the CQS, in: Ang, S, Van Dyne, L (Eds), Handbook of Cultural Intelligence M E
3, 4 Earley, C P, Mosakowski, E (2004) Cultural Intelligence, Harvard Business Review hbr.org./2004/10/cultural-intelligence (archived at https://perma.cc/GG4U-NPBC)
5 Earley, P C, and Ang, S (2003) Cultural Intelligence: Individual Interactions across Cultures. Standford University Press, Palo Alto
6 Gozzoli C, Gazzaroli D (2018) The Cultural Intelligence Scale (CQS): A Contribution to the Italian Validation, Frontiers in Psychology, 9. doi.org/10.3389/fpsyg.2018.01183 (archived at https://perma.cc/RT73-4NWM)
7 Uhlmanni, E L, Heaphy, E, Ashford, S J, Zhu, L, Sanchez-Burks, J (2013) Acting professional: An exploration of culturally bounded norms against nonwork role referencing, journal of Organizational Behaviour, 10.1002/job.1874 www.jeffreysanchezburks.com/blog/wp-content/uploads/Acting-Professional.pdf (archived at https://perma.cc/8S2P-4UUW)
8 SHRM (2015) Cultural Intelligence: The Essential Intelligence for the 21 Century www.shrm.org/hr-today/trends-and-forecasting/special-reports-and-expert-views/Documents/Cultural-Intelligence.pdf (archived at https://perma.cc/EV5L-Z3AN)
9, 10 El-Sharif, F (2019) Jacinda Ardern's solidarity with Muslims should be the norm, not the exception, CNN edition.cnn.com/2019/03/25/opinions/new-zealand-jacinda-ardern-leadership-muslim-community-el-sharif/index.html (archived at https://perma.cc/9C3L-U9PS)
11 Included (2021) Apetito: Inclusive Leadership Programme www.included.com/project/apetito-inclusive-leadership-pogramme/ (archived at https://perma.cc/5Z7B-P5W7)
12 Included (2021) Gatsby Africa: Developing Inclusive Leadership www.included.com/project/developing-inclusive-leadership/ (archived at https://perma.cc/Q58S-S75T)

PART TWO

Unlocking your team

Introduction

STEPHEN FROST

When Desmond Tutu visited the London Olympic and Paralympics 2012 he told us, 'diversity is important so that we know our need of one another'. London 2012 relied on the ultimate team. No matter how brilliant the venue managers were, they couldn't do it without the ticketing experts. And no matter how skilled the ceremonies designers were, they couldn't stage the opening ceremony without thousands of volunteer performers. Tutu was right, we need each other.

So now it's time to turn our attention to teams.

It was critical to start with you. Without self-awareness, and an acknowledgement that this is your work, not someone else's, we can't make environments inclusive. With this clearly stated, it's now time to acknowledge that work doesn't happen in isolation. Even a solitary pursuit such as writing or lecturing involves a team, be it researchers or others with different skill sets.

Teams can be the best of times and the most frustrating of times. Good teams lift you up. They can complement your skill set, teach you something new, cover your blind spots. They are the foundation for how work gets done. How can we maximize the positives and minimize the frustrations?

Every boss wants a high performing team, and inclusive teams perform better. That's generally because people are happier and deploy discretionary effort. People enjoy higher morale, are more creative and share more knowledge.

There is a plethora of inclusive actions from prioritizing face-to-face interactions whenever possible, to getting to know your colleagues on a human level, to considering how you allocate work. These are not ends in themselves. They are critical to creating high performing, inclusive teams that contribute to overall organizational agility. We are moving away from the era of 'departments' and into the era of swarming project teams. Agility is key. And an adaptive, inclusive mindset is key to this.

If you're the executive in charge, be empowering. Provide support and air cover, but then step away and hold the team accountable for outcomes, not inputs or method. If you're a team manager, define those outcomes and take part as one of the team rather than reinforce hierarchy, joining in the problem solving as an equal, coaching and sharing learning. If you're a team member, ask for forgiveness, not for permission and be part of the solution you seek.

The interdependency between you and your team is critical to inclusion working. So, in addition to you, your leadership and your behaviour, there are three critical components that are key to creating inclusive teams.

1 **Understand:** Acknowledge and celebrate differences – when you assemble a team, take the time up front to perform a mini SWOT – work out where people's strengths lie and play to them. Also be alive to any deficiencies or gaps in the team and how you will account for them. Many organizations take this further and conduct a team audit so everyone is aware of what everyone else brings from the get go.

2 **Lead:** We have two ears and one mouth in that ratio for a reason, so listen more than you talk. Communicate clear goals that everyone is aware of, understands and is committed to. Check this, don't assume. Then be prepared to be vulnerable and uncomfortable – the more you can lead by example, the more you elicit reciprocity among your team members. This is critical for creating psychological safety in the team so you can air issues, deal with them and move on rather than getting bogged down in destructive and inefficient politics and drama. Some organizations even go as far as creating dissent channels – ways of channelling disagreements to a good outcome.

3 **Deliver:** Deploy good protocol and measure progress – distribute an agenda in advance to especially benefit colleagues whose first language isn't English or the dominant language in the team, as well as introverts and reflective thinkers. Consider tech and how remote workers can be

pre-emptively included. Rotate meeting times to account for different time zones or childcare or other caring needs. Give credit, rotate the chair, appoint a devil's advocate…

The Key to Inclusion starts with you, but now it's time to translate that into the reality of team work. We'll start with good management practice, discuss various models of deploying team working and finally consider all this in the realm of technological change and different ways of working.

04

Inclusive management practices

DEIRDRE GOLDEN

The Black Mambas are 'the world's first all-female, anti-poaching unit, and, together with 30 other local women, they are saving South Africa's endangered rhinos and elephants'.[1] The Mambas patrol South Africa's Kruger National Park, protecting wild animals from poaching and snaring, a dangerous occupation by anyone's standards. Despite this, they don't carry weapons, instead they are subjected to months of intensive training and survival skills and critically they rely on tight teamwork. Since their founding, in 2013, they have reduced poaching and snaring incidents by 76 per cent.

The Mambas' consistency in team working and their successes enables them to be described as a high performing team. R Katzenbach and Douglas K Smith describe a high-performance team as 'a small number of people with complementary skills who are committed in a common purpose, performance goals, and approach, for which they hold themselves mutually accountable'.[2] Inclusion in the team is an important part of this. It's the glue that creates and binds a successful team together in a situation where the manager ensures that all team members feel valued and that their contribution matters in achieving the overall goal.

However, not all teams work in harmony, particularly where there are different thinking styles, ideas and personalities. While diversity undoubtedly brings benefits, it can also introduce a layer of complexity in team management, and this can be made harder in the context of social and cultural divisions in society when views become polarized.

Creating diverse and inclusive teams

Following the publication of the book, Culture Wars: The Struggle to Define America,[3] Hunter described a dramatic realignment and polarization of American culture encompassing abortion rights, gun laws, gay rights, and more recently with the emergence of the #Blacklivesmatter movement and the #MeToo movement.

In Britain the discussions on many topics have similarly shifted dramatically from what were differences in opinion to polarization on important issues including Britain's vote to exit the European Union in 2016, issues around race and Britain's colonial past, and the interface of women's rights and trans rights.

These social and cultural divisions in wider society inevitably seep into the workplace, and the challenge for many managers is to navigate a path to mutual understanding in the team and nurture inclusion. In this chapter, we'll look at some specific practices to support leaders nurture team diversity and inclusion against a backdrop of wider social disruption. We'll complete an Inclusive Management Checklist starting with hiring, then establishing the right culture, how to manage disagreement and how to socialize inclusively.

Hire for diversity and manage inclusively

Building a diverse team requires taking a strategic, long-term approach, rather than the traditional shortcuts to getting people into the organization. This should be embedded in the organizations recruitment and selection policy. It means everyone involved in the recruitment process should be trained in how to hire diverse talent, and committed to seeing it through even when being pushed back by recruitment agencies or managers citing tight timescales.

1. Build a diverse talent pipeline

- Expand the scope of the traditional pool of colleges or universities beyond those normally visited to include those in more ethnically and socially diverse locations.
- Recruit for potential rather than only looking at what immediate skills and qualifications are needed.

- Undertake an internal review of the talent profile of existing employees and identify diverse talent with the potential to be retrained. This could involve asking employees if they would like to be considered for other roles as well as using psychometric and skills tests.

- Tap into Employee Resource Groups (ERG) to identify diverse talent and to use their knowledge to outreach to local communities to build trust and familiarity with the organization, as well as explaining recruitment and selection processes.

- Where a team is homogenous prepare it for diversity, this is particularly important when welcoming new team members. This could include unconscious bias and diversity training for the team.

- Take regular soundings in the team, either through pulse surveys or one to one discussion to check on the health of the team culture and whether anyone needs some support.

2. Measure performance

Measuring outputs accurately captures what has been produced or actioned, for example, a training initiative measures how many people go through the training; whereas measuring outcomes allows you to see the change that occurs as a result of the training initiative.

Transparency in decision making, fairness in dealing with all team members, encouraging different opinions and listening to team members concerns, as well as regular and honest feedback, help to create confidence in the performance measurement system.

Establish psychological safety and lead by example

An important element that can contribute positively to inclusion and performance is creating psychological safety. According to David Altaman, COO Centre for Creative leadership, psychological safety at work is:

> 'the belief that you won't be punished or humiliated for speaking up with ideas, questions, concerns, or mistakes. When you have psychological safety in the workplace, people feel comfortable being themselves. They bring their full selves to work and feel okay laying all of themselves on the line.'[4]

But how realistic is a state of psychological safety for everyone when people may hold very different views? In today's world this is a difficult path for managers to tread.

When we talk about safe spaces in a work context, it should not only be about hearing what you want to hear, it's also about making a safe place to disagree. Likewise, respect is often mentioned in organizational values, and means having due regard for someone's feelings, wishes, or rights. However, what it should not mean is that you have to totally agree with someone else's view, but rather that you can hear another's view.

This aspect needs attention if managers are to manage inclusively. Clearly, if words or behaviour are blatantly racist, sexist, disablist etc. then it is not acceptable and can be the subject of disciplinary action; but ignoring views and silencing them because they are different can lead to undercurrents of discontent and exclusion which will not go away.

The role of the manager is key to creating an environment where different views that are relevant to the team can sit alongside each other. This can include setting ground rules around participating with positive intent and mutual trust, hearing from everyone, listening without interruption, and not defaulting to the use of labels.

It may also be that a manager has to bring a little less of themselves into the room in order to allow the team members to truly grow and be themselves. This may at first sound counterintuitive, when the idea is that everyone can bring their whole selves to work, but a manager has position and power in relation to the rest of the team, and as such may need to prioritize the needs of the team in that particular situation.

1. Establish norms of behaviour

Set norms of behaviour based on the organization's norms as well as positive intent and trust that can act as touchstones for a team. They can also provide a baseline against which individual and team behaviour can be measured.

- Be transparent and share information with all members of the team.
- Aim for balance when facilitating discussions and ensure that both sides of the argument are presented and heard.
- Draw on facts gathered from reliable, established sources, not hearsay.

- Use a clear decision making process to allocate secondments and opportunities for high profile projects rather than relying on informal networking.
- Ensure fair and equal access to training and development resources, check has everyone heard about them, and whether they need additional support to put themselves forward.

2. Promote dialogue within the team

Recent social developments including #Blacklivesmatter, violence against women and other movements has catapulted inequality into sharp relief, and as a result many organizations in the UK are endeavouring to get a better understanding of the needs and concerns of their employees. Good practice promotes open dialogue about topics such as race in the workplace. Initiatives such as 'Let's talk about race' create a space for employees to discuss their feelings and concerns in the aftermath of George Floyd's murder, with an opportunity to share their own experiences working in the organization.

Lloyd's of London ran a number of open sessions for all colleagues. They advertised them as listening sessions with Pauline Miller, former Head of Culture. Their approach involved creating 90 minute virtual sessions broken into three parts, comprising around 15-20 employees in each session from across the organization (self-selecting).

a Employees were encouraged to discuss their feelings about the death of George Floyd and the impact it had on them personally.

b The second part started a dialogue about their experiences in the organization either from their own individual perspective or as an ally etc. The sessions heard both positive and negative experiences.

c The third part of the session asked employees what types of things they would like to see the organization doing going forward, and in this section they invited two members of the Executive team to be part of the solution.

Following the sessions, Pauline reviewed the comments, aggregated and anonymized them for the leadership committee, which was then turned into a longer term strategy. One interesting finding was that some of the actions were already underway in the organization, but communication hadn't been as effective as it could have been in sharing this.

3. *Measure and report on inclusion*

Monitoring inclusion in the team is important to ensure that no-one is left out or disengaged. This can be done through a variety of measures, drawing on hard data or soft data (see an upcoming section), as well as using a bespoke Inclusion Diagnostic, which allows in-depth assessment of how the team is feeling and enables comparison over time. Chapter eight has further information on the Inclusion Diagnostic.[5]

- Create regular check-ins with the team particularly following virtual meetings, for example asking people to score how they are feeling; this can then be drawn on at the start of the next meeting or discussion to try and pinpoint what did not go well.
- 360 feedback in the team.
- Quarterly pulse surveys measuring employee engagement;
- One tech company has launched an employee resource group called an inclusion collective (see chapter 14, Inclusion in Tech), focused on exploring ways of being more inclusive, for example, how to balance remote and in-person working, allyship and inclusive communication.
- There are also a growing number of platforms, such as In Chorus, that provide an opportunity for employees to informally and anonymously report unacceptable comments and behaviours which enables the organization to measure and resolve such incidents.

Manage dissent and disagreement proactively

Conflict or disagreement is not unusual in a team and can arise for any number of reasons, so it needs to be recognized and managed proactively and not swept under the carpet. For example, conflict can arise when a team member believes that the views of another in the team are very different to their own. The manager needs to understand from the individual exactly why they feel like they do and what exactly has occurred.

The role of the manager is key in setting ground rules that allow everyone to be heard. Ground rules such as participation with positive intent and mutual trust, hearing from everyone, listening without interruption and not defaulting to the use of labels.

Where feelings are high they must be acknowledged, but rather than rush to judgement, a more considered or thoughtful approach needs to be taken to cut through the emotion and get to the bottom of the issue. An experienced Global D&I practitioner once told me that the first thing to do in situations of conflict or intense disagreement is to separate out the heat and the light from the topic and get to the facts of the situation, rather than reacting to heightened emotion.

Establishing the facts can be difficult to do when someone is angry or upset, and it requires the manager to respond by creating a safe space to listen to the complainant; to clarify exactly what was said and by whom; to hear the context of the situation; then to hear from the other party; identify any witnesses etc. and then allow some time for the heat of the emotion to settle. It may mean getting the two parties together and facilitate a discussion, or where a more serious complaint is made to follow a formal investigation process.

The reality is, for learning to take place we need to hear each other's viewpoints even if they are not aligned with our own. The aim is not to agree with everything that is being heard, but to enable people, particularly those in a team, to hear each other and critique the views and behaviours, rather than the person.

1. Take action when things go wrong

A key source of dissatisfaction for employees is when poor behaviour results in nothing to be done. While the ultimate responsibility lies with the manager or leader, every individual team member should also be empowered to call out unacceptable behaviour. This is easier said than done. It requires trust in the process, and a belief that an employee will be listened to.

Witnessing unacceptable behaviour and not acting can be construed as colluding in the behaviour, or acting as a bystander, which brings its own stress. If someone feels powerless or intimidated they may choose the line of least resistance and keep their head down which reinforces a toxic culture.

Speaking up about unacceptable behaviour, or 'speaking truth to power' by taking a stand about something that goes against prevailing opinion, requires courage, particularly as a lone voice. The situation is exacerbated where the unacceptable behaviour comes from a more senior source. In a situation which is moving beyond the manager's ability to manage dialogue and collaboration between team members, it may be most appropriate to seek advice and help from the HR department.

Many organizations have a whistle blowing service, but this route tends to focus more on financial irregularity or misconduct, rather than on cultural issues. Speaking to an Ally can of course provide vital support to an individual who may find it difficult to speak up.

Organizations use different methods to listen to employees' concerns: Standard Chartered Bank holds an open session with employees through an annual webinar providing employees with the opportunity to ask the Board questions; Chanel uses listening groups to tap which act as a useful way to allow the organization to tap into employee concerns.

However, where there are deep rooted issues that people feel they cannot speak about in an open session, a different approach is needed. For example, the Guardian Service is being used in some National Health Service Trusts (NHS). It was set up in 2013 in response to the Francis Investigation into failures of care, leadership and culture at Mid Staffordshire NHS Foundation Trust.[6]

The service is a 24/7 confidential service to encourage and support staff to speak up about their issues, concerns and discover ideas to form resolutions. It provides employees access to trained people from an external independent organization, providing a confidential opportunity for employees to raise specific work related or work culture issues and seek advice, support, and identify solutions.

2. Managing diverse perspectives

In 2018, James Damore, a software engineer at Google's headquarters in Silicon Valley posted a document in an internal on-line discussion forum. The document entitled 'Google's Ideological Echo Chamber' questioned the company's diversity efforts. In a memo, Damore outlined in detail his ideas and evidence to support his views.

One of the more contentious points he asserted was that women are underrepresented in the technology industry not because of bias and discrimination but because 'preferences and abilities of men and women differ in part due to biological causes'.[7]

As the memo went viral the backlash was swift and Google reacted by firing Mr Damore. In turn, Mr Damore sued Google for firing him, arguing that he was punished for 'heterodox political views and for being a white male'.[8]

In common with many organizations, Google champions a culture of openness, diversity of thinking and courage to speak up, principles we would all agree with. But what happens when someone says something that doesn't align with what is perceived as the right message? Presenting a view that sits in between the stated philosophy or creed of the organization, and a total rejection of it, what I call the 'grey areas'.

In an email to all employees, Google's chief executive, Sundar Pichai clarified Google's course of action and said that portions of the memo had violated the company's code of conduct and crossed the line 'by advancing harmful gender stereotypes in our workplace'.[9]

As seen in Chapter 1, cognitive diversity includes people with different perspectives, ideas, lived experience, problem solving methods etc. It therefore opens up the potential for many different viewpoints being shared, some of which may be not align with the corporate viewpoint, and however difficult, everyone has the right to have an opinion and express it.

This provides a challenge for managers seeking different thinking, and to ensure that the views expressed are coming from a constructive perspective and don't cross the line into views that are contrary to organization values and policies, or the law. Regularly reminding the team of the organization values, and the requirement for positive intent in all discussions will help set the tone.

It also means ensuring that the organization's work on diversity and inclusion is regularly revisited and communicated to employees to ensure consistency of understanding, accepted behaviours re-maintained and reminding why D&I work is so important. It is easy for myths to develop if left unchallenged.

Earlier in my career, I ran an employer's network comprising senior DEI specialists who met to discuss DEI developments, share practices and learn from each other in a confidential environment. Naturally the Google case generated a lot of discussion, but what was clear was that many, not all, felt that perhaps Google could have taken a different course, drawing on the situation to generate a controlled discussion of the issues in the organization, sharing its own data in real time and lead facilitated discussion drawing on expert opinion on the issues raised. This would have upheld the organization's values of openness and difference providing an opportunity for the organization to put into context its data and its perspective on the issue as well as explore why some employees felt their views weren't being heard.

Work and socialize inclusively

1. Practice inclusive meetings

In-person situations afford the opportunity to be aware of body language, general engagement and to see if team members are paying attention, as well as enable the manager to pick up on whether a team member is not OK. But in the virtual world, this is much more difficult; for example, if someone's camera is switched off, how do you pick up on any of this? The issue isn't about the camera per se, nor is it about whether someone crochets in a meeting to aid their concentration, but about doing things that are non-work related.

- Meetings should last no longer than necessary and space out virtual meeting calls to ensure people have a break between calls to prevent fatigue.
- Establish ground rules up front, including protocols around camera use and how questions and discussion will be coordinated.
- Take a few minutes at the start of the meeting to ask how people are/what is going on in their lives, with the team manager leading by example. Replicate things people do naturally when they meet in person to help to create a sharing environment.
- Ensure every member of the team speaks, for example go round the virtual room as you would do in an in-person meeting.
- Be aware of your own affinity bias when asking questions and responding to people, and take steps to guard against it.
- After the meeting check in with each participant in the meeting to ask them how it felt for them.
- At each meeting change the order of who speaks first.

2. Managing inclusion in a remote environment

In 2013, Yahoo! CEO Marissa Mayers ended Yahoo's remote-working 'experiment' when she mandated that all employees return to the office to work in person.[10] It was one of a number of actions taken by the new CEO and was part of a drive to reset the culture. Yahoo felt that the collaboration and interaction from in-person working was diffused by remote working and having a negative impact on the culture of the organization.

An inclusive culture is formed by norms of behaviour that set expected behaviours and engender trust. Moving to a remote environment, without compensating for the loss of in-person connectedness can change the norms of behaviour and affect team morale and productivity.

This is one of the most important learnings from the lockdown experience. Social connectedness and in-person relationships are fragile and cannot be taken for granted. People are subject to emotion and sensitive to the conditions they find themselves in and may require some additional measures to support inclusion in these circumstances.

- With advance notice, introduce regular 'all-in days', where the whole team comes together.

- Use a round robin technique to hear from everyone on the screen/in the office. Let team members know in advance you are going to ask them to share something personal etc. Start with yourself as manager and then onto reflectors or introverts to ensure their voices are heard.

- Use a technique such as a Hackathon to create an event which could be a half day or day, where the team can come together to solve a specific problem(s). While it is used extensively in the IT industry it can be applied in most environments enabling a problem to be continually reviewed and refined to solution. Its usefulness lies in its ability to bring all team members together to work towards a solution.

- Cameras switched on should be the default position, unless someone has a particular issue in which case they should raise this with the manager in advance.

- Deploy regular pulse surveys to take the temperature of the team; create a feedback loop; and share feedback with the whole team to ensure everyone has the opportunity to hear what is being said and facilitate discussion.

3. Team building

Socializing together is important to teambuilding, however consideration needs to be given to ensuring everyone can partake. In the UK, drinking alcohol is a big part of socializing, but for others this may not be the case. This doesn't just apply to those who do not drink because of religious or cultural reasons, but for anyone who prefers not to partake in an alcohol-based event. Alcohol can often fuel unacceptable behaviours; this can leave some people feeling exposed and vulnerable to the kinds of actions that can follow on from this.

Taking a more considered and inclusive approach to socializing and team building events means being more creative in what it could be.

Good management is inclusive management

In the wake of the pandemic, employee attrition rates have been increasing. Employees are reassessing their lives; many have endured unprecedented disruption, possibly illness and personal pain or bereavement, as well as job insecurity or job loss. However, inclusive managers can be the critical factor in persuading talent to stay.

For example, recent events such as the impact and aftermath of the #Blacklivesmatter movement could have led people, particularly those from Black and minority communities to question how their own organization responded to these events, and possibly finding them lacking in their response, leaving them feeling not heard and disengaged.

Many employees juggling multiple responsibilities may also have rated their employer unfavourably in their support for them.

These reassessments may have led people to think more deeply about what they want from an employer. The old psychological contract may not hold the same attraction it once had. The pandemic has brought opportunity as well as hardship, and people may now be looking to shape a new psychological contract.

The reset button has been pushed in a multitude of ways, and it has also presented an opportunity to rethink how we work, where we work, and when we work. If managers don't get ahead of these trends and lead their teams in an inclusive fashion, they may simply not have performing teams in the future.

Key takeaways

- Suggest ideas for team events or ask the team what they would like to do. Consider individual preferences; this does not mean for example that an event with alcohol is no longer allowed, it could mean alternating events and venues so everyone has the chance to participate.

- Ensure any events are managed with consideration of people who have caring, parental or other responsibilities that impact them attending events outside of working hours.

- Remind everyone attending a work social event that they are representing the company and appropriate respectful behaviour is required.

Further reading

The Chartered institute of Personnel and Development (2021) How to talk about race at work www.cipd.co.uk/knowledge/fundamentals/relations/diversity/conversations-race-work#gref (archived at https://perma.cc/3GXN-5G6S)

References

1 Goyanes, C (2017) These Badass women are taking on poachers – and winning. National Geographic www.nationalgeographic.com/adventure/article/black-mambas-anti-poaching-wildlife-rhino-team (archived at https://perma.cc/JK8G-FBBU)

2 Katzenbach, R Smith, D K (1992) The Wisdom of Teams: Creating the High Performance Organization. Harvard Business Review Press, Brighton

3 Hunter, J D (1991) Culture Wars: The Struggle to Define America. Basic Books, New York

4 Altaman, D (2020) What is psychological safety at work? Center for Creative Leadership www.ccl.org/articles/leading-effectively-articles/what-is-psychological-safety-at-work/ (archived at https://perma.cc/467H-EWYX)

5 Included (2020) Impact Report www.included.com/impact-report/impact-report-2020/ (archived at https://perma.cc/CM44-RB6B)

6 Francis, R (2013) Report of the Mid Staffordshire NHS Foundation Trust Public Enquiry: Executive Summary [PDF] assets.publishing.service.gov.uk/government/uploads/system/uploads/attachment_data/file/279124/0947.pdf (archived at https://perma.cc/T7DS-3723)

7, 8 Damore, J (2017) Google's Echo Chamber. Gizmodo. gizmodo.com/exclusive-heres-the-full-10-page-anti-diversity-screed-1797564320) (archived at https://perma.cc/B3NE-BTF7)

9 NBC News (2018) Revolution: Google and Youtube Changing the World [Video] www.youtube.com/watch?v=_M_rSFBYEe8&list=PLDIVi-vBsOExzqg6JEfk35vd5AUrLFYf_ (archived at https://perma.cc/E942-PH9G)

10 Goudreau, J (2013) Back to the Stone Age? New Yahoo CEO Marissa Mayer Bans Working from Home, Forbes www.forbes.com/sites/jennagoudreau/2013/02/25/back-to-the-stone-age-new-yahoo-ceo-marissa-mayer-bans-working-from-home/ (archived at https://perma.cc/SE82-BBAT)

Acknowledgements and thanks

Pauline Miller
Barbara Pryce
Maria Angelica Perez
Mary Walsh
Sinead Daly
Jill Rothwell
Lt Michael Golden RN

05

Employer models

PRIYA RADIA

While based in Iraq, in 2003, General Stanley McChrystal of the Joint Special Operations Task Force (JSOTF) took a rather unusual approach to leading his team. Al Qaeda's speed of change was keeping them two steps ahead, and McChrystal understood that no increase in capacity or technology was going to help. The JSOTF team desperately needed internal change.

Military organizational structure is known for its disciplined, hierarchical frameworks, but McChrystal transformed his task force into a network of smaller groups or a *team of teams*. Interconnected, transparent, and agile, these teams were able to function more effectively, and react quicker to change.[1]

In the corporate world, some of the biggest organizational transformations have also been initiated by drastic changes in missions and visions. A key element of their successful execution has been a deliberate focus on designing core team structures and foundations that underpin day-to-day activities.

Employer models and inclusion

Organizational models and team structures are a way of dividing up work. They consist of elements such as roles and responsibilities, managerial structures, and decision making power. Culturally, they also inform communication methods, levels of collaboration, autonomy, and employee relationships. This impacts culture, levels of employee engagement, trust, and perceptions of inclusion. We begin this chapter by examining some common employer models and their impacts on inclusion. We will then look at recent influencing factors, as well as ideas to consider when incorporating inclusion into your organizational model.

Tried and tested: traditional employer models

There is an endless list of types of team structures in existence today – from hierarchies, to function-based, process-led, circular, or even *flatarchies*. While newer models have surfaced from trends in technology or changing cultural demands, traditional models emerged from one of the biggest events in business history: the Industrial Revolution. Let's recap some of the most common models:

FIGURE 5.1 Common team models

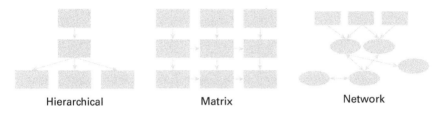

Hierarchical   Matrix   Network

Hierarchical team structures

Perhaps the most traditional of all is the hierarchy. An authoritarian approach where individuals have an identifiable chain of command, processes are formalized, and regulations clearly defined –with all of these pillars held up by a foundation of strict discipline. Initially developed in manufacturing, it proved extremely beneficial for standardization, consistency, rationalization and low-cost operations.[2] Its natural rigidity and one way flow of communication and decision making power, however, has proven to be unsustainable in many cases.[3]

We still see a strong presence of hierarchical tendencies in governmental and military organizations, but efforts have been made to move away from these. The UK National Health Service (NHS) is one such example that has been a thoroughly heated political debate with millions invested in structural transformation – for example, through the establishment of teams of Clinical Commissioning Groups to decentralize decisions on healthcare budgets.[4]

From a DEI lens, standardized processes and regulations could be beneficial for equality, especially if these processes are less biased. For example, if all employees must follow the same hiring and promotion processes, it might reduce the chances of preferential treatment through networking, or the impacts of in and out groups. But what about individuals who need adjustments? Inclusion is, after all, about organizations and teams adapting to meet the needs of people – not the other way around. The concentration of power at the top of a hierarchy can also make it trickier to collaborate well, communicate transparently and, perhaps most importantly, build a sense of psychological safety between teams and leadership that can exist beyond the distinct barriers of 'us and them'.

Matrix team structures

Globalization and the rise of service work has increased the popularity of matrix structures, reaping the benefits of both hierarchical and flat structures. A halfway point – moving towards more decentralized decision making and cross-coordination of resources between different functions, departments, products, or geographies. From a DEI perspective, while these elements can make it easier for teams to adapt to changing demographics, or increase the range of perspectives and skills accessible for projects, it can also add another layer of complexity and grounds for greater internal conflicts.[5]

Imagine, for example, that your role as Hiring Manager has positioned you in the HR department as well as the Research and Development function. This could be useful for inclusive recruitment as you have access to insights from both teams to support decision making, such as inviting diverse individuals to an interview panel. The dual nature of your position might also mean, however, that you have to co-ordinate and communicate with twice as many people, or even balance conflicting strategic directions. This can complicate, and bias, decision making, and make clear communication more difficult – two key factors influencing perceptions of team inclusion. Furthermore, *your own* experience in HR might be very different to colleagues at the same level but in a different arm of the business; the matrix makes it more difficult to maintain equity across the organization.

Network team structures

Flatter in structure, this model leans towards shared responsibilities, decentralized decision making, and autonomy within each team. Networks focus less on rules and processes, and more on teamwork and agility which can bring huge benefits from a DEI lens. Less stringent processes can make it easier to more quickly adapt to employee needs, and increase the pace of change around DEI initiatives. Open, collaborative cultures can support psychological safety in both teams and leaders where opinions from different seniority levels are equally valued. Broader participation in decision making lends itself to greater transparency and objectivity, and access to a more diverse range of voices.

But what happens without strong visionary leadership? Without an accountable, inclusive culture? Lack of structural discipline could result in negative consequences where bias or discrimination is present – allowing it to manifest more easily without intervention. Computer game development company Valve is a theoretically flat organization, whose viral employee handbook initially earned its 'no management structure' high praise.[6] In recent years, however, interviews have revealed its 'pseudo-flat culture', with a 'hidden layer of powerful management structure'[7] which has led to favouritism being more valued than skills. This is a prime example of where bias is given free rein, and exclusionary groups of employees can lead to low levels of transparency, objectivity and psychological safety.

Team of teams

This final model stems back to agile methodology. Infamous in the world of software development, agile ways of working have been dramatically reshaping the technology sector over the last two decades. In its simplest form, agile methodology strives to enable people, projects, and businesses to adapt quicker and more efficiently.[8] A particular example is the team of teams model[9]:

FIGURE 5.2 Team models

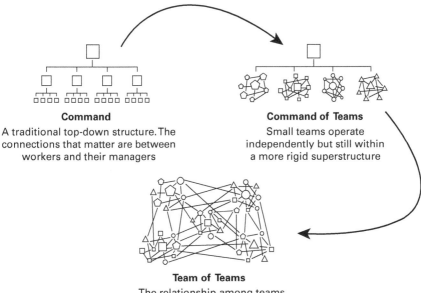

Command
A traditional top-down structure. The connections that matter are between workers and their managers

Command of Teams
Small teams operate independently but still within a more rigid superstructure

Team of Teams
The relationship among teams resembles the closeness among individuals on those teams

Team of teams has seen significant success in times of crisis. We discussed McChrystal's story, who states that launching and empowering small teams that can function without the barriers of organizational structure, enables organizations to 'respond more quickly, communicate more freely, and make faster and better decisions'. Many larger organizations (including Cisco, Google, and Apple) use elements of this at scale through a 'command of teams'.[10] Jeff Bezos's rule that any team should be small enough that it can be fed with two pizzas is a major contributing factor to Amazon's flexibility and innovation - with teams working towards a common, shared goal.[11] Smaller team sizes have also been linked to enhanced employee motivation, engagement and creativity.[12]

How might this structure impact DEI? Cross-functional teams (across departments or seniority levels) can capture greater diversity of thought. Sourcing teams by skills rather than hierarchies can support employees feeling valued if they are recognized for their strengths and not bypassed because of other characteristics. The self-managing and self-organizing nature can also help employees to bring their ideas, expertise, and initiatives to the table and make their voices heard.[13]

California-based The Morning Star Company operates with c. 600 permanent staff and over 4,000 seasonal workers. Their secret to success? Zero managers. Instead, they operate on a principle that structures will come and go according to the organization's needs.[14] Employees are empowered to define their own roles, collaborate among teams and even manage topics such as compensation or internal conflicts through a peer-review process. The business has seen good employee engagement, loyalty and transparency; they are proof that self-managing structures are in fact, scalable.[15]

Current trends affecting team structures

Change can quickly escalate the complexity of an organizational model. A range of macro-environmental factors have influenced the way leaders structure their teams; from political and economic events such as Brexit and COVID-19 lockdowns, to more social and technological trends such as the growth of e-commerce, remote work, and increasing awareness of a healthy work/life balance.

Of these, there are three influences we believe have had a far-reaching impact, most significantly when it comes to workplace inclusion:

1. Digital transformation: the fourth industrial revolution

Technology has seen exponential growth in the last few decades – the AI industry alone is expected to be worth $190 billion by 2025.[16] From applicant tracking systems in HR, to Customer Relationship Management platforms in Sales, we have access to a wealth of smart technology and the data it provides. Structurally, some jobs will continue to see machines replacing people.[17] Technology has also made it easier to naturally move towards more inclusive structures.

Take for example – instant messaging. Interactions are no longer confined by geographical office locations or who you might sit with in the cafeteria. Employees now have access to search for and message any employee – in any location, any team, and at every seniority – through a couple of clicks on Teams, Slack, or Hangouts. This can support inclusion from a psychological safety perspective, both with leaders (who are more accessible) and within teams (through quicker, easier collaboration).

2. The future workforce

If you've stumbled across a restaurant, gallery or tourist attraction in 2021, you've likely witnessed someone filming videos for TikTok – the latest social media app taking the post-pandemic world by storm. Its key driver? Gen Z.[18] Millennials (born 1981 – 1996) and Gen Z (born 1997 onwards) have increasingly become majority groups in the workplace and their expectations have changed.

TikTok's catapult into popularity is a perfect example of how exposure to global and digital interconnectedness has changed needs and behaviours. A 2018 McKinsey study showed that expression of individual truth, the need to be 'radically inclusive' and have dialogue over confrontations, are key characteristics of this group.[19] TikTok users can explore their creativity through short videos and interact with peers globally. Amidst the ever-growing noise of the world, ultimately – they want their voices to be heard.

In the workplace, there is a higher demand for autonomy, creativity, collaboration, communication and inclusion. For Millennials, inclusion is 'a culture of connectedness that facilitates teaming, collaboration and professional growth'.[20] These elements lean towards a flatter model; rigid processes can not only make it more difficult to satisfy these needs, but also lead to widening generational divides.[21] In contrast, previous generations defined inclusion as 'the acceptance and tolerance of demographically diverse individuals', indicating views less intertwined with culture, ways of working, or cognitive diversity.

Toronto-based chatbot provider Ada is one company improving generational inclusion through improved flexibility and autonomy – such as unlimited holidays and flexible hours.[22] Dating app Thursday is another example, tasking a 22-year-old student intern with a £25 budget and a goal to reach 1000 downloads.[23] Her creative marketing activities led to a viral social media post and contributed to the app jumping from 154th to 7th place in the Global App Store Charts in 6 hours.[24] The diversity of thought that led to these outcomes might have been more difficult to access in a hierarchical environment – where decision making power is more concentrated among senior roles.

3. COVID and the rise of hybrid work

Remote and hybrid work are rapidly on the rise (see Chapter 6), bringing a flexibility that means teams no longer need to physically work from the same place, or even in the same time zones. This affects everything from reporting structures and recruitment processes, to personal and professional communication styles.

From an inclusion lens, the impact has been mixed. A recruitment benefit is access to a more diverse pool of candidates beyond geographical limitations. However, this could alter reporting structures. Managers overseeing cross-cultural teams will subsequently need to be more aware of the significance of cultural intelligence in building an inclusive environment. Another impact is on psychological safety; insights into everyday lives (and children/pets screaming in the background) have blurred the once more distinct lines between personal and professional worlds. One of *Included's* pharmaceutical clients said to us that virtual work has enabled leaders to engage with their teams 'human to human' for the first time.

The *future* of hybrid work must be carefully considered to ensure there is equal inclusion of those in the office or working virtually. As a team leader, how can you be conscious of the fact that women are likely to have higher workloads (on average – 15 hours more a week) than men? Or if more women opt to continue remote working, how can you ensure their progress will not be hindered by bias that favours men with extra face time in the office?[25]

Building inclusive teams

This section is divided according to *Included's* five service areas: Strategy, Data, Governance, Leadership and Systems. As we move through each, we will explore actions you can take as a team leader to incorporate inclusivity into your immediate environment and various client examples. Keep in mind that company size, industry and existing models will no doubt influence some of the below ideas.

Strategy

In an organizational design survey by Deloitte, over 80 per cent of respondents said they were either currently restructuring or had recently completed one.[26] If organization-wide transformation plans are already underway, think about how a new structure will impact your team. For example, consider conducting interviews with direct reports around DEI expectations – what impact will your proposed model have on inclusion? Will it help or hinder it?

If structural transformation is not on the roadmap, there are still actions you can implement into your existing teams as shown in Table 5.1:

TABLE 5.1 Improving inclusion in your team through strategy

Your current structure	Ways to improve inclusion in your team
Hierarchical	• If you are part of the senior leadership team, consider designing an action plan with targets to ensure appropriate diversity among senior leadership. A 2019 McKinsey study found that 'companies in the top quartile for gender diversity on executive teams were 25 per cent more likely to have above-average profitability than companies in the fourth quartile' – diverse senior leaders will support both your moral and business case for inclusion.[27] • Transparency and psychological safety may be more difficult to achieve. For example, where decisions are made exclusively at the top, employees can feel left in the dark. Consider developing a strategic communications plan, which includes frequent, honest, two-way communications from you to your immediate reports.
Matrix/ mixed	• Increased complexity can cause misalignments in DEI strategic directions between subsidiaries, departments, and teams. At a team level, something as simple as reaching out to peers in other teams can help you to understand if everyone is on the same page. Employee resource and network groups are also helpful to lean on if they sit across all the different teams of the business.
Flat	• Where roles are less clearly defined, accountability for a DEI strategy is essential (see also Governance) – is there a dedicated DEI team? In your immediate team, is there an awareness of what this strategy is?

EXAMPLE:

In 2021, *Included* conducted a Strategy Alignment Workshop for a function of a management consultancy. Participants recognized that the existing organization-wide, hierarchical nature contributed to its culture and created barriers to inclusion. Together, we assessed the team's DEI maturity, upcoming actions, and further recommendations on how to improve inclusion in their function, while maintaining their broader core structures. Ideas included pilot projects where teams were chosen based on individual strengths, and an alternative approach to project planning through which expectations around working hours were set up front. The aim was to empower the team to move from a fast-paced, stressful, 'System 1' mode to one where they could successfully leverage their unique mix to deliver high quality client deliverables while maintaining a suitable work/life balance.

Data

Data is a crucial supporting pillar across all DEI efforts; it enables you to measure the success of initiatives, highlight existing gaps, predict future trends, and guide more targeted interventions. Leveraging a combination of quantitative and qualitative data (focus groups or interviews) can give you rich insights into existing levels of inclusion, as well as finding out whether any structural issues might be causing feelings of exclusion. Other ideas are included in Table 5.2:

TABLE 5.2 Improving inclusion in your team through data

Your current structure	Ways to improve inclusion in your team
Hierarchical	• Thinking about the impacts of newer generations and the pandemic, consider combining future workforce projections with a strategic horizon scanning exercise to anticipate potential structural changes. E.g., if your team needs to adapt to hybrid working permanently.
	• Analyse data insights with a structural lens. E.g., if promotion rates in women or ethnic minority groups is an issue, are hierarchical practices hindering equal opportunities?
	• As a team manager, lead by example on data gathering efforts to support strong response rates. Another simple action is to reach out to direct reports to check if your team structures are contributing to any feelings of exclusion.

(continued)

TABLE 5.2 (Continued)

Matrix/ mixed	• In more complex structures, communicate with other teams to ensure you have a consistent methodology across the business. This will provide the most accurate, comparable data and support knowledge sharing on best practice inclusion initiatives.
	• Reaching out to direct reports is also recommended here.
Flat	• In more open structures, confidentiality may be a concern for employees when providing data. Define and communicate to your team who holds the data to boost psychological safety and data collection rates.
	• As teams have smaller populations, be careful what you report on to ensure individuals are not identifiable. E.g., with 100 employees, not publishing results for groups with less than 5 individuals would be a good threshold for maintaining confidentiality.

EXAMPLE:

The Bank of England is an organization with an established structure, protocols and traditions. *Included* partnered with the Bank to run an Inclusion Diagnostic which highlighted a variation in inclusion by seniority levels for both gender and ethnicity. While legacy hierarchy still existed in the Bank, *Included* recommended a Sponsorship Programme to help senior leaders work towards decreasing this barrier. This included participation from the Governor, and resulted in impact across all different teams of the organization.

Governance

Roles and responsibilities are a key element of organizational structures. In any type of structure, networks such as Employee Resource Groups (ERGs) can provide employees with a support route for specific DEI matters. These should be open to and accessible by **all** teams and seniority levels. Table 5.3 shows some further ideas:

TABLE 5.3 Improving inclusion in your team through governance

Your current structure	Ways to improve inclusion in your team
Hierarchical	• How do reporting structures work? Consider factors such as how many direct reports each manager has – too many can dilute a leader's attention and weaken team bonds.
	• Who is accountable and responsible for key business decisions? How are these communicated? Where decision making is centralized, ensure there is a clear path of communication from decision makers to your team members – this could be as simple as hosting Q&A sessions, or encouraging decision makers to be more open on internal communication channels.
Matrix/ mixed	• Both suggestions above will be equally important here.
	• For employees with multiple managers, does each individual have access to someone they can raise questions and concerns to? Ensure communication channels are clearly defined so there are fewer barriers to an employee feeling able and empowered to speak up.
Flat	• With less stringent structures, pay close attention to how you form teams. Is diversity of thought (demographics, perspectives, experiences) present in each team? Challenge teams that are formed purely through networking, or 'in groups' and develop skill-based criteria instead.
	• Do you have an appropriate accountability culture in place to avoid bias or discrimination in processes/decision making? Consider developing a team RACI or leaning on cultural initiatives to encourage team members to own and share their mistakes in a safe space.

EXAMPLE:

In 2021, *Included* partnered with a national regulator to develop their governance frameworks. The firm had complex internal structures, a vast range of stakeholder groups involved, and nine ERGs that were more in competition with each other than aligned through a common goal. The Executive team had 'Champions' and 'Sponsors' – however, the People function found that the titles were more ceremonial and actions were being isolated as a 'HR activity'.

Through a redesigned framework and recommendations, we identified ways to strengthen and clarify roles and responsibilities. This resulted in stronger governance around how stakeholder groups were managed, clearer communications strategies, and greater accountability that supported DEI outcomes in both the workplace as well as the firm's outward-facing position as a regulator.

Leadership

A client once said to me that 'leaders are the system' – ultimately, their behaviours are a reflection of the organization and will impact how employees experience their working life. For any type of structures, it is key to engage *all levels* and teams in activities such as allyship, unconscious bias or psychological safety training. More ideas are included in Table 5.4:

TABLE 5.4 Improving inclusion in your team through leadership

Your current structure	Ways to improve inclusion in your team
Hierarchical	• Hierarchical leadership does not automatically mean not inclusive; in your immediate teams, consider borrowing characteristics of flatter structures such as more open collaboration and communication to boost psychological safety, or implementing Amazon's team size rule. If you manage a large team, can you split them up into smaller, informal working groups?
Matrix/mixed	• If you are a team leader with reports across geographies, pay close attention to cultural intelligence. How can you ensure that your language, actions and ways of working are appropriate for different cultures?
Flat	• Even flatter structures can see exclusionary behaviours develop, making it even more important for *all* individuals to be leaders in the DEI space. Emphasize the idea that all employees need to own their actions and impact in order to create a truly inclusive environment.

EXAMPLE:

I started my own career in a quite hierarchical front office investment bank, and over the years made my way to the current 15-person *Included* team. At each job change, I moved to a slightly smaller, flatter business and the changes I've seen and felt when it comes to personal feelings of inclusion, perceptions of leadership and culture have been quite significant. It's much easier to feel psychologically safe with a leader who is almost a team member – and walks the walk when it comes to inclusive leadership behaviours.

Systems

Clear, unbiased processes are a key starting point. This includes recruitment, promotions, hiring and redundancies – as well as embedding inclusion into processes such as product design (Table 5.5).

TABLE 5.5 Improving inclusion in your team through systems

Your current structure	Ways to improve inclusion in your team
Hierarchical or matrix/mixed	• In cases of discrimination or microaggressions, are lengthy bureaucratic processes disincentivizing employees to report these or talk about them? Consider assigning ownership to an employee within your own team who can directly handle such cases. An anonymous alternative is also useful for collecting open and honest feedback.
Flat	• Hiring for team 'cultural fit', or bias arising from networking and personal relationships is a risk to DEI progress. Ensure there is appropriate training for your hiring managers, as well as the tools and technology to support them (e.g. blind CVs, applicant tracking systems, access to diverse job boards and agencies). Individually, think about how you can challenge day to day behaviours that contribute to exclusive environments. • Define appropriate support routes for any cases of discrimination, and a fair process to resolve these. These can often be less clear in flatter organizations and disincentivize employees to speak up.

EXAMPLE

Included worked with a consultancy with inclusion and retention issues for women and younger employees. As part of the process re-engineering recommendations, we suggested improvements to internal recruitment processes which enabled employees to move laterally throughout the organization. Using a tool such as Profinda, leaders were able to search the database by skills and not by name. This not only reduced waste, but also ensured teams were formed based on skills and not purely through networking.

Summary

Organizations have naturally developed in very different ways over the years. Extreme versions of any model, hierarchal of flat, can be a risk when building inclusive workplaces. Hierarchical structures present barriers through bureaucracy, and flatter structures need to be more carefully designed to ensure full participation from all employees. Considering the changes we have seen culturally and technologically, combined with the key elements that form perceptions of inclusion – it is more evident that characteristics of flat structures make it easier to foster an inclusive environment.

No team structure is fixed. Regardless of what your organization-wide structure is, as a team leader you can implement solutions in your immediate environment to meet the needs of the business, your team, and your clients in the most effective and inclusive way.

Key takeaways

1 Types of team models range from tall and hierarchical to completely flat and agile. While it is possible to build inclusive environments in each, **characteristics of flatter structures lend themselves more towards inclusion.**

2 The size of your business, industry and macro-environmental changes will also impact both your structure and levels of inclusion; **being able to** *adapt* **in your team is an essential characteristic.**

3 There are a number of practical steps you can take without dramatic restructuring, such as communications plans or data collection. Being aware of and able to mitigate any structural disadvantages (such as centralized decision making in a hierarchy) is key to achieving an inclusive team.

Further reading

Brozovich, B G, John Golden III, and Stephen and Brozovich, B G, John Golden III, and Stephen (2019) *Inside Day 1: How Amazon Uses Agile Team Structures and Adaptive Practices to Innovate on Behalf of Customers* SHRM. www.shrm. org/executive/resources/people-strategy-journal/Spring2019/Pages/galetti-golden. aspx (archived at https://perma.cc/VFQ2-C6UZ)

Gino, Francesca, Bradley R Staats, Brian J Hall, and Tiffany Y Chang. The
    Morning Star Company: Self-Management at Work. store.hbr.org/product/the-
    morning-star-company-self-management-at-work/914013?sku=914013-PDF-
    ENG (archived at https://perma.cc/979P-MWNJ) Harvard Business School Case
    914-013, September 2013. (Revised June 2016)

References

1   McChrystal, S A (2015) *Team of teams: the power of small groups in a
    fragmented world.* London: Portfolio
2   Serpa, Sandro and Ferreira, Carlos. (2019) The Concept of Bureaucracy by
    Max Weber International Journal of Social Science Studies. 7. 12. 10.11114/
    ijsss.v7i2.3979
3   Morgan, J (n.d.) (2015) *The 5 Types Of Organizational Structures: Part 1, The
    Hierarchy* Forbes. www.forbes.com/sites/jacobmorgan/2015/07/06/the-5-types-
    of-organizational-structures-part-1-the-hierarchy/ (archived at https://perma.
    cc/QXW3-T3WH)
4   Crisp, N (2011) *24 hours to save the NHS: the chief executive's account of
    reform 2000 to 2006* Oxford: Oxford University Press
5   Slack, N, Chambers, S, Johnston, R, Hicks, C, Lewis, P and Yang, Y (2011)
    Operations management Harlow: Pearson Education Ltd
6   Kelion, L (2013) Valve: How going boss-free empowered the games-maker
    BBC News. 23 September. www.bbc.co.uk/news/technology-24205497
    (archived at https://perma.cc/4Z95-EKXY)
7   Spicer, A (2018). *No bosses, no managers: the truth behind the 'flat hierarchy'
    facade | André Spicer* The Guardian. www.theguardian.com/commentisfree/2018/
    jul/30/no-bosses-managers-flat-hierachy-workplace-tech-hollywood (archived at
    https://perma.cc/A3MF-ZYTH)
8   Atlassian (2019) *Agile best practices and tutorials* Atlassian. www.atlassian.
    com/agile (archived at https://perma.cc/8A7P-NZFR)
9   Alexander, A, De Smet, A, Kleinman, S and Mugayar-Baldocchi, M (2020) *To
    weather a crisis, build a network of teams | McKinsey.* www.mckinsey.com/
    business-functions/people-and-organizational-performance/our-insights/to-
    weather-a-crisis-build-a-network-of-teams (archived at https://perma.cc/
    EL5N-3W52)
10 Deloitte (2019) *Organizational performance: It's a team sport* Deloitte
    Insights. www2.deloitte.com/us/en/insights/focus/human-capital-trends/2019/
    team-based-organization.html (archived at https://perma.cc/3GJD-P4TE)
11 Hern, A (2018) *The two-pizza rule and the secret of Amazon's success* The
    Guardian. www.theguardian.com/technology/2018/apr/24/the-two-pizza-rule-
    and-the-secret-of-amazons-success (archived at https://perma.cc/8JBS-DF3W)

12   Mueller, J S (2012). Why individuals in larger teams perform worse. *Organizational Behavior and Human Decision Processes,* 117(1), pp. 111–124

13   Hamel, G (2017) *First, Let's Fire All the Managers* Harvard Business Review. hbr.org/2011/12/first-lets-fire-all-the-managers (archived at https://perma.cc/V3HX-HJ6B)

14   Morgan, J (2015) *How Morning Star Farms Operates Without Any Managers* Forbes. www.forbes.com/sites/jacobmorgan/2015/06/04/how-morningstar-farms-operates-without-any-managers/ (archived at https://perma.cc/VA6T-MK2G)

15   Corporate Rebels (2016). *Morning Star's Success Story: No Bosses, No Titles, No Structural Hierarchy* Corporate Rebels. corporate-rebels.com/morning-star/ (archived at https://perma.cc/E5CJ-JW2Y)

16   Costa, C D (2021) *How Technology Will Change The Way Business Is Run In 2021* Forbes. www.forbes.com/sites/celinnedacosta/2021/04/04/how-technology-will-change-the-way-business-is-run-in-2021/ (archived at https://perma.cc/CBR4-SPHT)

17   Chui, M, Manyika, J and Miremadi, M (2016). *Where machines could replace humans-and where they can't (yet)* McKinsey & Company. www.mckinsey.com/business-functions/mckinsey-digital/our-insights/where-machines-could-replace-humans-and-where-they-cant-yet (archived at https://perma.cc/KV49-8QX3)

18   Muliadi, B (2020). *Council Post: What The Rise Of TikTok Says About Generation Z* Forbes. www.forbes.com/sites/forbestechcouncil/2020/07/07/what-the-rise-of-tiktok-says-about-generation-z/ (archived at https://perma.cc/MCJ2-72ZU)

19   Francis, T and Hoefel, F (2018) *'True Gen': Generation Z and its implications for companies* McKinsey & Company. www.mckinsey.com/industries/consumer-packaged-goods/our-insights/true-gen-generation-z-and-its-implications-for-companies (archived at https://perma.cc/J8EC-MCD5)

20   Smith, C and Turner, S (2015) *The Radical Transformation of Diversity and Inclusion The Millennial Influence for inclusion.* www2.deloitte.com/content/dam/Deloitte/us/Documents/about-deloitte/us-inclus-millennial-influence-120215.pdf (archived at https://perma.cc/7PUK-J4LW)

21   PwC (2011) *Millennials at work Reshaping the workplace.* www.pwc.com/co/es/publicaciones/assets/millennials-at-work.pdf (archived at https://perma.cc/B3A8-PTD5)

22   Case, T (2021) *How Gen Z is handling the workplace generation divide, and how it can be fixed* Digiday. digiday.com/media/how-gen-z-is-handling-the-workplace-generation-divide-and-how-it-can-be-fixed/ (archived at https://perma.cc/9N2Q-MTMR)

23 Firstpost. (2021). *Dating app company handcuffs woman to pole as part of world's most embarrassing internship.* www.firstpost.com/world/dating-app-company-handcuffs-woman-to-pole-as-part-of-worlds-most-embarrassing-internship-10046261.html (archived at https://perma.cc/36LU-7DWN)

24 McNeill Love, M. (2021). Matthew McNeill Love on LinkedIn: To even feature on the Global *App Store Charts is monumental for | 115 comments.* www.linkedin.com/posts/matthewmcneilllove_to-even-feature-on-the-global-app-store-charts-activity-6859416965669257216-dZy8 (archived at https://perma.cc/94CA-UXYH)

25 Krentz, M, Kos, E, Green, A and Garcia-Alonso, J, 2020. *Easing the COVID-19 Burden on Working Parents* BCG Global. www.bcg.com/publications/2020/helping-working-parents-ease-the-burden-of-covid-19 (archived at https://perma.cc/XFT3-E9L9)

26 Miller, D, Okamoto, T and Page, T (2016) *Organizational design* Deloitte Insights. www2.deloitte.com/us/en/insights/focus/human-capital-trends/2016/organizational-models-network-of-teams.html (archived at https://perma.cc/QN4E-M9ZX)

27 Dixon-Fyle, S, Dolan, K, Hunt, V and Prince, S, 2019. *Diversity wins: How inclusion matters.* www.mckinsey.com/featured-insights/diversity-and-inclusion/diversity-wins-how-inclusion-matters (archived at https://perma.cc/M242-TH83)

06

Teaming with the machine: Inclusion in the age of industry 4.0

NICK BASANNAVAR

Introduction

Generative Pre-trained Transformer 2 (GPT-2) is an artificial intelligence (AI) language tool, launched in 2019 by San Francisco research organization OpenAI. It is capable of predictive language modelling, such as writing whole news articles when prompted by a headline, or continuing novels and stories when fed an extract.[1]

When journalists from *The Guardian* experimented with GPT-2 in 2019, they asked it to reimagine, based on the first lines, the opening passages of classic novels such as George Orwell's *1984* ('It was a bright cold day in April, and the clocks were striking thirteen…') and Jane Austen's *Pride and Prejudice* ('It is a truth universally acknowledged…').[2]

The ensuing results certainly didn't represent great pieces of literature. They contained confusing sentence constructs, illogicalities, and peculiar plot formulations. AI technologies like GPT-2 (and now GPT-3 and GPT-4) are still in early development, generally lacking in contextual awareness and incapable of human artistic expression.

However, they are bound to reach a high level of technical story-telling sophistication before long. In the coming years and decades, it won't be unusual for humans to read novels written by machines. Indeed, we already observe AI-created art in galleries[3] and by humanoid-robot artist-poets.[4] We already consume journalism produced by algorithmic computer programmes.[5] We already rely on everyday automated services and AI tools – from the chatbot helping us to resolve a customer service issue, to the piece of code making our working day a bit more efficient.

What marks our current era, more than anything else, is the staggering pace of technological change. And in the working world, this is having a huge impact on how we design, manage and develop teams.

Industry 4.0

Many commentators have observed that we are living through a technological revolution, popularized by Karl Schwab of the World Economic Forum as the 'Fourth Industrial Revolution', or 'Industry 4.0'.[6] This chapter argues that we urgently need to stop and think about the impact of (conscious and unconscious) bias in this rapid change moment. Without doing this we will fail to serve our teams well, and they will fail to fulfil their potential.

Industry 4.0 contains powerful implications for diversity and inclusion for the wider working world, and for the organizations that populate it. We build on the previous two chapters, which featured inclusive management and new employer models, to offer perspectives on how, as leaders, we might think about mitigating the visible and invisible risks of Industry 4.0 to successfully integrate and harness technology within our teams.

We start by exploring some of the key features and definitions relating to this technological change. We will see that automation and AI are not distant concepts, but live issues in all aspects of our lives. We will explore the implications. What is the impact for inclusion of getting automation and AI wrong (and right)? How can we build technology that is truly accessible and that does not entrench existing inequalities? What are the consequences of having hybrid human/non-human teams, and should we be catering for robots like we would human workers? We will explore ways that we can manage technological revolution in positive ways, creating included, happy and integrated teams.

ECHOES FROM THE PAST

Concepts such as AI and automation are not new. They have been prevalent in human myth, art, science and speculation since ancient times. 12,000 years ago, the Yoruba people of West Africa worshipped Ogun, a god of iron with powerful creative intelligence and the ability to call on automaton armies to defeat foes.[7] In the Taoist text Liezi, dating to 5th century BC, 'a technician named Yan Shi made a humanlike robot that could dance and sing and even dared to flirt with the king's concubines'.[8]

The Jacquard weaving loom, invented in 1804, was a major landmark in automation and a key feature of the industrial revolution.[9] It fundamentally reshaped the nature of a 'team', sending many skilled workers to unemployment, creating joint human-machine teams, and redrawing the roles of many workers who remained: from expert weavers to lower skilled machine operators.[10]

Later, AI took a huge turn towards becoming reality with Alan Turing's 'Turing Test' composition at the University of Manchester (1950) and his colleague Christopher Strachey's work on 1951's Ferranti Mark 1, the first working AI computer which created the possibility for autonomous machine play in checkers and chess.

Technological change is a perpetual feature of human history, belonging to the past, the future and the present. It is a continuous human-led process. As the historian Eric Hobsbawm observed in 1962, 'the Industrial Revolution was not indeed an episode with a beginning and an end… It is still going on'.[11]

Current context and definitions

It is not surprising that the Fourth Industrial Revolution causes so much fear and anxiety, given the sheer number and complexity of features and terms. This includes the Internet of things (IoT); robotic process automation; artificial intelligence; quantum computing; genetic engineering; augmented, virtual and extended reality; metaverses like Mark Zuckerberg's reshaped Facebook venture; 3D printing; cloud computing; big data; big analytics; smart sensors. Fears about robots – some justified – have abounded for centuries: that they will take human workers' jobs, or that they will rise up, surpass the intelligence of, and overthrow their hitherto-dominant overlords.[12]

The fact is that everything in that confounding list above exists in our lives today, to one degree or another. Automation and AI already intersect with inclusion, and this has implications for teams and managers. These two technologies are predicted to have the most profound impact on the lives of the world's citizens in the next fifty years.[13]

Automation is a broad category which encompasses repetitive, predictable processes, performed by machines (or *robots*) instead of humans.

AI is a more specific form of technology whereby human, non-repetitive, non-predictable behaviours (such as speech, image, text, analysis, creativity) are analysed and mimicked.

Both are highly prevalent already in our home, social and working lives – particularly in the Global North (the traditional West, plus economically advanced Eastern nations such as China, Japan, South Korea and Taiwan).

There are many well-documented potentially positive impacts to these technologies: efficiency; productivity; increased leisure time; freeing up humans and teams to engage in more strategic or interesting tasks; quick reskilling and upskilling, and more. In the domestic sphere, this looks like smart meters, robotic cleaning devices and home assistance and entertainment systems. In the social sphere, we may encounter autonomous transportation, facial recognition technology, automated medical procedures, or robot-made art. In exploration and response, machine learning has been used in space missions and viral-outbreak predictions. The COVID-19 pandemic has brought about rapidly accelerated, mass adoption events in all these settings.

Here, we think specifically about work and teams. In Table 6.1, we introduce some (non-exhaustive) extant and emerging examples in the working world (employers and organizations), along with implications for inclusion:

TABLE 6.1 Industry 4.0 examples and potential implications on inclusion

Industry 4.0 example	Potential benefits for teams and inclusion	Potential risks for teams and inclusion
Pandemic-propelled, accelerated digitization of business tools such as Zoom and Microsoft Teams	Democratization of company and team cultures; flattening of hierarchical structures; efficiency; higher productivity; global teaming	Remote work disproportionately benefits already wealthy senior staff/ homeowners; insecure low-income WFH conditions; introverts suffer from video call overload; burnout and mental health crisis
Hybrid human-robot teams	Smarter, more efficient teams; increased wellbeing	Ethical implications of robot workers
Automated customer-facing interactions, including robot or drone mail/food/package delivery services such as Starship.xyz	Convenience; targeted services that work for every individual; customer experience	Privacy; data risk; security risk; impact on gig economy/ zero-hour workers (usually those from marginalized backgrounds)
Automated and smart talent management systems such as smart workloading and role allocation – see eightfold.ai or Profinda.com	Reduction in recruitment and internal mobility waste; equal access; debiased skills-based matching; better project outcomes	Biased algorithms or language which exacerbate lack of diversity in senior positions/performance

(continued)

TABLE 6.1 (Continued)

Industry 4.0 example	Potential benefits for teams and inclusion	Potential risks for teams and inclusion
AI-enabled sentiment analysis for employers to better understand their workers and customers' views	Fairer, more tailored and team-centric insights and decision making	Biased or discriminatory algorithms that misunderstand employee sentiment; diminished trust of employees
AI-powered customer insights, for example in banking, trading and financial services	Greater, more tailored customer experience	Biased or discriminatory algorithms that misunderstand customer sentiment; superintelligent AI which surpasses the human-led markets themselves
AI-powered business analytics, including in fraud detection in financial services; language analytics of contracts in legal firms; selection of participants for clinical trials in pharmaceutical firms	More accurate and efficient compliance and security systems; greater access to services previously denied to minority groups	Biased, incomplete or discriminatory algorithms leading to entrenchment of wealth and/or health inequalities

Humanity has always had to contend with issues relating to technological advancement. However, the above list suggests that we are in uncharted territory. Its range demonstrates the positive and exciting aspects, as well as the highly hazardous and far-reaching implications of Industry 4.0 (see also Zhang et al, 2019)[14].

Leaders of teams in organizations of all kinds need to think hard about their own roles. Here, we point towards how that might be done by exploring critical areas pertaining to the intersection of Industry 4.0 and inclusion.

Ineffectiveness and inequality

When steaming ahead into the application of new technologies, teams might be unconsciously (or consciously) missing key concepts, missing blind spots, and creating unintentionally unequal outcomes and worse products and services. This is not a concern of the future; unfortunately, biased design is already leading to dramatic failures in effectiveness and safety, from sexist hiring algorithms to racially biased AI.[15]

Take driverless cars. In 2019, the Georgia Institute of Technology in the US deployed the Fitzpatrick scale (used to classify human skin colours) and found that AI models used to detect objects and pedestrians in driverless cars returned reduced accuracy of around five per cent when looking at images of pedestrians with darker skin tones.[16] The implications for universal road safety are horrifying. Similar ethical problems apply in many areas of life where facial recognition technology is used as image analysis.[17] As the researcher Shira Schneider puts it, 'algorithms are intended to make life easier, but these types of algorithms are concerning because they amplify systemic racism'.[18]

One of the most troubling features of Industry 4.0 is the startling lack of diversity among the teams of programmers and managers at its vanguard. This contributes to blind spots in design processes, and ultimately in faulty, uninclusive products and services. According to data scientist Steve Nouri, 'due to the lack of diverse engineers and researchers, the products that are developed and used by billions of users may result in the propagation of bias on a large scale'.[19] When it comes to AI, the Eritrean computer scientist Timnit Gebru claims that there are 'almost no Black researchers' and 'we are in a diversity crisis'.[20] Even if we *do* factor in and successfully utilize diversity, the nature of AI is such that 'you are bound to have some sort of bias in your data set. You cannot have a data set that perfectly samples the whole world'.[21]

The damaging risk we are left with is that due to biased repetitive programming, outcomes could be less accessible and less equal technology, when the intention is to create the opposite. A lack of diversity and inclusion in our teams can and will create rotten consequences. Thankfully, the inverse is also true: if we can design with diversity and inclusion genuinely at the centre, we can create great outcomes.

Of course, there are currently many limitations to AI. In practice, AI machines do not yet demonstrate self-awareness, nor an appreciation of environmental factors. But they will surely get there – and at some stage, experts from the Max Planck Institute for Human Development believe, they will surpass human thought and reason, and move beyond our control.[22] If this supersession is predicated on biased, ineffective human inputs, we could be irreversibly and catastrophically damaging the future of humankind.

Industry 4.0 is also seeing the reinforcement of existing economic and labour inequalities within economies, cultures and organizations. Automation, contrary to popular opinion, is unlikely to create a mass (human) unemployment event. In 2017, McKinsey found that while 50 per cent of *tasks* performed by workers could be automated, only five per cent of actual *jobs* could be fully automated.[23] Nonetheless, many jobs will be surpassed. And as the World Economic Forum stated in 2020, 'inequality is likely to be exacerbated by the dual impact of technology and the pandemic recession. Jobs held by lower wage workers, women and younger workers' were harder hit.[24] Deloitte and the Institute for Public Policy Research found in a joint report that 'twice as many women as men work in occupations with a high potential for automation'.[25] And we know that it is predominantly marginalized ethnic and socio-economic groups who occupy the lowest-paid, highest-risk roles. Organizational leaders need to think deeply about this if they have the ambition to build diverse and inclusive teams.

This is analogous to – and indeed tied up with – the climate disaster facing the planet. The Global North has been disproportionately responsible for environmental crises, yet the Global South suffer most from it. At the same time, the majority of those involved in trying to *fix* climate change also come from the Global North, particularly from white privileged elites.[26] Many of the presumed benefits of Industry 4.0 – greater tech advances, convenience and increases in productivity and efficiency – lead in only one direction: towards greater growth. This in turn, if we follow the logic of climate theorist-activists such as Jason Hickel, is highly likely to mean an ever-greater extraction of resources at just the time we need to rein it in.[27] The grim starting point is that the Global South, constituted to a large degree of marginalized people of colour, will continue to bear the brunt of tech-fuelled excess.

Ethics: building and leading hybrid human-robot teams

I hate my robot vacuum cleaner. He hates me too. We don't get on; we never have. He seems to go out of his way to attack my feet. I do go out of my way to put pieces of fruit and cans of beer on his head. (He can't reach to take them off and he looks stupid.) But amidst the discord, I clearly care enough to have anthropomorphized him. That's *him*, not *it*, after all. And – in our shared vision of a spotless floor – we form a domestic team of sorts, albeit a dysfunctional one.

My experience is anything but unique. The reality is that humans are increasingly sharing our workplaces and social spaces with robots. Many love their machines as if they were pets or, in some cases, children. Amazon's 2021 release of the household robot Astro is a case in point.[28] Robots and AI tools have become family members, colleagues, and even friends.

Does it follow, then, that automated robots and our AI machines should receive and offer the same level of care and dignity as human beings? If not now, then what about in 20 years when they might resemble humans more in terms of their physical appearance and their thought sophistication, having had more time to mimic us? As the philosopher Carmen Krämer has argued, 'robots are becoming increasingly autonomous and rational', and one of the key tenets of dignity is autonomy.[29] This is a two-way street. In a setting such as healthcare, human dignity is an integral part of the experience. It is the quality of dignity which helps to provide comfort to the care recipient. But how can robots be expected to truly replicate their human counterparts when they themselves are supposedly incapable of human emotions?[30]

As leaders of teams, we need to come to terms with the realities and consequences of hybrid human-robot teams. We need to ensure that humans who work with robots are properly included, and we need to think about the inclusion of machines themselves. Part of this might mean treating them with dignity, but it's also about how we fit them into functioning units and ensure they are productive, supportive, and supported. When composing teams, we need to also think about the diversity of the robots. Who wrote the code that it uses for its activities? What biases or blind spots are inherent?

There are other inclusive and ethical considerations at play. In 2021, a student from Concordia University in Montreal, Canada, searched out his Art History professor online to ask a question after a lecture, only to come across an 'in memoriam' page that stated he had been dead for some time. That hadn't stopped Concordia from using the professor's pre-death recorded lectures as learning content for their courses.[31] Elsewhere, lectures have been delivered with holographic representations of the speaker.[32]

Not only does the impact of combining human (living and dead), robot and AI workers together mark one of the biggest shifts in the ways that humans convene, debate, and learn since Fatima al-Fihri founded the world's first university (in what is now Morocco) in the 9th century. Here we have examples of how the university benefits from 'free' digital labour. It is also denying work to young professors in deeply competitive fields, further entrenching inequalities in the higher education sector. In a short-termist, technology-driven effort to cut costs and digitize the curriculum, universities are likely to worsen long-term inequalities. Similar ethical logic, with different examples of consequences for human and non-human workers, applies in all professional fields.

Unlocking teams in the age of Industry 4.0

The happy news is that if we get it right, technologies such as AI and automation can be a force for inclusive good.

At *Included*, we break down complex challenges using a simple but powerful intervention model that has helped leaders to categorize and catalyse diversity and inclusion work for more than a decade. This mutually exclusive, collectively exhaustive (MECE) framework is constituted of strategy, data, governance, leadership and systems work. Ideally, these are approached sequentially, in that order.

The prize is great. Businesses have a lot of waking up to do, but they will continue to have a huge role to play in our communities. We know that accessible products and services are better for everyone. We know that diverse and inclusive teams are happier and stronger performing. Indeed, as we will see in Chapters 7 and 12, it is inclusion that could be the path through the staggering changes the planet is undergoing. Here are practical examples of how we can interact with Industry 4.0 from a position of calm strength, rather than stress, to unlock the vast potential of our teams.

1. STRATEGY

In the era of Industry 4.0, the uncomfortable reality for many organizations is that top-down purpose statements and strategies often fail to inspire. Indeed, many workers in large organizations wouldn't even be able to say what their company's stated purpose is. Instead, purpose and happiness in a work context is derived from their immediate, fast-shifting organizational neighbours, environments and touchpoints: their boss, their colleagues, their team. It is in digitally enabled teams, after all, that corporate workers spend most of their time – often more time than is spent with families.

Many organizations, as we will see in Chapter 7, have spent enormous amounts of time and money in retrofitting a 'purpose' to their corporate identity and activities. This can feel instinctively phoney in contexts like accountancy or corporate finance, where organizations which for decades or longer had been concerned with profit suddenly embraced concepts such as impact, purpose, social good, and 'giving back'.

Wellcome, the world's second largest funder of medical research, has shown how inclusive strategy in Industry 4.0 might look. It has positioned DEI not only as an internal 'employer' issue, but as a critical enabler of 'better science and more equitable health solutions'.[33] For science and non-science teams, this means that they think about DEI in everything that they do. Wellcome actively funds research that looks at the intersection of Industry 4.0 and better science research, including AI in the clinic and governing AI safety in healthcare. And in 2019 it announced a £75m fund to look at how everybody could benefit from AI and data advances and innovations in health.[34] This means that every team in Wellcome, regardless of function or seniority, can connect with the organization's purpose in a highly specific way.

The Wellcome example suggests that by putting inclusion at the core of our purpose and strategy, we can enable teams to find their own diverse, localized meanings. This has important implications for those leading on inclusion strategies. AstraZeneca, one of the world's leading pharmaceutical companies, has found success by crafting strategies with the input of their people, asking the whole organization what the future should look like in the fact of likely innovative upheaval. DEI itself became a central theme of the strategy.

New technologies can both help and hinder the strategy process. Once we have both broader and localized strategic directions clearly set, empowering local teams to forge their own paths, we can ensure that any Industry 4.0 interventions in our organization are meaningful and supportive. Don't implement new technologies for implementation's sake. Consider why it is that we are introducing this technology, and what they can do to help.

2. DATA

Taking an evidence-led approach is the second critical step in getting DEI work right in the age of Industry 4.0. We must first hold up the mirror to our teams. Who are we in terms of diversity right now? Who are we going to be in three, five or ten years? How are we doing in terms of inclusion? And how are we going to leverage technology to keep monitoring progress?

Industry 4.0 advances can help here. There are myriad useful evidence-building techniques that it throws open, such as smart engagement and pulse surveys to track employee inclusion; modelling to understand the future diversity of the organization; and even virtual reality tools which claim to help leaders experience life in the shoes of others and build empathy.

There are ethical issues to overcome. While ethical data gathering (such as building good data structures and deploying anonymous surveys) is a good step, we should avoid rushing headlong into adopting tools such as AI-based sentiment analysis or virtual reality without first considering the implications for privacy, employee safety, and actual effectiveness.

UCB, headquartered in Belgium, is a leading global pharmaceutical company specializing in immunology and neurology. Since 2020, with the support of *Included,* they have been carefully building a leading approach to DEI strategy and data. They started by making a baseline, running diversity projection models to understand who was in their current global population, and what that would look like in future years should current hiring and retention trends continue. They then conducted a survey to understand, quantitatively, the current global levels of equity and inclusion. Finally, drawing on smart Industry 4.0 cloud analytics tools such as Qlik, they brought those datasets together to build a DEI dashboard and index.

Together, these interventions are providing actionable insights, helping UCB managers around the globe (and in different functions) to understand key DEI performance metrics, and giving the organization a benchmarkable lens on how they are performing overall. Taking a truly collaborative approach, UCB leaned on the expertise of its various teams to make progress.

3. GOVERNANCE

Governance is the third critical determinant in building inclusive organizations. This refers to formal governance structures such as boards of directors and C-suite groups, semi-structured approaches to employee groups, and informal governance that occurs among the networking and influence-building in the day-to-day work of organizations.

What is clear is that those who look after organizational governance cannot be passive when it comes to reconciling Industry 4.0 and inclusion. This means ongoing self-education: listening to your organization and external expertise to truly understand the risks, challenges, and long-term benefits that will arise from the intersection of technological change and inclusion. It means providing the oversight needed to empower teams to experiment and to control new technologies, rather than being controlled or led by them. And it means holding the organization to account on progress.

AstraZeneca has had an extraordinary couple of years, leading the global pursuit of the COVID-19 vaccine. In among this, they have enacted market-leading DEI governance steps. The firm's Senior Vice President of Reward and Inclusion, Rebekah Martin, explains how in recent years they had established a Global Council for Inclusion and Diversity. A key active member is the CEO, Pascal Soriot. The Council is an example of active listening and ongoing education, with key governors working together with employees to forge long-term ambitions and strategy. It is a top-down *and* a bottom-up approach, with senior leaders mixing with junior staff to share best practice and make a genuine difference. The approach has already made a positive impact on addressing the representation of women globally, and diversity in markets such as Japan.

The firm tracks against annual ambition measures, covering metrics such as gender representation, and national and ethnic representation in senior leadership. Ultimately these accountable structures help deliver the key aims of the organization: serving diverse patient populations by building high-performing inclusive and diverse teams. As Martin pointed out, 'inclusion and diversity in action built our strategy – something that normally happens behind closed doors in the boardroom'.

4. LEADERSHIP

In his 1935 essay, In Praise of Idleness, the British philosopher Bertrand Russell wrote that 'modern methods of production have given us the possibility of ease and security for all [but] ... we have continued to be as energetic as we were before there were machines'. 'In this,' he reckoned, 'we have been foolish, but there is no reason to go on being foolish for ever.'[35]

Just because we have better tools doesn't mean we have to go on with foolish energy, to drive our teams to work harder on other, less important stuff. For leaders, the most powerful feature of a pandemic-heralding Industry 4.0 is not robotic process automation or augmented reality. It's empathy. People are burned out by overwork, by the pandemic, by climate change, by inequalities, by failures of global leadership everywhere. The direction of travel and the source of corporate excitement with Industry 4.0 seems to be frictionless productivity. This is a very dangerous place to go without thought for the human consequences.

In its simplest form, inclusion is adaptation. And leaders need to adapt to teams, rather than expecting teams to solely adapt to them. The global pandemic showed us the importance of great leadership and inclusive cultures. In some ways, people struggled. Those at the start of their careers, having moved to urban areas and occupying small flats or rooms, had a tough and isolating time. Technology was both a support, and a compounder of existing difficulties. Meanwhile, the reframing by some leaders of corporate working as a kind of ersatz 'family life', replete with 'family dinners', blurred boundaries between home and work, and longer working hours, has been deeply unhealthy.

Elsewhere, however, the rapid adoption of modern technologies helped to foster inclusive working cultures. Suddenly, through tools like Zoom and Teams, people were visible at their most human moments. Busy domestic kitchens were visible. Cats jumped on keyboards. Children ran around in the background.

AstraZeneca showed the importance of empathic leadership in a COVID-disrupted, technology-saturated global working structure. Crowdsourcing is a key part of the firm's leadership culture, with initiatives such as tech-enabled, global 'Culture Jams' launched to shape corporate direction in a science-focused, innovative environment. A key aim here, says Rebekah Martin, is to foster an open environment where contributors feel safe to challenge and share. When it came to building a new corporate strategy, the executive canvassed the entire organization with questions to shape the strategy: a powerful example of adapting to teams, rather than the other way round.

In this way, leaders can work hard on behaviours and how they show up, creating more comfortable, psychologically safe and inclusive teams in which people work alongside machines to do their best work.

5. SYSTEMS

Systemic challenges require careful, systemic approaches. Institutional racism has been a centuries-long process; we cannot dismantle it overnight. The fifth key approach to DEI is to build it into all our teams, functions, processes and activities, whether in talent and HR, marketing, procurement, investments, operations or product design, or anything else.

Industry 4.0 has a huge role to play here. Its emergent technologies are themselves being systematically introduced into all imaginable categories of work processes, and if we can get the inputs right, we can harness these advances to accelerate systemic change and to create inclusive teams.

Let's take talent. Typical recruitment processes have long been recognized as holding bias at almost every turn – in value-laden CVs, in attraction techniques, in interview design and more. Applied is a growing tech start-up which grew out of the Behavioural Insights Team in the UK. It is now one of the world's most innovative recruitment tools. At heart a debiasing, anonymization tool, it supports recruiters to hire more ethically, more inclusively, and more successfully by intervening at every stage of the hiring system. Applied's job description analysis tool helps recruiters to identify gender or other bias in postings and to rewrite them.

Applied's approach to job application screening – anonymized and built for skills-based questions, rather than experiences and identities – helps recruiters get to the right candidates, not just the most convenient ones. It does away not only with CVs, but with blind CVs, which can still contain misleading, value-laden signals for reviewers. Applied's revolutionary approach has led to example-setting impact for its users: reduced time on the hiring process; a 93 per cent retention rate after one year; and up to four times the attraction of ethnic minority candidates than previously achieved (Applied, 2021). It is a great example of how we can leverage emergent technologies and machine learning to rethink our established processes and ultimately create better outcomes.

Conclusion

It is tempting to glance at the multi-layered, complex features of Industry 4.0 and to despair. How is the manager supposed to understand the vast array of changes and risks that are coming down track, let alone control and harness them to create success?

This chapter has aimed to serve as an awakening to some of those difficult challenges (such as in-built tech bias, reinforced inequalities and ethical considerations), but also to comfort by showing that there are approaches we can take to be successful. By breaking it down (using the five-step model above of strategy, data, governance, leadership and systems) we see how many organizations are already getting ahead of Industry 4.0 to build inclusively and empathetically for success.

Key takeaways

1 Industry 4.0 innovations including automation and artificial intelligence are having a profound – and likely irreversible – impact already on domestic, social, professional, and geopolitical settings. These innovations come with important implications for inclusion.

2 Leaders in organizational settings cannot ignore Industry 4.0, an age in which they will be managing hybrid human-machine teams. We must be aware of, lean into, and take control of the issues to mitigate bias and stop inequality becoming widespread.

3 By taking a systemic approach that considers strategy, data, governance, leadership, and systems, we can turn risk into opportunity, get ahead of the challenges heralded by Industry 4.0 and ultimately reframe it to help us to create successful, diverse and inclusive teams. Successful examples can be seen in contexts such as big pharma, medical research, and tech.

References

1 Vincent, J (2019) OpenAI's new multitalented AI writes, translates, and slanders, *The Verge*, 14 February www.theverge.com/2019/2/14/18224704/ai-machine-learning-language-models-read-write-openai-gpt2 (archived at https://perma.cc/R7PN-MQR8)

2 Hern, A (2019) New AI fake text generator may be too dangerous to release, say creators, *The Guardian,* 14 February www.theguardian.com/technology/2019/feb/14/elon-musk-backed-ai-writes-convincing-news-fiction (archived at https://perma.cc/5B8U-3P78)

3 ARTFIX (2021) 'deeep' disrupts London's art scene with first AI art fair (14 – 17 October, 2021), *ArtfixDaily*, 6 October www.artfixdaily.com/artwire/release/2105-%E2%80%98deeep%E2%80%99-disrupts-london%E2%80%99s-art-scene-with-first-ai-art-fair-(14-%E2%80%93- (archived at https://perma.cc/NJK9-LURA)

4 Flood, A (2021) Robot artist to perform AI generated poetry in response to Dante, *The Guardian,* 26 November www.theguardian.com/books/2021/nov/26/robot-artist-to-perform-ai-generated-poetry-in-response-to-dante (archived at https://perma.cc/Y7UE-EQMN)

5 BBC News (2020) Microsoft 'to replace journalists with robots', *BBC News*, 30 May www.bbc.com/news/world-us-canada-52860247 (archived at https://perma.cc/H548-YDW6)

6 Schwab, K (2017) *The Fourth Industrial Revolution* London: Penguin UK

7 Adams, N R (2019) The Curious History of Artificial Intelligence | An African Perspective, *Medium*, 1 November becominghuman.ai/the-curious-history-of-artificial-intelligence-an-african-perspective-46002515934e (archived at https://perma.cc/ASA7-8A4A)

8 Bourne, J (2021) The Ancient Imagination Behind China's AI Ambition, *NOEMA*, 22 April www.noemamag.com/the-ancient-imagination-behind-chinas-ai-ambition (archived at https://perma.cc/3QZ8-4XG6)

9 Morais, B (2013) Ada Lovelace, the First Tech Visionary, *The New Yorker*, 15 October www.newyorker.com/tech/elements/ada-lovelace-the-first-tech-visionary (archived at https://perma.cc/U7R8-8REQ)

10 Geselowitz, M N (2019) The Jacquard Loom: A Driver of the Industrial Revolution, *IEEE Spectrum,* 1 January spectrum.ieee.org/the-jacquard-loom-a-driver-of-the-industrial-revolution (archived at https://perma.cc/Y2FE-YTYY)

11 Hobsbawm, E (2003) *The Age of Revolution: Europe 1789–1848.* London: Abacus

12, 17 Colback, L (2020) The impact of AI on business and society, *Financial Times*, 16 October www.ft.com/content/e082b01d-fbd6-4ea5-a0d2-05bc5ad7176c (archived at https://perma.cc/PMD7-34G2)

13 Spotlight (2021) AI and automation: how can the UK prepare for the future of work? *New Statesman*, 4 November

14 Zhang, H. et al. (2019) The role of AI in mitigating bias to enhance diversity and inclusion. New York: IBM Smarter Workforce Institute. Available at: https://www.ibm.com/downloads/cas/2DZELQ4O (https://perma.cc/FP34-99RJ) (Accessed: 27 December 2021)

15 BBC News (2018) Amazon scrapped 'sexist AI' tool, *BBC News,* 10 October www.bbc.com/news/technology-45809919 (archived at https://perma.cc/Z2S3-7TMF)

16 Wilson, B, Hoffman, J and Morgenstern, J (2019) Predictive Inequity in Object Detection, *arXiv:1902.11097* 1 arxiv.org/abs/1902.11097 (archived at https://perma.cc/Q66Y-U929)

18 Schneider, S (2021) *Algorithmic Bias: A New Age of Racism*, Thesis. Yeshiva University repository.yu.edu/handle/20.500.12202/6887 (archived at https://perma.cc/T7PF-6M2D)

19 Nouri, S (2021) Diversity And Inclusion In AI, *Forbes*, 16 March www.forbes.com/sites/forbestechcouncil/2021/03/16/diversity-and-inclusion-in-ai/ (archived at https://perma.cc/X9VR-DZ4Q)

20, 21 Snow, J (2018) 'We're in a diversity crisis': cofounder of Black in AI on what's poisoning algorithms in our lives, *MIT Technology Review*, 14 February www.technologyreview.com/2018/02/14/145462/were-in-a-diversity-crisis-black-in-ais-founder-on-whats-poisoning-the-algorithms-in-our/ (archived at https://perma.cc/T6SH-47CK)

22 Alfonseca, M et al. (2021) Superintelligence Cannot be Contained: Lessons from Computability Theory, *Journal of Artificial Intelligence Research,* 70, pp. 65–76

23 Manyika, J and Chui, M (2017) *A Future That Works: Automation, Employment, and Productivity,* McKinsey Global Institute www.mckinsey.com/~/media/McKinsey/Featured%20Insights/Digital%20Disruption/Harnessing%20automation%20for%20a%20future%20that%20works/MGI-A-future-that-works_Full-report.pdf (archived at https://perma.cc/U9CN-SKU7)

24 WEF (2020) *The Future of Jobs Report 2020* World Economic Forum www.weforum.org/reports/the-future-of-jobs-report-2020/in-full/executive-summary/ (archived at https://perma.cc/GU9K-YZ69)

25 Deloitte (2020) *Fast forward to the past: Is automation making organisations less diverse?* www2.deloitte.com/content/dam/Deloitte/uk/Documents/public-sector/deloitte-uk-diversity-and-automation-brochure-landscape.pdf (archived at https://perma.cc/B2J8-NYN3)

26 Williams, (2021)

27 Hickel, J (2020) *Less is More: How Degrowth Will Save the World.* London: Random House

28 Basu, T (2021) Amazon's Astro robot is stupid. You'll still fall in love with it, *MIT Technology Review*, 4 October www.technologyreview.com/2021/10/04/1036413/amazons-astro-robot-pet/ (archived at https://perma.cc/9JHY-M3WZ)

29 Krämer, C (2020) Can Robots Have Dignity? *Artificial Intelligence*, pp. 241–253

30 Zardiashvili, L and Fosch-Villaronga, E (2020) 'Oh, Dignity too?' Said the Robot: Human Dignity as the Basis for the Governance of Robotics, *Minds and Machines*, 30(1), pp. 121–143

31 Kneese, T (2021) How a Dead Professor Is Teaching a University Art History Class, *Slate*, 27 January slate.com/technology/2021/01/dead-professor-teaching-online-class.html (archived at https://perma.cc/W4QH-TBLM)

32 McKie, A (2019) Holograms on campus: good for teaching, good for the environment?, *Times Higher Education (THE)*, 15 October www.timeshighereducation.com/news/holograms-campus-good-teaching-good-environment (archived at https://perma.cc/GSM6-43FS)

33 Couch, L (2021) How we're putting culture, diversity and inclusion at the heart of our strategy, *Wellcome*, 26 March wellcome.org/news/how-were-putting-diversity-equity-and-inclusion-heart-our-strategy (archived at https://perma.cc/AXD7-V259)

34 Thomas, J (2019) New programme to explore how innovation in health data can benefit everyone, *Wellcome*, 28 June wellcome.org/news/new-programme-explore-how-innovation-health-data-can-benefit-everyone (archived at https://perma.cc/N7P9-WTRW)

35 Russell, B (1935) *In Praise of Idleness and Other Essays.* London: George Allen & Unwin Ltd www.newstatesman.com/spotlight/2021/11/ai-and-automation-how-can-the-uk-prepare-for-the-future-of-work (archived at https://perma.cc/AP5C-AHCG)

PART THREE

Unlocking your organization

Introduction

STEPHEN FROST

We've covered you and your team. It's now time to focus on the key to organization-wide inclusion. For this, we need to consider five mutually exclusive, yet collectively exhaustive factors.

We'll start with organization strategy, as current challenges are unprecedented in terms of the speed of disruption and change. We'll suggest that merely tweaking the existing system is wholly inadequate. It's time now for wholesale system change. This might sound dramatic or overwhelming, but as we'll demonstrate, it's simply necessary for organization survival. Rather than an 'add on', that adds limited value, and may even be net cost, how can inclusion be strategic? How can inclusion be a method that answers varied, and seemingly intractable, problems, from talent and customer acquisition and retention, to team productivity and the need to be constantly agile and adaptable?

We'll then look at data. As we explored earlier, we are living through a data explosion, yet in the midst of this sea of information, we are failing to pick the trends that matter. Our cognitive capacity is failing to keep up with what we are supposed to be analysing. Diversity is important, but it's inclusion that determines long-term organization performance, otherwise it's diversity in, diversity out. We can now accurately measure inclusion, and we'll explore how this is critical to building an inclusive organization.

Next is governance. From the Board down, we need to be clear on who is actually going to do the work. We need clarity on who will be responsible and accountable for its success. We'll look at what good governance actually means, how it is executed, and how this is critical to inclusion. Gone are the days of the Board demonstrating a passing interest in inclusion or requesting some ad hoc information. It's now a case of how this is a constant management tool and how inclusion adds to good governance, being of catalytic value.

Leadership is the penultimate chapter of this section. We will explore what inclusive leadership actually means, how behaviour change actually happens, and how our theory of change, *understand, lead, deliver,* has led to sustainable, scalable and meaningful change in organizations worldwide. As we've stated earlier, leadership can't be outsourced. In an era of greater transparency and accountability, how we behave matters even more than it did before. Rather than doing this because we know we have to, it's about reflecting deeply on what our core, intrinsic motivations might be, and unlocking them for enlightened self-interest.

Last, we will look at systems, the essential engineering organizations are now undertaking to debias their processes, from recruitment to marketing and from procurement to talent management. Debiasing systems is the sustainable, scalable way to impact change throughout the organization – and it doesn't rely on training. Instead, we make use of behavioural economics and nudge theory – how can we encourage inclusive behaviour naturally? What kinds of behaviours do we want to see more or less of in the organization? We can design processes intentionally to help us create the kind of organization we, and potential candidates, actually want to work in.

To put all this in context, it's important to be aware of where your organization currently is, and work from there. We review *Included's* maturity model, from Diversity 101 (compliance paradigm) through Diversity 2.0 (marketing paradigm) to Inclusion 3.0 (embedded inclusion). We introduce a new paradigm, Inclusion 4.0 which is about changing the system. This sounds ambitious, but we'll show through some case studies how this is already occurring.

Inclusion 4.0, changing the system, is the future. Post pandemic, BLM, and in the midst of multi-variable change, this is the way forward for organizations who want to be inclusive and thrive in the new age. There's much talk of the new normal, but we suggest this is the new difference.

07

Rethinking inclusion, rethinking strategy

STEPHEN FROST AND NICK BASANNAVAR

On 26 March 2020, the global tobacco firm Philip Morris International Inc. (PMI) publicly released a proxy statement to its shareholders. The accompanying letter from the board restated to its readers the firm's revamped corporate purpose, originally trailed in 2016:

> '…to deliver a smoke-free future by focusing its resources on developing, scientifically substantiating and responsibly commercializing smoke-free products that are less harmful than smoking, with the aim of completely replacing cigarettes as soon as possible.'[1]

Critics have pointed to the fact that while firms like PMI busy themselves with brand management and altruistic mission statements, they continue to propagate harmful nicotine addiction to the young, through both traditional cigarettes and 'next generation products' such as e-cigarettes.[2]

Whatever one's views on Big Tobacco, the PMI statement is an extraordinary document. Here is one of the world's largest companies, now ostensibly rewiring its own purpose and activities *against* the very thing that has brought it so much success. In this bright new world, PMI self-represents as a good corporate citizen, a purpose-led organization that puts public health and the reduction of adverse environmental impact at its core.

Other tobacco companies such as Imperial Brands (committing to 'next-generation products')[3] British American Tobacco (building 'A Better

Tomorrow')[4] and Altria ('Moving Beyond Smoking')[5] have taken similar approaches to their public purpose messaging in recent years.

Fossil fuel firms are a parallel here. Royal Dutch Shell plc, which by 2019 had extracted from the planet 11.1 billion barrels of oil equivalent, claims 'to power progress together with more and cleaner energy solutions'.[6] British Petroleum meanwhile (20 billion barrels as of 2019), is 'reimagining energy for people and our planet'.[7] Both now present themselves as climate-first organizations.

These examples raise important questions about how far organizations go to transform themselves, whether that's to continue being profit-making concerns, to better reflect or lead their markets and their communities, or to become enterprises that truly create and contribute to inclusive social change movements.

We live in extraordinary times. Patience is growing thin with polarization, racism, environmental damage, inequality and injustice, just as those same issues continue to ossify and cause harm. Beyond notions of greenwashing or pinkwashing, organizations are increasingly under the microscope for their contributions towards bettering our collective state. Rather than inclusion being an add on, inclusion should be core to their future strategy, in ways we have not fully appreciated yet.

Inclusive strategy

Strategy. One of the most used words in modern organizational life. But what is it? According to business theorist Max McKeown, strategy is simply about 'shaping the future':

> 'use strategy to figure out how to achieve your purpose and ambitions. You move between where you want to go (ends) and what you need to do to get there (means). Great strategy is the quickest route from means to ends to shape your future.'[8]

So far, so logical. But how does it apply to inclusion? Until now, organizations have tended towards having distinct DEI strategies that often (though not always) sit underneath an overarching organizational strategy. A DEI strategy will often be internally focused, a 'these four walls' approach to an organization's own population, falling under the brief of the overburdened CPO or HRD.

Of course, organizations need to think deeply about their people, from improving the diversity of the workforce, to ensuring psychological safety is present and that everyone feels truly included. To some extent, distinct strategic workstreams are inevitable and indeed desirable.

However, here we argue that it's time to rethink inclusion. Rather than having distinct inclusion strategies, detached from organizational purpose and objectives, organizations might think about repositioning inclusion *as* strategy. Repositioning inclusion *as* purpose. Inclusion is the ends; it is also the means.

We introduce the *Inclusive Purpose Organization* (IPO). Organizations are not islands. They do not exist in isolation to global issues, and in many cases they unfortunately exacerbate them. But the working world is also a key part of the solution, holding a critical middle ground between governments and activists. It is incumbent upon organizations to remould, reinvent and rethink their parameters, purposes, strategies and business models in order to help repair broken global structures, to seek and champion diversity, and to create inclusion within and beyond their own walls. As we will discuss below, this is at the heart of Inclusion 4.0, an approach that goes beyond *embedding* inclusion in the current structure or system, to changing the structure or system instead.

What's clear from the tobacco and fossil fuel examples is that pure brand management and optics are not enough. Recalibrating purpose for inclusion is not simply about rewording a mission statement on the website. It's about strategic change *and* systemic change. It's high-level direction, and it's on-the-ground, sleeves-rolled-up practicality. It must be humble, meaningful, and sincere. Logically, there are therefore important considerations regarding who can legitimately lead this work, and how those leaders might do it.

FIGURE 7.1 Purpose > strategy > implementation (*Included*, 2022)

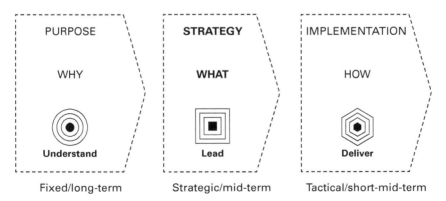

Strategic shifts in response to external shocks

Netflix used to make money by posting DVDs to customers in dog-eared red envelopes. In 2021, it won more Academy Awards than any other studio.[9] Amazon started out in the 1990s as an online bookstore, run from Jeff Bezos' garage. Now it is in effect the world's largest logistics company, plus much more besides.[10] Toyota started out making automatic looms in 1924. Now it is the world's largest automotive company.[11] Colgate did not start off making toothpaste; they made soap and candles.[12] Tiffany & Co., founded in 1837 as Tiffany, Young and Ellis, were stationers many years before they changed their hand to jewellery.[13] And Nokia used to make paper.[14]

The history of global business is full of examples like these. The world changes; we change with it. Organizations adapt all the time. As Heraclitus suggested two thousand years ago, the one absolute certainty in life is change. However, McKeown reminds us that while 'change is inevitable, progress is not'.[15]

In the 1920s, the average life expectancy of an organization listed in the US S&P 500 index was 67.[16] In 1958, it was 61; by 2016 it was around 18 years.[17] Seen another way, only 28 companies which were in 1984's launch edition of the FTSE100 (the UK's leading indicator of companies with the highest market capitalizations) were there in 2017.[18] Only 53 companies present on the US's Fortune 500 index in 1955 were there again in 2018.[19] This does not, of course, present a complete picture. Many organizations survive without necessarily appearing in indices year after year; different geographies tell different stories (such as Japan where turnover in the Tokyo Stock Exchange is at 89 years); and some organizations increasingly consider success not to be measured by market capitalization but by other metrics.[20] Nonetheless, the current long-term trend is that businesses are experiencing shorter lives, or at least shorter times spent on particular specialisms.

We're now at a moment where organizations need to change again, and this time quite dramatically. We cannot disentangle businesses from the world in which they operate, and that world is experiencing profound disruption in almost every location and by almost every available consideration. Take the classic PESTLE analysis, originally conceived by the Harvard scholar Francis Aguilar in 1967, and then developed and expanded by subsequent theorists.[21] This model is designed to help organizations craft strategies with due consideration given to political, economic, socio-cultural, technological, legal, and environmental factors. Typically, if even one of those factors is in a state of high flux or disruption, it can create a chaotic impact on business planning. Right now, we are experiencing a global moment where every single one of those factors is in flux.

The pace of change is startling, from the polarized global political scene which has seen the rise of reactionary far-right and populist governments; to the damaging economic impact caused by the COVID-19 crisis (itself a multiplication of the economic hangover from 2008-09's financial crisis); to the growth of social justice movements championing inclusion and gender, racial and minority equality; to the digitally-driven Industry 4.0 era that we are now in and which was explored in Chapter 6; to fast-changing legislative contexts brought on by political crises such as Brexit; and to the imminent existential crisis we all now face in relation to environmental change.

Contextual influences on strategy

It's important to situate any strategy in the context within which its success will be determined. In Table 7.1, we consider some of the major trends influencing corporate strategy and inclusion.

TABLE 7.1 PESTLE analysis of trends influencing corporate strategy and inclusion

PESTLE factor	Key features: how a lack of inclusion manifests
Political	• Polarization and the loss of the political centre ground
	• Disruptions to peace or to long-standing international consensus or alliances
	• Reactionary and/or authoritarian governments (e.g. Brazil, Japan, China, India, US, UK, Poland)
	• The political environment that previously created a more certain operating environment is now part of the flux
	• Organizational need to bring polarized parties together to get work done
	• Organizations cannot rely on existing norms and protocols
Economic	• Typical economic cycles (boom and bust) and long-term Kondratiev waves now interspersed with irregular and short-term additional shocks such as pandemics, accelerated stock market volatility, faster, more frequent and more far-reaching technological innovation
	• Swing away from economic behemoths and towards social finances (cryptocurrencies, challenger banks, mobile economics)
	• Demographic shifts – declining birth rates and longer lives
	• Growth of African markets
	• Chinese economic uncertainty
	• Vast economic inequalities between and within nations
	• Rising wealth and changing consumer purchasing decisions

(continued)

TABLE 7.1 (Continued)

PESTLE factor	Key features: how a lack of inclusion manifests
Socio-cultural	• Global institutional racism, sexism, ableism and homophobia, mutated by social media and globalization • Social awakening and movements fighting for inclusion and equality such as #MeToo and Black Lives Matter • The backlash: wars on culture • Huge demographic changes • Employee activism and challenge to established hierarchies • Changing consumer preferences and heightened activism • Real-time brand and reputational challenges on social media in an age of greater transparency that can expose failings quickly
Techno-industrial	• Industry 4.0 (see Chapter 6) and exponential technological change • Pandemic-accelerated digital change • Hybrid working models • Greater opportunities for disabled participation, less excuse for denying varied working styles • Unintended consequences such as mass female exit from labour market and promotion opportunities • Segregation in workforce experience and opportunities
Legal	• Breakdown of shared global legal principles • Legislative crises caused by administrative failures • Erosion of hard-won equalities legislation
Environmental	• Existential climate change crisis • Divestments of fossil fuels • Race for clean energy • Green growth' myth (Hickel, 2020) • Climate change activism as the preserve of white, privileged elites • Coupling or decoupling of inclusion and climate agendas

The global COVID-19 pandemic is a major event that runs across and influences all of these factors, creating a highly unpredictable, disruptive and exacerbating effect. For example, the pandemic had a disproportionate effect on already-marginalized minority groups, as drawn out by the Lawrence Review in the UK.[22] Throw in demographic issues like declining birth rates across much of Europe, Asia, and North America,[23] paired with improvements in health provision which have led to the '100-year life' and accordingly long working lives,[24] and the implications for the organization are profound.

DEI today: the model for change

The good news is that there is a path through. We believe that the kernel of all these weighty change issues is inclusion. As you can see in Table 7.1, it is inclusion that has been the missing ingredient in many of the global structural challenges we now face. If we agree with that premise, it stands to reason that by reengineering our purposes and our systems with inclusion at the core, it is also inclusion that can help us tackle these seemingly intractable problems. For the avoidance of doubt, in this model inclusion does not replace other important strategies around topics such as sustainability. Rather, inclusion is the *method* which helps an organization to plot a path for the future to achieve those goals.

One thing social movements have done is to urge major (and smaller) global organizations into action on topics like race, ethnicity and gender. At the time of Stephen and Raafi's previous book in 2019, many organizations and their leaders were still exploring the *why*: why should we care about DEI? Now, while not a *fait accompli*, many of those same organizations and leaders have evolved their thinking. They recognize that institutional inequalities exist; they recognize that change needs to happen. Many – though by no means all – increasingly get the *why*; they are now grappling with the *how*. How do they acquire diverse talent? How do they adapt their workplaces to a completely different working pattern? How do they avoid backlash? How do they challenge hierarchy without throwing the baby out with the bathwater? How do they convince increasingly activist employees that the organization genuinely cares about them and their concerns? More and more, organizations are thinking and talking about and seeking to bring about truly embedded inclusion.

Collectively, many of us have reached a critical next step on the journey to inclusive cultures. Let's think back to Stephen's previous books that introduced the concepts of Diversity 101, Diversity 2.0, and Inclusion 3.0 – concepts that together constitute a maturity model for D&I work and which are pillars of the work we do at *Included*.

To recap these concepts:

- **Diversity 101** is the compliance-driven, legislative approach to diversity, incorporating box-ticking exercises and achieving a 'minimum'.
- **Diversity 2.0** is the world of 'taking a stand', manifesting in corporate messaging, visible social campaigning, and smart marketing on D&I.

- **Inclusion 3.0** is where inclusive thought and action are truly 'embedded' in decision-making and practised throughout all layers, functions, and behaviours of an organization.

We've now analysed organizations through these paradigm lenses for the best part of a decade, a decade when DEI has accelerated to be a top organizational priority. Does this mean that all organizations are now at Inclusion 3.0? Absolutely not.

Diversity 101 has been emboldened by gender pay gap legislation and the increasing interest of regulators in DEI as a soft power tool in their armoury. For example, many large organizations are now measuring and closing the gender pay gap, and starting to measure the ethnicity pay gap also.[25] Most financial services organizations are diligently attending regulator briefings on their 'cultural expectations'. Shareholders and boards are increasingly asking their executives for meaningful metrics.

Diversity 2.0 has seen the largest growth, especially so in the heated media environment of Black Lives Matter and other social justice causes. Employees and consumers expect organizations to have a point of view on these issues. They may or may not directly relate to their trading, but regardless they matter to stakeholders. And in a hyper-connected world, brave is the organization that fails to acknowledge the work needed in this area.

More of Inclusion 3.0 is happening than people realize. We've been encouraged that there are now multiple examples of organizations incorporating and embedding inclusion in their work. For example, Cloudflare, the internet services firm, undertook a detailed analysis of their engineering design and incorporated an 'inclusion step' to pre-emptively embed inclusion awareness into product design. This came from a prior misstep when coding errors led to exclusion of certain users from important online resources. But with a combination of expert advice, engaged employees and inclusive managers, they were able to turn this into a future proofing exercise that stands Cloudflare in good stead for all future design.

What has become increasingly clear to us over the years is that this maturity model is not an either/or proposition. We must not leave Diversity 101 behind when we evolve to Diversity 2.0. Legislation and human rights are obviously critically important tenets of life. Likewise, we must not forget about taking a stand or visibly marketing our D&I work (Diversity 2.0) just because we think we have it embedded (Inclusion 3.0). How we show up to the world and communicate our commitments truly matter.

We might instead think of the model like a house. Diversity 101 represents the foundations. Diversity 2.0 represents the outer walls and appearance. Inclusion 3.0 is the lifeblood: the interior structures and features. We need all of them.

By reframing inclusion away from being purely an internal HR, legal or marketing issue, and instead looking again, hard, at inclusion in our strategies, data, governance, leadership behaviours, and systems, we believed that Inclusion 3.0 could help to truly embed inclusive change on a systemic level. And we still believe that.

Inclusion as strategy: Inclusion 4.0 and the Inclusive Purpose Organization (IPO)

In addition to the above, the time has come for organizations to address an even more fundamental challenge. Further to compliance, marketing and embedding inclusion in everything they do, organizations need to confront the reality that the very behaviours and systems into which they are embedding D&I may be no longer fit for purpose.

Take for example, a female talent development programme. If the success of the programme is measured by the number of women promoted, yet the environment into which they are being promoted is still largely male, will this success be sustainable? Take a race sponsorship programme. If the success of the programme is promotions, or changes in representation, will this endure if the very norms and protocols needed to navigate the culture remain the preserve of certain groups? Take a comprehensive marketing and PR campaign in support of Black Lives Matter. No matter how genuine, authentic or successful that campaign, how credible is it if the core products of the same organization are still contributing to racial inequality?

Inclusion 4.0 is about changing the system, not embedding inclusion in the existing (unfit) system. In this way, inclusion needs to be strategic, otherwise it will be insufficient to shift the system and bring about the change required. In Inclusion 3.0, we saw that inclusion needs to be strategic to add value. If it's an initiative unlinked to and unembedded in the CEO's strategy, it will fail. Inclusion 4.0 is about determining what the overall organizational strategy is and articulating why it needs to be inclusive.

Let's take the example of the police. What if the reaction of police forces to examples of systemic racism was to change the notion of what policing is? In the UK, it's policing by consent, not force. What if police *forces* became police *services* and partnered with communities who could genuinely influence strategy and be joint agents in crime reduction? US police forces overall have a terrible reputation for race relations, yet there are examples of innovative community policing that are correlated with above-average reductions in crime.[26] Such movements could help to address long-standing, deep issues pertaining to the recruitment and experiences of minority police officers, which were so well summarized in Parm Sandhu's 2021 account of her career in London's Metropolitan Police.[27]

What about if, post-COVID, pharmaceutical companies reimagined drug development? Instead of clinical trials composed of certain groups in certain locations, they might think about calculated risks as part of an overall de-risking strategy. LifeArc, the British life sciences charity, is using its £1.6 billion endowment to focus on rare diseases that have largely been overlooked by traditional companies. With rapid technological advancements, and a compelling proposition attracting top talent, it is quite conceivable this emphasis on inclusion will lead to some breakthrough drugs that are commercially successful to boot.

What about if technology companies made the reduction, or even elimination, or bias a core part of their purpose? Imagine the effect on employee morale of Amazon's facial recognition software being used to decrease the racial incarceration disparity instead of fuelling it.

The street we live on

The state of the world, outlined above, is in no small part due to exclusion of particular people from decision making. Organizations have blindly advocated for more women to get into senior leadership positions, without first questioning whether the leadership structures themselves are sound (see, for example, outdated partnership models at big consultancy firms). If a given corporate system is built purely to create profit for majority white, male, already wealthy shareholders, why would we continue to propagate it with inclusion as an enabler? We are in danger of releasing a vaccine (inclusion) into an already doomed body. Worse, we risk compounding extant broken structures. We risk people misunderstanding what inclusion is about and eliding the critical requirements of marginalized minority groups in their ongoing struggle for equal access.

It is this problem that has sparked for us the concept of the Inclusive Purpose Organization, the major feature of Inclusion 4.0 in our refreshed

TABLE 7.2 Concepts on the journey to inclusion

(See also Frost and Alidina, 2019)	Diversity 101 'diversity for diversity's sake'	Diversity 2.0 'diversity for social responsibility'	Inclusion 3.0 'diversity as business strategy'	Inclusion 4.0 'inclusion as organizational purpose'
Definition	Compliance-based programmes designed to raise awareness of difference, meet legal standards and achieve a minimum	Marketing and reputation-led programmes designed to 'take a stand'	Integrated systems designed to embed inclusion in and throughout organizations	Recalibration of systems to frame inclusion as both purpose and strategy (ends and means)
Origins	Ensuring basic rights in the face of historical injustices.	Shareholder pressure, HR and marketing functions and corporate social responsibility	Recognition of unconscious bias, egocentricity and leadership deficit	Advanced awareness of global inequalities, climate crisis, organizational shifts
Education method	Diversity training, unconscious bias, simple internal action plans	Diversity workshops, internal DEI strategies	Strategic, structured conversations and interventions, external and internal DEI strategies	Inclusive strategic planning, impact-led, community-centred approaches
Leadership approach	Top down, authority led, compliance driven	Top down, authority led, auditing approach	Bottom up, top-level support, creative group leadership, peer review	Vulnerable, humble, networked, servantship, citizenship (interconnected-ness)
Delivery mechanisms	HR or L&D delivery teams, equality impact assessments	Marketing, DEI team, needs assessments	Whole organization, benchmarking and information sharing	Executive-led (purpose and strategy), whole organization delivery
Measurement	Quotas, legal reporting	Marketing campaigns, voluntary targets, corporate social responsibility reporting/PR	Target zones, high-frequency real-time reporting and individual accountability	Impact (external and internal), advanced digitally enabled reporting, individual accountability

maturity model. If Inclusion 3.0 is embedding inclusion in the organization as it is, Inclusion 4.0 is changing the organization to be inclusive. If Inclusion 3.0 is ensuring balanced slates, independent scoring and consistent questions to all interviewees, Inclusion 4.0 is moving the location of the interview to a location that empowers the candidate and forces the organization to adapt to a new crop of talent. What many executives have yet to grasp is that adapting to others is not simply a nice thing to do, it's the ultimate client-centricity that futureproofs the organization you are running.

If Diversity 101, Diversity 2.0, and Inclusion 3.0 are the house, Inclusion 4.0 is the street we live on. It's our purpose, the environment we choose to inhabit, the systems we create and participate in. The locale we are dependent on to meet our basic survival needs. Table 7.3 shows some of the key features of the IPO.

TABLE 7.3 Key features of the IPO

	Traditional organization	Inclusive Purpose Organization
Purpose	Commercial	Inclusion
Performance metrics	Revenue and profitability	Impact
Stakeholders	Shareholders	A wider circle – people and communities
Growth	Year-on-year growth	Stability and return on investment in terms of people, planet, profit
Structure	Hierarchical, command and control	Flat, networked, hybrid
Culture	Certain Employee adapts to employer	Humble Inclusive, employer adapts to employee
Outlook on inclusion	Internal	External and internal

CASE STUDY
Ofcom: making communications work for everyone

Some organizations already have naturally inclusive purposes. Take Ofcom, the regulator for communications (including television, radio, and now online content) in the UK. Their purpose is to 'make communications work for everyone'. Mission statements don't get much more inclusive than that. The challenge that Ofcom has been exploring is how to turn their purpose into lived reality for their 900 people (internally) and their stakeholders (externally) – the entire UK population – all the while navigating rapid changes in digital consumption, and so-called 'culture wars' played out in the UK political and media spheres which threaten the rights of marginalized groups.[28]

The logic for inclusion as strategy for Ofcom is simple. To make 'communications work for everyone' they have to include everyone. That means making their staff base as diverse as possible but then including them in decision making. That entails a series of staff networks, brought together with a series of summits with senior management to directly influence policy, internally and externally. That means holding their regulated entities accountable for DEI. Recently, Ofcom published its fifth Diversity in broadcasting report that showcased comparative DEI data from the major broadcasters. We could see from the five-year trends that progress had been mixed. Ofcom was able to adapt and highlight further work needed in certain areas (such as race and disability) to inform strategy – for itself and its stakeholders. Of course, it's not always easy and they have to make decisions that not everyone is going to agree with. However, they have adapted to their diverse clients (the broadcast sector and the UK population) in a way that brings their staff base into decision making and fosters a sense of belonging. This means that they are well placed to make inclusive decisions in the future.

CASE STUDY
AstraZeneca: COVID-19 vaccine development

AstraZeneca was one of the first major pharmaceutical companies to develop a COVID-19 vaccine. How they developed it is interesting in terms of adapting strategy to an inclusive purpose.

Pharmaceutical companies do not always enjoy the best reputation among important stakeholders, not least the general public, only marginally better than the tobacco and oil companies we started the chapter with. 'Big Pharma' has often been seen as profiting from illnesses and restricting and controlling drug supply to maintain high prices and margins.[29] At the same time, there are legitimate and significant research costs to recoup, alongside the necessity of incentivizing further research, innovation and drug development that has wider societal benefits.

When it came to the COVID-19 pandemic, AstraZeneca took an interesting approach. They agreed with Oxford University to develop the vaccine at cost price, in other words to not profit from its development and distribution. The key scientist at Oxford, Sarah Gilbert, said 'we're a university and we're not in this to make money'.[30]

This is in contrast to other pharmaceutical companies that adopted a more conventional approach. While AstraZeneca has not lost money, it has not profited either. Oxford and AstraZeneca agreed to supply the vaccine on a not-for-profit basis and 'in perpetuity for low and middle-income countries'[31]. However, the result in terms of staff morale, talent acquisition, stakeholder relations and other discretionary efforts has been remarkable, and has clearly contributed to other successes too.[32]

The clinical trials involved over 24,000 diverse participants in Brazil, South Africa and the UK. Further trials took part in Kenya, Japan, India and the USA. This is in stark contrast to previous clinical trials that used relatively homogenous easily accessible groups and ended up with drugs that were inequitable for certain groups[33].

Pascal Soriot, AstraZeneca CEO said that 'the vaccine's simple supply chain and our no-profit pledge and commitment to broad, equitable and timely access means it will be affordable and globally available'.[34]

By rethinking how vaccines should be developed, and pre-emptively considering inclusion, AstraZeneca has achieved significant competitive advantage against competitors and positioned itself well for the future among important stakeholders.

CASE STUDY

Bank of England: racial equality as fiscal strategy

In September 2020, senior leaders at the Bank of England – the central bank of the United Kingdom – commissioned a Court Review on ethnic diversity and inclusion to measure progress and better understand barriers to a more inclusive Bank. Court Reviews have historically been reserved for matters of the highest strategic importance, commissioned rarely. That the Bank's leadership decided to conduct such a process reflected the critical and urgent nature of this topic, in a year marked by COVID-19 and social campaigning. As Chair of the Review Diana Noble put it, diversity and inclusion 'will lead to better outcomes for the Bank, and better outcomes for the people of the United Kingdom'.[35]

The Review's findings were published in July 2021. The Bank found that there had been many failings and much work to do, particularly across three major areas: the career experiences of colleagues, the lived experiences of minority ethnic colleagues, and the frameworks and systems that would help to improve ethnic inclusion.

These findings in themselves are nothing surprising. The challenges facing the Bank can also be seen in many other sectors and organizations. Indeed, there is not a single organization that we have come across that has got DEI perfectly right.

What felt different about the Bank's approach was the extremely public, visible nature of its self-assessment. The Bank went public with its own failings, going as far as to highlight to national newspapers some of the most problematic trends, tendencies and 'material disparities' they had uncovered within themselves.[36] This set a powerful, proactive example not only to other regulators, but to organizations of all kinds. Leadership like this is what distinguishes Inclusion 4.0 from other models.

Humility of this kind has been a long time coming in public organizational life. The Bank's example shows us a clear demarcation from the now-tired roadshow of D&I awards ceremonies, Instagram campaigns and PR sheen. The Bank has historically propagated racial injustice, propping up aspects of the British empire and housing governors with links to the slave trade.[37] It has work to do, but it has vulnerably acknowledged this fact and is now setting about doing it.

Conclusion

We started with the challenging examples of tobacco and fossil fuel organizations trying to repurpose themselves. Greenwashing or not, what is clear is that in addition to these organizations, there are many others, in many sectors, from public services to pharma to tech, that are now revisiting their very purpose. While the case studies of Inclusion 4.0 organizations are still significantly fewer than those we can cite from Diversity 101, 2.0 or Inclusion 3.0, the opportunity is there for the taking. We look forward to partnering with visionary professionals who want to make inclusion a force for good for themselves, their teams, their organizations and the wider world.

Key takeaways

1 To navigate the current global environment, organizations need to radically rethink their strategy. A PESTLE analysis demonstrates that inclusion can be the missing piece of the jigsaw to help them better succeed.

2 Beyond compliance, marketing and even embedding inclusion in everything an organization does, Inclusion 4.0 is the new paradigm for how organizations consider their very purpose. Inclusive Purpose Organizations (IPOs) change their systems to be more effective in the future.

3   There are already proof points and case studies of organizations repurposing towards becoming IPOs and inclusion 4.0 entities. This chapter sets out the framework for others to seize the opportunity.

References

1   Philip Morris International (2020) Letter from the Board of Directors philipmorrisinternational.gcs-web.com/static-files/9119cdbc-0f37-4235-87d0-1a79e50684cd (archived at https://perma.cc/M4WR-DGTM)

2   Truth Initiative (2021) 4 ways the tobacco industry is attempting to rebrand itself, *Truth Initiative: Inspiring Lives Free From Smoking, Vaping and Nicotine*, 10 June truthinitiative.org/research-resources/tobacco-industry-marketing/4-ways-tobacco-industry-attempting-rebrand-itself (archived at https://perma.cc/C7G6-V7R7)

3   Imperial Brands (2018) *From Tobacco to Something Better: Our Approach to Next Generation Products.* Imperial Brands plc www.imperialbrandsplc.com/content/dam/imperial-brands/sciences/About_Us/NGP/Imperial%20Brands%20NGP%20Report.pdf (archived at https://perma.cc/79DN-S92Q)

4   British American Tobacco (2020) *News Release: Building A Better Tomorrow.* British American Tobacco plc www.bat.com/group/sites/UK__9D9KCY.nsf/vwPagesWebLive/DOBMSP7L (archived at https://perma.cc/2388-VQJ7)

5   Altria (2021) *Reducing Harm and Preventing Underage Use: Moving Beyond Smoking.* Altria Group, Inc www.altria.com/-/media/Project/Altria/Altria/responsibility/corporate-responsibility-reports/reducing-harm-and-preventing-underage-use-2020-2021.pdf?src=moving-beyond-smoking#page=5 (archived at https://perma.cc/Y3L3-Q54E)

6   Shell (2020) *Energy For A Better Future: Annual Report and Accounts for the Year ended December 31 2019,* Royal Dutch Shell plc reports.shell.com/annual-report/2019/servicepages/downloads/files/shell_annual_report_2019.pdf (archived at https://perma.cc/58C8-A9WT)

7   BP (2018) *Growing the business and advancing the energy transition,* British Petroleum plc www.bp.com/content/dam/bp/business-sites/en/global/corporate/pdfs/investors/bp-annual-report-and-form-20f-2018.pdf (archived at https://perma.cc/5E9J-DWS3)

8   McKeown, M (2013) *The Strategy Book: How to Think and Act Strategically to Deliver Outstanding Results.* London: Pearson UK

9   Spangler, T (2021) Netflix Wins Seven Oscars, Biggest Haul Among All Studios This Year, *Variety*, 26 April variety.com/2021/awards/news/netflix-oscars-most-wins-1234959949/ (archived at https://perma.cc/DK47-94DN)

10 Neerman, P (2019) Amazon world's largest and quickest parcel deliverer, *Retail Detail,* 4 December www.retaildetail.eu/en/news/general/amazon-worlds-largest-and-quickest-parcel-deliverer (archived at https://perma.cc/YFN8-6XGR)

11 OICA (2017) *World Motor Vehicle Production: World Ranking of Manufacturers,* International Organization of Motor Vehicle Manufacturers www.oica.net/wp-content/uploads/World-Ranking-of-Manufacturers.pdf (archived at https://perma.cc/67XE-X27L)

12 Colgate-Palmolive (2021) *Our History, Colgate-Palmolive* www. colgatepalmolive.com/en-us/who-we-are/history (archived at https://perma.cc/ G4FN-SL27)

13 Biron, B (2019) Tiffany & Co. was just acquired by LVMH, *Business Insider,* 26 November www.businessinsider.com/tiffany-and-co-history-iconic-luxury-brand-2019-11 (archived at https://perma.cc/7WDE-E9RR)

14 Pascoe, W. (2001) Charting the rise of Nokia, *BBC News,* 23 August news.bbc. co.uk/1/hi/business/1505703.stm (archived at https://perma.cc/B8TA-AAWJ)

15 McKeown, M (2008) *The Truth about Innovation.* London: Pearson Education

16 Gittleson, K (2012) Can a company live forever? *BBC News,* 19 January www. bbc.com/news/business-16611040 (archived at https://perma.cc/5YMG-QQVA)

17 Garelli, S (2016) Top reasons why you will probably live longer than most big companies, *IMD Business School,* December. www.imd.org/research-knowledge/articles/why-you-will-probably-live-longer-than-most-big-companies/ (archived at https://perma.cc/UYC5-DCVQ)

18 Brett, D (2017) FTSE 100 history: how the index has changed over 33 years, *CityAM,* 3 July www.cityam.com/ftse-100-history-index-has-changed-over-33-years/ (archived at https://perma.cc/6UL2-2XGM)

19, 20 Wei, W (2019) Corporate Longevity, *Brunswick Group,* 4 June www. brunswickgroup.com/corporate-longevity-i10173/ (archived at https://perma. cc/M5BE-ASXV)

21 Aguilar, F J (1967) *Scanning the Business Environment,* New York: Macmillan

22 Lawrence, B D (2020) *An Avoidable Crisis: The disproportionate impact of Covid-19 on Black, Asian and minority ethnic communities* www. lawrencereview.co.uk/ (archived at https://perma.cc/5WEQ-YDHX)

23 McBain, S (2021) The baby bust: How a declining birth rate will reshape the world, *New Statesman,* 7 July www.newstatesman.com/politics/2021/07/ baby-bust-how-declining-birth-rate-will-reshape-world (archived at https:// perma.cc/P4PL-M3M7)

24 Gratton, L and Scott, A. (2020) *The 100-Year Life: Living and Working in an Age of Longevity.* London: Bloomsbury Publishing

25 LSE (2021) Gender pay gap closes by one fifth after reporting introduced, *London School of Economics and Political Science,* 26 March www.lse.ac.uk/News/ Latest-news-from-LSE/2021/c-March-21/Gender-pay-gap-closes-by-one-fifth-after-reporting-introduced.aspx (archived at https://perma.cc/5TNA-ANMM)

26 City of Plymouth, MN (2014) *Pillar 4: Community Policing & Crime Reduction* www.plymouthmn.gov/departments/public-safety/police-/21st-century-policing/pillar-4 (archived at https://perma.cc/6BXV-3XUP)

27 Sandhu, P (2021) *Black and Blue: One Woman's Story of Policing and Prejudice.* London: Atlantic Books

28 Ofcom (2021) *Making Ofcom work for everyone: Ofcom's diversity and inclusion strategy 2021–26.* Ofcom. www.ofcom.org.uk/__data/assets/pdf_file/0012/210900/diversity-and-inclusion-strategy-report-2019-20.pdf (archived at https://perma.cc/77FR-6VFS)

29 Anderson, R (2014) Pharmaceutical industry gets high on fat profits, *BBC News*, 6 November www.bbc.com/news/business-28212223 (archived at https://perma.cc/5LCZ-C89V)

30 *BBC News* (2020) Prof Sarah Gilbert: The woman who designed the Oxford vaccine, 23 November www.bbc.com/news/uk-55043551 (archived at https://perma.cc/5ZZA-HNZQ)

31 Beaumont, P (2020) Oxford AstraZeneca vaccine to be sold to developing countries at cost price, *The Guardian,* 23 November www.theguardian.com/global-development/2020/nov/23/oxford-astrazeneca-results-covid-vaccine-developing-countries (archived at https://perma.cc/N8LD-DXVJ)

32 The Telegraph (2021) Winners of the WorkL Workplace Awards 2021 revealed, *The Telegraph,* 26 October www.telegraph.co.uk/business/2021/10/26/winners-workl-workplace-awards-2021-revealed/ (archived at https://perma.cc/8REN-5GH5)

33 University of Oxford (2020) Oxford University breakthrough on global COVID-19 vaccine, 23 November www.ox.ac.uk/news/2020-11-23-oxford-university-breakthrough-global-covid-19-vaccine (archived at https://perma.cc/W7MX-X876)

34 Boseley, S and Sample, I (2020) Oxford AstraZeneca Covid vaccine has up to 90% efficacy, data reveals, *The Guardian,* 23 November www.theguardian.com/society/2020/nov/23/astrazeneca-says-its-coronavirus-vaccine-has-70-per-cent-efficacy-covid-oxford-university (archived at https://perma.cc/3YXF-9925)

35 Noble, D (2021) *Court Review of Ethnic Diversity and Inclusion,* Bank of England www.bankofengland.co.uk/report/2021/court-review-of-ethnic-diversity-and-inclusion (archived at https://perma.cc/247A-RW6X)

36 Strauss, D (2021) Bank of England's minority ethnic staff face 'material disparities', review finds, *Financial Times,* 21 July www.ft.com/content/846ecd58-e971-450d-ba44-6a6b1e210b6a (archived at https://perma.cc/3HGB-X9WJ)

37 Jolly, J (2020) Bank of England apologises for role of former directors in slave trade, *The Guardian,* 18 June www.theguardian.com/business/2020/jun/18/bank-of-england-apologises-for-role-of-former-directors-in-slave-trade (archived at https://perma.cc/82CP-UKZN)

08

Data and measurement

RAAFI-KARIM ALIDINA

At this point in time, we know more about each other than ever before in human history. According to Data Never Sleeps, an organization that tracks how much data is created across the globe, 90 per cent of all data that exists was created in the past two years.[1] Through online shopping, social media, sharing of pictures, streaming tv and videos, and just searching the internet, humanity produces more than 2.5 quintillion bytes of data every day.

With this rapid increase in the availability of data, organizations are seeking to make data-driven decisions in previously unimaginable ways. For many years, this reliance on data to make decisions somehow skipped the DEI field. The world has wasted about $8 billion per year on diversity programmes because organizations never measured their impact or effectiveness.[2] But data is one of the most critical components of building more inclusive workplaces.

This chapter will define why D&I data is so important, what types of data to collect, and how to leverage that data to develop concrete, effective, and sustainable D&I interventions and embed an inclusive lens in an organization.

Why data is critical for DEI work

Collecting, analyzing and applying insights from data has become a key element of how businesses drive success. Data is used in everything from predicting customer trends, to assessing credit risk. Similarly, data also brings several benefits to a strong DEI programme. When collected accurately and leveraged well, diversity and inclusion data can help you understand your organization's past, assess your present, and prepare for the future.

With comprehensive and accurate data, organizations can look back at different initiatives to assess what worked and what didn't – and most importantly, what worked or didn't work *for whom*. For almost any programme introduced in an organization, some groups will benefit more than others. What's important, though, is to understand if there are systematic patterns in the groups that weren't benefiting. If there are patterns, then we can provide appropriate supports for those groups. However, without understanding the differences between people – their genders, races, disabilities, etc. – we won't be able to see if any of those patterns exist or identify gaps to deliver targeted initiatives. This baseline assessment helps us to understand where the problems are so that our initiatives focus on those areas, rather than developing solutions before we know what the problem is.

Finally, having comprehensive data allows us to prepare for the future by helping us analyse longitudinal trends to predict where our organizations might be in coming years. For example, with adequate diversity data, we can see if with current hiring, termination, and resignation rates we are becoming more or less diverse in different ways and why. This allows us to course-correct now, so that don't have those issues in the future.

Measuring diversity vs measuring inclusion

Most organizations have begun to measure diversity. This often starts with gathering data on those characteristics many of us often think about when we hear the word *diversity*: gender and race/ethnicity. Often, because most large organizations gather birthdate information as part of HR onboarding, organizations can measure age diversity as well. These are critical pieces of information for understanding our people better.

However, these are only the beginning. While gender-, age-, and race-based discrimination are essential to measure and correct, bias and discrimination exist across many other aspects of diversity. Also importantly, these are not the only aspects of our identities that inform the way we think and make our teams more cognitively diverse. Organizations are becoming more cognizant of this, understanding that cognitively diverse teams perform better. As such, they are beginning to put more effort in measuring other demographics such as disability (both visible and invisible), sexual orientation, and religion. This may not be possible in all contexts – there may be legal or cultural barriers to asking some of these demographic questions – but increasingly organizations are asking *how* they can get diversity data rather than *if* they can get it. This is a positive trend as biases against marginalized groups exist everywhere, regardless of the hurdles in counting those groups.

Furthermore, organizations are expanding the scope of cognitive diversity and are measuring things like introversion/extraversion, socioeconomic background, educational background, and work style. When measured correctly with statistically validated tools like the Big 5 Personality Index or the Bridge Group's social mobility measurements, these are extremely useful data for understanding and leveraging diverse teams.

Yet, while many organizations have become mature in measuring diversity, very few are measuring inclusion. *D* and *I* are very different. Diversity is about the mix of people we have, the different identities represented by the people in the room. Inclusion, however, is about the environment in which the group works. It's about whether different people, regardless of their backgrounds, feel like they can speak up, like their voice is heard, like they can be themselves without a fear of backlash.

Inclusion is essential because diverse teams only perform better if each individual feels they can actually bring their diverse perspectives, approaches and solutions to the table.

Measuring diversity *can* begin to help us understand how included employees feel – if large proportions are answering 'prefer not to say' to diversity characteristics, that could indicate a lack of psychological safety to disclose that information. But beyond these basic inferences, measuring inclusion requires further inquiry.

Inclusion can be more difficult to quantify as it measures people's perceptions, but you can do so by measuring elements like transparency, microaggressions, and trust and belonging. *Included* finds many clients are already gathering data in these areas through employee engagement or well-being surveys, they just aren't thinking of them as aspects of inclusion. However, once we take that data and combine it with diversity data, we can better understand trends of which groups are feeling less included and develop interventions targeted for them.

We also find that qualitative inclusion data is useful for moving forward in organizations. Building intrinsic motivation around often requires more than just rational argument. It also requires leaders to empathize with those who feel less included. Qualitative data often allows for this much more easily than quantitative data does. Additionally, listening and focus groups to gather qualitative data create spaces for marginalized employees to express themselves and often serve as positive interventions in and of themselves.

You've got data, now what?

Organizations often let their data sit around without doing much with it. Data solutions company Splunk found that on average 55 per cent of data that companies collect is unused.[3] For over a third of the companies surveyed, more than 75 per cent of their data is unused. This is so common that this unused data has its own name: Dark Data. So the question is, once an organization has collected information on the diversity and inclusion of their employees, how do we ensure that this doesn't go to waste and become dark data?

One of the main reasons Splunk found for unused data was that organizations didn't know *how* to use their data. But when DEI is embedded in organizational strategy, we become much more specific about what data we're gathering and why. For example, if our goal is to increase ethnic diversity, then logically we gather ethnicity data on hiring, termination, and resignation rates to see where we can improve. A similar approach can be taken with inclusion data – if we find that psychological safety is low for disabled employees but high for non-disabled employees then we can focus on those areas.

While collecting data is critical, before we do so it's crucial to know what we want to do with that data.

How leveraging data helps us become more mature in our DEI initiatives

While leveraging DEI data is often used with business outcomes in mind, it can follow that our organizations mature in our understanding and implementation of DEI initiatives.

We have worked with clients at all stages of the DEI journey. Some are just beginning, collecting data because they're required to report it. Others are extremely mature, using insights from inclusion data to drive changes in their systems and processes, behaviours, and the way they do their work. Most are somewhere in the middle, still in the process of understanding the power of inclusive workplace cultures and how they can use that to drive their business goals. Just by starting to measure DEI, organizations realize what they *could* know – and they want to know more.

Often, this starts with measuring mandatory diversity characteristics, such as gender, age, and sometimes ethnicity. But often, once leaders see this data they want to know more about their employees. So they begin to gather data about more diversity characteristics, like disability, sexual orientation, and others.

Using data to drive important questions

Once organizations have and begin sharing this data, it often leads to questions. Some questions *Included* has experienced from clients include, 'Why do we have so few disabled employees?', 'Why is the proportion of women at upper levels so low?', 'Why are so many of our recruits from upper socio-economic backgrounds?' These questions are important ones, and they all have one thing in common: They start with *Why*.

Diversity data asks *what* does our organization look like, or *who* works there. But once we know that, it's natural for us to ask *why?* This is what inclusion measurement seeks to answer. And as we begin getting answers to those questions, we start to ask *How?* How do we solve these problems we've identified?

Once we've started asking *how*, we begin developing and embedding interventions. While your organization might just be beginning, and you might feel stagnated because you're not doing deep work yet, taking the first step in DEI measurement can be the catalyst towards embedding inclusion throughout the entire business.

The critical role of public policy in organizational DEI

Many countries have long lists of protected characteristics, but organizations often don't collect data on all of them. In the UK, the 2010 Equality Act identified eight different characteristics to be protected from workplace discrimination by law.[4] However, over a decade later, many organizations in the UK don't even measure those characteristics to ensure they aren't discriminating. They deal with cases as they come up, rather than taking a preventative approach.

What does help, though, is when policy requires some reporting on this data. If an organization has to report something to the government, they have almost no choice but to measure it. In the US, the Equal Employment Opportunity Commission requires organizations to report their ethnicity data to ensure there is no racial discrimination occurring. The UK's gender pay gap reporting law required all companies of 250 employees or more to report their gender pay gaps to the government. This policy led to many more organizations measuring their gender pay gaps for the first time.

Policy interest in D&I data is only increasing – for example, regulators in the UK are talking more and more about the importance of D&I and have begun to ask firms they regulate about their D&I data collection practices or to share their diversity data. This is just the beginning of sector-wide pushes for public D&I measurement.

With this data being publicly available, anyone can see who is doing better on their salary gaps, or who is employing more people of colour. This is critical more now than ever before as young people are increasingly interested in working for companies that align with their values. In fact, one survey by the Institute for Public Relations found that '47 per cent of millennials think diversity and inclusion are important criteria when looking for a potential employer'.[5] This public data allows candidates to ask important questions to their potential employers about what they care deeply about. And if organizations don't have a good answer for why their gender pay gap is so large, or why their company is so undiverse, they'll lose out on good candidates.

This leads to the biggest reason why policy around public reporting on DEI is so critical: it forces organizations to look at why gaps might exist. This data gets discussed in the press. It's referenced on Glassdoor. It's discussed within the company. As such, organizations are forced to justify their results. And if they can't, there's pressure to review the reasons behind them. And sometimes, this can lead to more systematic changes in how organizations make remuneration, recruitment, or promotion decisions.

The business case controversy: why inclusion data is so important

The business case for DEI – that organizations that are more diverse make more money, are more innovative, and make better decisions overall – is one of the main reasons organizations engage in this work. One oft-cited study is a 2015 McKinsey report (and their follow-up reports) showing that organizations with more gender-diverse boards had better returns, and that organizations in the top quartiles of gender and ethnic diversity had financial returns that were 15 per cent and 30 per cent above the industry median, respectively.[6]

This is powerful data for any organization – get more diverse and you'll make more money. However, recent scholarship has found that these claims may be exaggerated. They state that they couldn't replicate the findings from the original report.[7] These studies do acknowledge that diverse teams don't have *worse* outcomes, but they find that the financial benefit from diverse teams is minimal at best.

So how do we make sense of these data? Do we still need to make the business case for DEI? Can we do so justifiably given these new findings?

When we look deeper, we can easily see the main reason these findings aren't incongruous: they're not actually about DEI – they're just about diversity. But we know that diversity without inclusion doesn't actually lead to positive results. If your diverse team members don't feel like they can speak up and express that difference, then you can't leverage it.

The research shows the importance of inclusion in teams. University of Texas professor Meghna Sabharwal has found that diversity management alone does not improve workplace performance. An approach that promotes greater inclusion of employees by taking their backgrounds and views into account and increasing transparency in decision-making leads to increased performance and productivity.[8] Further research has shown that diversity is more likely to lead to feelings of workplace well-being, trust in the organization, and employee engagement when inclusion practices are also incorporated into the organization.[9]

These are only two of the studies showing that diversity is insufficient, but they also emphasize the importance of doing more research on inclusion rather than just diversity. While we may know that inclusion is critical for performance, we still don't know enough about what aspects of inclusion are most critical or whether inclusion is more important for certain groups.

Additionally, we need to know more about which inclusion techniques work. There are myriad nudges and interventions that can help create more inclusive processes, like using strictly structured interviews[10] or setting inclusive meeting norms.[11] However, we also know that nudges like these are highly context-dependent and often only work for a short period of time because people get used to them. More research needs to be done to see what works in different workplace contexts, and what interventions can stick long-term.

Thus, while there is a debate about the business case for diversity, there isn't really one about the business case for inclusion. The focus shouldn't be on trying to make the case that inclusion matters, but instead on understanding what interventions are most effective to implement.

Quantitatively measuring inclusive cultures: the inclusion diagnostic

Most organizations, when they begin to measure inclusion, ask employees questions like, 'Do you feel like our company culture is inclusive?' or 'Do you feel like your voice is heard?'. These questions and can give helpful information about how employees feel overall about an organization. If this is paired with diversity data, then we can disaggregate that information by demographic group to understand if different groups have different opinions in these areas.

However, while these questions provide an overview, they don't tell us anything about *why* employees feel included or not. Moreover, these questions are quite abstract and nebulous, making them difficult for employees to answer. If someone asked you, 'do you feel included here?' most likely, your answer would be 'sometimes yes, sometimes no' or 'in some ways yes, but in other ways no'. It leaves the definition of what it means to feel included up for personal interpretation, which can lead to inconsistent and unreliable results.

To solve this problem, *Included* developed our Inclusion Diagnostic (ID). This survey tool asks employees specific, tangible questions about the behaviours they experience related to inclusion and exclusion. By reviewing the academic literature on DEI – everything from sociology and anthropology to organizational behaviour and economics – we were able to identify key questions about behaviours that make people feel included. Instead of asking, 'do you feel your voice is heard?' we ask, 'how often are you interrupted in meetings?' and 'do you feel you can express dissent without a fear of backlash?', among other similar questions. These questions are much more concrete for employees to answer, providing much more reliable results.

Moreover, when we pair these questions with outcome measures like job satisfaction or likelihood of turnover and with demographic questions, we can run statistical analyses that show which behaviours affect which outcomes, and how that might differ for different groups. This allows organizations to target their interventions much more specifically, increasing the likelihood of success and efficiency.

CASE STUDY
Global tech scale-up

Challenge

This organization was a rapidly expanding technology company for whom DEI was already a critical part of enabling the business to grow successfully. Their rate of growth meant that DEI was essential for recruitment and inclusion of new hires. While the organization had already launched several initiatives, they had noted a few blind spots within their approach and some employees had raised concerns around issues they were facing.

They required support in gathering the right diversity data to understand their current structure and what this might mean for the future of the organization's diversity. They were keen to investigate how this structure varied according to seniority levels. This diversity data would subsequently enable them to define the most targeted, effective interventions. They also needed help gathering baseline data on inclusion for a clearer understanding of which groups were feeling most excluded and how to best implement measures to improve inclusion.

Actions

Included first ran a Diversity Projection Model to establish what the company might look like from a diversity standpoint in one, three, and five years under different scenarios. If they continued their existing actions, they would get slightly more gender- and age-diverse, but could they have a huge impact with even just moderate changes in recruitment and retention strategies?

We then ran our Inclusion Diagnostic to understand how different groups experienced inclusive or exclusive behaviours at the organization. The data revealed that improving psychological safety, reducing microaggressions, and increasing transparency and objectivity in decision-making were the biggest drivers of inclusion, and that groups experienced these differently.

Finally, we ran focus groups to delve more deeply into the findings of the previous work, specifically focusing on these key behaviours and the demographic groups who were most disproportionately being affected by these behaviours.

Impact

This data work led to an increased understanding about where the company was lacking diversity and inclusion. This allowed leaders to set achievable as well as stretch targets on diversity in an informed way. Moreover, the inclusion data allowed them to set priorities for what interventions they would introduce. For example, one of their focus areas was improving inclusion levels for women who were not experiencing the same levels of psychological safety as other groups. Similarly, LGBT+ employees had lower perceptions of transparency in personnel decisions than others, which has led to more clear and structured promotion requirements. As a growing firm, they had limited resources to spend on DEI initiatives, and this data ensured that they were allocating those resources in the most efficient way to create impact on inclusion.

In similar organizations these interventions have resulted in more diverse hiring as they have grown. Feedback from candidates indicated that part of why they joined the organization is the company commitment to DEI. The data collected ensured that the commitment the company had stated both internally and externally, was backed up by evidence and appropriate actions too.

Recap, techniques, and tips

Choosing the right interventions

As mentioned earlier, there are many evidence-based interventions that could help make your organization more inclusive. Two examples mentioned were strictly structured interviews and inclusive language norms in meetings, but these techniques run the gamut from organizational-level structured programmes (like a sponsorship or reverse mentoring scheme) to more individual-level changes like having a dedicated devil's advocate in meetings.

Many of these could be helpful in your organization, but their effectiveness is very context-dependent. If you work in a culture where disagreement with a manager is considered taboo, then having a dedicated devil's advocate may be too aggressive at first. If you work in a small start-up, sponsorship might not work as a structured programme.

For this reason, it's important that you understand the methodology behind any intervention you attempt. If you understand why the intervention is meant to work – the problem it tries to solve and the critical parts of that solution – you'll be better able to adapt that intervention for your specific context. Otherwise, you run the risk of changing an essential component of the intervention making it doomed to fail from the start.

Having a dedicated devil's advocate tries to normalize dissent so that people from marginalized groups feel they can bring up opinions or ideas based on their minority experience even if that idea contradicts the prevailing opinion in the room. Knowing this, the critical component of this technique isn't just that someone (the devil's advocate) expresses disagreement, but that the leader in the room *responds positively to that disagreement.* This means that you could adapt this method so that it's multiple devil's advocates, or you create structured devil's advocate time in your meeting for everyone to dissent, or you create an anonymous dissent box where people can write down their disagreements without a fear of it being traced back to them. All of those are fine adaptations because the critical components are still there: disagreement, and positive responses from the leader to that disagreement.

DEI interventions are rarely simple 'plug-and-play' initiatives. But with the right understanding of those interventions, you can easily adapt them to be as effective as possible for you and your specific context.

Setting targets and benchmarks

Earlier in this chapter we discussed using diversity data to build projection models of what an organization might look like in the future. These projection models can be an extremely effective way of setting realistic targets for an organization. For example, when one organization *Included* worked with hired a new CEO, he very quickly posted on social media that the company would reach 50 per cent women overall and 30 per cent women in leadership in 3 years. However, when *Included* built a projection model based on their diversity data, we found that these targets were literally impossible to reach in that time-frame without dramatically expanding the company, even if all hires and no terminations or resignations were women. As a solution, we used the model to set more realistic targets and reframed the original ones as stretch targets. This allowed the organization to keep their ultimate ideal in mind while still setting a more reachable target for leaders to strive for.

Another way to set targets is to benchmark against other organizations. However, while comparing to other companies can be useful it can also lead to inadequate targets and industry-wide stagnation. Take the tech industry: organizations may compare themselves to large tech firms like Google, Apple, or Facebook. However, those organizations all hover around 30 per cent women.[12] If that number is used by tech companies as their benchmark, once they reach 30 per cent women they are unlikely to push for more equal representation. Organizations can use other sources for benchmarks that might help push them beyond the industry giants, such as industry-level workforce data, university graduation rates, or workforce population data. Google may be 30 per cent women, but women make up 53 per cent of STEM undergraduates in the US and 57 per cent of the US workforce population.[13] Using those benchmarks is much more likely to push companies beyond their stagnating industry standards.

Prioritizing your interventions

Even when DEI is embedded in an organization's strategy, we know that there are limited resources – human, monetary, and time. We may conduct an ID and realize that we have a lot of interventions we'd like to implement. But we can't do everything. So how do we decide which interventions to prioritize?

At *Included*, we suggest three approaches to prioritizing your DEI interventions:

1 Prioritize based on the outcomes you care most about. Set up your inclusion measurement correctly to ask questions about the inclusive and exclusive behaviours people experience as well as the outcomes you care about like job satisfaction or collaboration. You can then run regression analyses to understand how these behaviours link to these outcomes. Once you've decided which outcomes you care most about improving, you can use those regressions to identify which behaviours affect those outcomes most and prioritize interventions accordingly.

2 Prioritize based on behaviours with the most room for improvement. Often when a company is measuring different aspects of inclusion, they'll find that there are one or two areas where they are performing particularly poorly overall. That could be around transparency, microaggressions, psychological safety, or something else. If you find that there is a particular area where your employees are giving you low scores, that might be a critical area to prioritize.

3   Prioritize based on demographic groups that need the most support. Most inclusion measurements we've run with organizations have found that there are groups that feel less included than everyone else in the company. Across the approximately 15,000 people we've surveyed on inclusion in over 20 languages in over 30 countries, one consistent finding is that disabled employees give lower scores across every metric of inclusion. This is also often true of Black women. When an organization has findings like this, they might prioritize interventions that provide particular support for these most excluded groups.

Most organizations use some combination of these prioritization methods, choosing one or two interventions from each method. Regardless of which method you choose – and all are valid methods – it's important that you communicate your reasoning for doing so. This will help develop buy-in for your strategy and increase transparency.

Whatever shape your strategy ends up taking, whatever interventions you choose, ensure they are driven by DEI data. Ensure you collect data on a broad swathe of diversity characteristics, but also about how included those diverse employees feel in the workplace. Leveraging that data properly can be extremely powerful, and will allow you to develop specific, targeted interventions. With this data-led strategy, you will be able to create effective and sustainable change for your organization.

Key takeaways

1   Collect both diversity and inclusion data. Without inclusion, you won't get the positive outcomes you're looking for. And without measuring inclusion, you can't identify the right levers or measure progress.

2   Know the method underlying the interventions you implement. This is critical for you to be able to adapt the interventions for your context effectively.

3   Ensure your targets and benchmarks are data-driven. This will help you set more realistic goals while allowing you to still see the big, long-term picture.

Further reading

Klein, K (2017) Does Gender Diversity on Boards Really Boost Company Performance? Knowledge@Wharton, 18 May knowledge.wharton.upenn.edu/article/will-gender-diversity-boards-really-boost-company-performance/ (archived at https://perma.cc/R9TG-C8ET)

References

1   Domo (2021) Data Never Sleeps 5.0, Domo Resource Center www.domo.com/learn/infographic/data-never-sleeps-5 (archived at https://perma.cc/TS9U-JVX6)

2   Kirkland, R and Bohnet, I (2017) Focusing on what works for workplace diversity, McKinsey & Company Featured Insights, 7 April www.mckinsey.com/featured-insights/gender-equality/focusing-on-what-works-for-workplace-diversity (archived at https://perma.cc/SQF5-AH7N)

3   Splunk (2019) Companies Collect a Lot of Data, But How Much Do They Actually Use? Priceonomics, 7 August priceonomics.com/companies-collect-a-lot-of-data-but-how-much-do/ (archived at https://perma.cc/W9LJ-NQUN)

4   Legislation.gov.uk (2010) Equality Act 2010 www.legislation.gov.uk/ukpga/2010/15/contents (archived at https://perma.cc/9LR8-U8XC)

5   Patrick, E and Washington, C (2018) 3 Ways Millennials Can Advance Workplace Diversity and Inclusion. Gallup Workplace, 30 November www.gallup.com/workplace/245084/ways-millennials-advance-workplace-diversity-inclusion.aspx (archived at https://perma.cc/D7H2-3GFH)

6   Dixon-Fyle, S, Dolan, K, Hunt V, and Prince, S (2020) Diversity wins: How inclusion matters, McKinsey & Company, 19 May www.mckinsey.com/featured-insights/diversity-and-inclusion/diversity-wins-how-inclusion-matters (archived at https://perma.cc/XR9H-QF5U)

7   Green, J, and Hand, J R M Diversity Matters/Delivers/Wins Revisited in S&P 500® Firms, Social Science Research Network ssrn.com/abstract=3849562 (archived at https://perma.cc/8HUY-25KL) or dx.doi.org/10.2139/ssrn.3849562 (archived at https://perma.cc/42XD-TVZJ)

8   Sabharwal, M (2014) Is Diversity Management Sufficient? Organizational Inclusion to Further Performance, Public Personnel Management, 43 (2), pp 197–217 (June)

9   Downey, S, Werff, L, Thomas, K, and Plaut, V (2015) The role of diversity practices and inclusion in promoting trust and employee engagement, Journal of Applied Social Psychology, 45(1), pp 35–44 (January)

10 Bohnet, I (2016) How to take the bias out of interviews, Harvard Business Review, 18 April hbr.org/2016/04/how-to-take-the-bias-out-of-interviews (archived at https://perma.cc/Y8UJ-SUE4)

11 Woolley, A W, Chabris, C F, Pentland, A, Hashmi, N and Malone, T W, 2010. Evidence for a collective intelligence factor in the performance of human groups. science, 330(6004), pp. 686–688

12 Johnson, J (2021) Distribution of Google employees worldwide from 2014 to 2021, by gender, Statista, 2 November www.statista.com/statistics/311800/google-employee-gender-global/ (archived at https://perma.cc/S5V7-PXY3)

13 Fry, R, Kennedy B, and Funk, C (2021) STEM Jobs See Uneven Progress in Increasing Gender, Racial and Ethnic Diversity. Pew Research, 1 April www.pewresearch.org/science/2021/04/01/stem-jobs-see-uneven-progress-in-increasing-gender-racial-and-ethnic-diversity/ (archived at https://perma.cc/8PTX-UV7V)

09

Governance

STEPHEN FROST AND KARL GEORGE

In May 2020, multinational group Rio Tinto decided to expand its iron ore mining operations in the Pilbara region of Western Australia. However, it failed to consider the importance of the 46,000-year-old, sacred, Juukan Gorge heritage site to the local indigenous community. It destroyed the site, which led to a public outcry and a national inquiry by the Australian Government.

The group's chief executive and two deputies left their jobs in September 2020, and in 2021, Rio Tinto's shareholders voted against the ex-CEO's exit package.[1] This incident demonstrates what happens when corporate objectives are pursued in isolation from an inclusion or inclusive governance strategy. These types of failures result from ineffective leadership and flawed decision-making by Boards and senior executives.

In this chapter, we will show you how corporate governance principles make inclusion possible. Good governance holds together purpose and performance; aspirations and accountability; objectives and outcomes. The better the governance, the better the performance, accountability, and outcomes. This starts at the Board. It then cascades down through the executives, who must be responsible and accountable, and all staff members who need to be informed and consulted. It involves employee resource groups (ERGs) and inclusion councils. These elements of good DEI governance cannot be separated from wider ESG (Environmental, Social and Governance) goals, if businesses are not to blunder into catastrophes.

Purpose and people, not just profit

ESG factors include corporate culture, ethical behaviour, sustainability, diversity, equality and inclusion. These have not been traditional elements of performance analysis, which has tended to focus on financial outcomes. Now, businesses are beginning to appreciate the financial repercussions of not focusing on ESG goals.

Investors have examined gender equality for some time, but the scrutiny has now widened to look at other aspects of diversity, such as race. The 2020 Parker Review found that 37 per cent of FTSE 100 companies surveyed (31 out of 83 companies) still did not have any ethnic minority representation on their Boards.[2] Later that year, one of Britain's biggest investment companies, Legal and General, warned that it wanted to see Boards of all FTSE 100 companies hire a non-white director by 2022 or it would start voting against them.[3]

Efforts to address the negative effects of climate change, along with steps to tackle social inequalities, are two important drivers that now link organizations to society and the environment. The definition of what makes a successful business has transformed. Sustainable investing has become a major force globally. It had reached assets of more than $30 trillion by the start of 2018. We can now measure the impact of businesses and organizations through reporting mechanisms that are global, sector-specific and issue-specific. The Global Reporting Initiative (GRI) is an independent, international organization that has developed global standards for sustainability reporting[4] Meanwhile, the World Economic Forum (WEF) has completed a year-long initiative to identify universal ESG metrics and recommended disclosures for all companies to report on to demonstrate how they deliver value in the long-term.[5]

At the same time, wrongdoing by companies is increasingly viewed as unacceptable by consumers and investors alike and frequently results in damaging publicity. The Chernobyl nuclear reactor accident of 1986 has cast a long and deadly shadow and the numbers who died as a result of participating in the clean-up operations may never be known.[6] The BP oil spill of April 2010, killed 11 crew members, injured 17 more and discharged an estimated four million barrels of oil into the sea over an 87-day period.[7] Explosions that devastated the port of Beirut in August 2020 were described as one of the planet's gravest industrial accidents. At least 218 people died, 7,000 were injured and an estimated 300,000 people were left homeless, alongside US $15 billion in property damage (BBC News, 2021).[8]

Biffa Waste Services Ltd, a familiar name in UK bin collections, was fined £1.5 million, plus costs and a proceeds of crime order in 2021 for shipping banned materials from household waste to India and Indonesia in 2018 and

2019.[9] In July 2021, Southern Water received a record £90 million fine after pleading guilty to thousands of illegal discharges of sewage which polluted rivers and coastal waters in Kent, Hampshire and Sussex between 2010 and 2015.[10] At the end of 2020, the UK's Department for Business, Energy and Industrial Strategy named and shamed 139 companies who had failed to pay national minimum wage between 2016 and 2018.[11] The total amount added up to £6.7 million that more than 95,000 workers had not received. The list included household names such as Tesco, Pizza Hut and Superdrug (GOV.UK, 2021).[12]

In June 2021, PricewaterhouseCoopers (PwC) published a report on linking executive pay to ESG goals.[13] The introduction said: 'Today, nearly half of the FTSE 100 companies set measurable environmental, social, and governance (ESG) targets for their CEOs, and have begun to introduce ESG targets in executive comp packages, and in a recent global survey by Willis Towers Watson, more than three-quarters of Board members and senior executives said strong ESG performance is a key contributor to financial performance.' Advances in technology and transparency make it easier than ever to gather and analyse data, meaning that scrutiny of organization performance against these types of measures is here to stay.

Three generations model of inclusion governance

Under the social section of ESG, we encounter diversity, equality and inclusion (DEI) along with health and safety, data privacy and protection, employee policy and the management of stakeholder relationships, wellbeing, working conditions, including slavery and child labour. The changes in mindset and approach that have got us to where we are today can best be explained by looking at a three generations model. This demonstrates how the thought process and the intention to 'do better' is moving forward.

The first generation of ESG environmental goals, Environment 1.0, was awareness of issues such as waste management and pollution, biodiversity and climate change. It's analogous to Diversity 101, and overwhelmingly a compliance issue. Businesses were concerned about the negative financial and reputational impact of non-compliance but not yet convinced about why this was an important business consideration. Profit maximization and shareholder capitalism left little room for social justice. For governance, Generation 1.0 organizations are led by powerful individuals with a lack of independence and diversity.

Environment 2.0 marked a move towards investigating what businesses could do about these challenges. Businesses began to recognize their culpability. This is analogous to Diversity 2.0, where stakeholders are increasingly important – a recognition that businesses could do more, beyond legal compliance, contributing to social cohesion and social justice. For governance, generation 2.0 organizations have more comprehensive governance principles and a diverse-by-function leadership.

Environment 3.0, today, is a committed drive by businesses to be Net Zero but also the recognition that taking care of the planet and being a prosperous business are not mutually exclusive. In summary, we move from awareness to empathy to action. This is analogous to Inclusion 3.0 where inclusion (and ESG) is embedded in the decisions the company makes about its day-to-day operations. This is about both an economic and ethical imperative. Karl has written extensively on Governance 3.0, which has flexible and adaptable governance structures and covers all aspects of diversity in leadership including neuro, social and ethnic diversity.

Who is governing?

Representation matters. There is a clear correlation between bad governance and lack of representation, as demonstrated in the introduction of this chapter.

Yet across every sector we see a lack of diverse representation. This is especially true in the Western world in terms of Black and ethnic minority people. Using the above generational model, Race 1.0 was about making sure you did not break the law. Race 2.0 is about being fair and nice and moral but Race 3.0 is about being competitive and getting the best people. Think about recruiting for a football team. Football club boards don't worry about where they get the talent from; they will have scouts everywhere looking for the best players. Similarly, businesses and organizations need to be using their networks, reaching out to different communities and using innovative way of finding the best people rather than making the excuse that there aren't people that they can get. If this starts to happen, then we can move the dial on representation.

Since the Davies Review of 2011, we have seen real improvement in female representation in governance.[14] There is still work to do, of course, but we now need to apply the same focus to race, disability and other areas.

Given current disruption in business, there is a whole generation of younger people who need to be included in leadership structures, leadership thinking and decision-making. Generation X, our generation, are mostly in charge. We come from the first generation of computers and the birth of Facebook. Yet Generation Y, the generation of the internet and smartphones, and Generation Z, from the fourth industrial digital revolution age, are not represented.

On the one hand, the lack of gender, race and age diversity in governance is a moral failure. However, it's more than this. As we see in the climate change debate, the people most affected are not making, or even inputting to, the decisions. We are now in an era, for the first time, where computers, robots and people are working together. Good governance requires us to profoundly consider who should be in the room.

The RACE Equality Code

Developed in the aftermath of the death of George Floyd in 2020. After a year of consultation it has provided a framework for addressing the lack of representation in the board room and in senior leadership teams. It is based on four key principles which are equally useful for addressing DEI and inclusion considerations: we should report on race so there is transparency; we should have clear actions and accountability; we should measure and drill down into data with clear targets for achievement and finally we should educate our stakeholders in what 'good' looks like and how to achieve it.

Good inclusive governance in practice

To embed inclusion, we need a clear understanding of the corporate governance principles that make inclusion possible. Governance is the glue that holds together strategy and performance while also ensuring that the organization stays on purpose and true to its values. The better the governance then the better is the alignment of the organization's key aspirations. We need systems, processes, rules and regulations to help.

There are 10 steps organizations need to take to embed inclusion into their day-to-day governance activities, which are outlined in Table 9.1.

TABLE 9.1 Steps for embedding inclusion in governance activities

Step	Explanation	Impact
1. Culture audit	• Survey to draw out key issues around behaviours, values, policies and structures that influence culture.	• Provides areas to test through boardroom or committee observation • Can be followed up with focus groups and interviews with stakeholders • Flags policies that are unintentionally promoting the wrong culture
2. Strategy review	• Check DEI strategy is part of overall ESG or corporate strategy • Check reporting and measurement systems complete these goals	• Determine extent DEI is integrated and embedded in the overall culture
3. Policy analysis	• Examine all polices to ensure they are supporting the goal of becoming an inclusive organization. • Policies should provide practical support, be accessible to all stakeholders and be supported by an appropriate review cycle	• Everyone in the organization can have confidence in the policy framework as a necessary first step, across bullying and harassment, an overall DEI policy, and a code of conduct and commitments around quality such as zero tolerance to racism.
4. Terms of reference	• Terms of reference must be consistent across each committee. • Terms must be effective, demonstrating the committee's purpose, duties, objectives, members, and level of authority. • Terms should support committee's efficiency by covering how decisions are made, the frequency of meetings, notice of meetings, performance reviews, and who the company secretary is.	• Reviewing these elements enables us to get terms of reference fit for purpose and measurement of the objectives identified for each committee to be monitored and actioned.

	• They should specify accountability, in decreeing what happens with meeting minutes, any matters arising, reporting lines and resourcing.	• Ensure the outcomes of organizations are identified effectively and people are accountable for achieving the performance criteria that have been agreed. It is critical to know where the responsibility lies for monitoring what happens
5. Roles	• Responsibility for inclusion should reside at Board level and be noted in role descriptions. • The executive sponsor for DEI should also be identified and all leaders understand that DEI is a collective responsibility and not, as is wrongly assumed, a HR function.	• A Board level sponsor with DEI responsibility makes sense in terms of accountability and focus. However, this doesn't mean that one person takes the responsibility from the rest of the Board. • Documenting the responsibilities of the sponsor, and demonstrating areas they will be responsible for, e.g. speaking at events or attending ERGs, helps provide a robust framework akin to other parts of the business. • An example we have seen is deciding the Chair would be the Board level sponsor on race and the CEO would be the executive level sponsor. This facilitated some targeted actions to shift the dial on very slow movement on representation at senior levels and therefore they would include it in the two most senior roles.
6. Statements	• It is important to get the balance right when publishing such statements, but your employees, your customers and society at large want to know your stance on key questions such as climate change and inclusion. We are starting to see more regulatory pressure on ESG reporting but what messages are you giving to all your stakeholders?	• What you do speaks more eloquently than anything you can say, however not saying anything also speaks volumes. • Carefully considered and crafted statements are important because they can help to support the values of the organization and introduce everyone to your culture and an acceptable, desirable code of conduct.

(continued)

TABLE 9.1 (Continued)

Step	Explanation	Impact
7. Actions	• We need a robust, specific action plan around DEI, but it cannot sit in isolation. It must be aligned with the overall strategic objectives of the organization. It has to be embedded into the business and SMART (specific, measurable, achievable, realistic and time-bound). • As part of the development of those actions it will be necessary to involve a wide range of stakeholders.	• A bottom-up approach should complement the work with the Board and senior leadership team. The people impacted by the decisions of the Board or leadership should have the opportunity to contribute to the discussion and help to set what the success measures will look like and what the consequences of non-performance are.
8. Transparency on reporting	• Reporting on DEI must be succinct, clear, timely and at the required level for Board members to be assured that they are equipped to make decisions. • When we have worked with organizations on inclusivity, we are always keen to see how they monitor success in achieving DEI objectives. • We need a reporting framework for inclusion, just as we have for every other area of business. In January 2020, the WEF published a White Paper called *Toward Common Metrics and Consistent Reporting of Sustainable Value Creationx (World Economic Forum, 2021)* This provides us with a methodology for reporting and an expectation that organizations define their purpose in a way that integrates social impact within the core of their business.	• One of our clients was able to demonstrate that in their Board and committee meetings they had a very comprehensive, balanced scorecard approach to monitoring their performance indicators. • I personally witnessed the challenge from the non-executives to the executives in reviewing adverse variations in financial performance targets. We then explained to them that they needed a similarly rigorous and transparent approach on reporting DEI measures.

9. Data	• We cannot move the dial on any part of inclusion unless we get the right data. We have to segregate it and think of intersectionalities: gender, race, sexual orientation. The WEF White Paper is a start here, but it lacks metrics on ethnicity and race. There are some good global metrics but it only refers to percentage of employees per employee category, by age group, gender and 'other indicators of diversity'. • The data should be disaggregated across various racial and diversity groups. Intersectionality of individuals also needed to be considered when trying to determine causality and underrepresentation. Records and data on DEI should be easily accessible and kept up to date.	• As discussed in Chapter 8, we sometimes find organizations collect data without thinking about how they are going to use it. As a result, they don't have enough data to make correct decisions with. For example, an Indian person could have completely different experiences to a person from Pakistan or Bangladesh. Sikhs have different experiences to Muslim people and Black Caribbean people have different experiences to Black African people. Younger women may have different experiences to older women.
10. Education	• We should create an environment where people are always learning, always developing themselves. • When we carry out diagnostics and identify learning needs, which could be as simple as how to recruit more effectively for diverse groups. If the required support and education is not in place, leaders can't be expected to deliver against these expectations. They will need a methodological and robust process for getting them up to speed.	• Inclusivity should lead to getting the best people, performing at their best and being rewarded and encouraged to be the best. It becomes a virtuous cycle of educating, getting the best talent and therefore the organization performs better. In that sort of environment, there are psychologically safe spaces for all parts of society to contribute easily.

The infrastructure of inclusive governance

Boards

Boards are key to inclusion and play a role no one else can. Whereas the Executive are operational, only the Board is truly strategic. Often inclusion fails in the operational day to day activity and needs strategic support to thrive.

Boards can consider all stakeholders and engage with them with a well-planned and all-embracing DEI strategy. The DEI strategy should align with the overall strategy and any action plans must also be aligned. The Board must not be afraid to make difficult and courageous decisions in order to move the dial on inequality and achieve inclusivity. These are strategic decisions the executive may shy away from. Board members must review performance objectives for management ensuring that DEI is the responsibility of all managers.

Terms of reference for the Board and committees must demonstrate comprehensive assurance on DEI and there should be adequate and clear lines of assurance between the Board and committees.

The Board should set goals for its own performance in regards to DEI objectives that are clearly identified. There should be clear role descriptions showing who is accountable for DEI. The Board should have DEI objectives as part of its own evaluation processes. We suggest a Board-level sponsor someone who, on behalf of the Board, would take responsibility for the monitoring and implementation of the identified DEI objectives. This should be written into the role description of the Board member, making it clear what they are accountable for.

We've found when working with boards that although they were carrying out the role, very rarely was it written into the role description of the Board member. It was also clear, when we looked at the performance management of the Board, that nearly all Boards now have a comprehensive evaluation process where they evaluate the performance of the Board; the individual members and the committees. But, in that performance evaluation we had to introduce to nearly all of the people that we have worked with, the concept of self-evaluation for the Board around DEI objectives. These could stretch from the composition of the Board itself, and its success in achieving previously identified targets, to how successful they have been in translating and cascading the responsibility for a fair and equal workforce being delivered by all leaders and managers.

Board recruitment

Given relative lack of Board diversity, recruitment to the Board is important, not least because it impacts the organization as a whole. The Board should be drawn from a range of backgrounds and perspectives. It should be well-balanced and cover all key competences and specific skills.

It is clear that having a balanced Board will ultimately lead to better decision making as a result of good discussions and contributions from people with varied life experiences. In order to get that diversity, there needs to be commitment and action towards tackling some of the systemic practices, culture and oversights when recruiting to the Board.

Start with raising awareness of the importance of diversity by educating the Board about the three generations of diversity (covered earlier) and also challenge the false dichotomy between increasing diversity and acquiring talent. Diversity is about getting the best talent.

Adopt a targeted recruitment campaign from diverse networks and recruit more than one position at a time to maximize your chances of diverse results. Check the language and images used in recruitment campaigns and the longlisting and shortlisting criteria.

Recruitment and interview procedures also need to be sensitive to traditional ways of recruiting that sometimes embody biases that can rule out potential candidates. Look at interview panels and questions to ensure they provide the best opportunity for all people.

Executives

Executives run the organization day-to-day. Many of the principles outlined above in relation to Boards and organizational strategy apply to Executives and organizational execution. Inclusion will thrive most when Executives lead on Inclusion in their daily work and the Board can add value strategically, rather than merely hold them to account.

It is important that someone at a senior level of the organization is responsible for inclusion. This could be an Executive Committee Champion, or a series of champions aligned to employee networks (see below). Robust mechanisms, such as the RACI framework – Responsible, Accountable, Consulted and Informed, should be used to ensure a process of accountability. DEI can sometimes be left to junior colleagues, or employees from a minority group, but an Executive-level sponsor must be involved in ERGs and committees and reflect their views when they report back to the organization through the Board.

Employee Resource Groups (ERGs) and inclusion councils

ERGs can be critical enablers of disseminating a good DEI policy, of facilitating two-way communication and of holding leadership to account. Terms of reference should be clear and consistent, there should be logic, transparency and fairness to funding, and all employees should be able to join all groups (with the caveat that communities may form within ERGs for reasons of privacy and safety, such as people not 'out' or wishing to disclose).

Many organizations will consolidate their Executive and Employee networks in an inclusion council. These take many forms but typically involve a committee of eight to 10 people drawn from all levels of the organization representing the diverse employee base. They will, as above, have robust terms of reference and clear goals and provide a forum to focus effort, energy and accountability in the organization.

For example, the security group G4S used its Council to educate the organization about its DEI aspirations. It convened senior Executives from its global businesses and brought them together with employee networks and other interested parties. This allowed expertise to flow both ways and provide air cover and attain buy in for employee initiatives.

Action

Organizations wanting to embed inclusive governance need to work through the 10-step comprehensive self-assessment process outlined above. It's then important to survey the leadership to understand their level of understanding and willingness to accept responsibility on issues of inclusion. The buck stops at the top and this will be covered in more detail in Chapter 10.

This then results in action, handily captured in the acronym ACT:

- The first A is Awareness. Do leaders see the importance of inclusion as a foundation stone for the entire performance of the business as successful, ethical, sustainable and responsible?
- The second A is Acknowledgement. Are leaders honest about where they currently are in terms of maturity and performance? Are leaders willing to face in to some uncomfortable realities, rather than brush issues under the carpet?

- The third A is Accountability. Do leaders have a genuine framework for accountability? What are the consequences of failing to hit their objectives?

- The first C is Concern. Do leaders care enough about underrepresentation of certain groups in the board and senior leadership team and other areas of inequality?

- The second C is Commitment. What have you done to demonstrate commitment? Have leaders made a non-generic statement and then followed through with concrete actions?

- The third C is Communication. This is about how open and transparent you are about the commitments you make. How widely are you willing to share?

- The first T is Target. This is about strategy, vision and strategic objectives. This is an area where many organizations struggle to align their DEI objectives with their overall objectives and create robust targets and indicators.

- The second T is Tenacity. What level of resource and commitment would the organization put in to make change happen? We need to benchmark across organizations how much resource, in finance and time, is going into DEI in the same way that we might do with IT.

- The third T is Training. Beyond compliance training, is there a programme that works and achieves impact? Is it measured, refined, and ongoing?

Conclusion

Good corporate governance principles make inclusion possible. Organizations lack inclusion when their governance structures are not representative and when responsibility and accountability are ambiguous. There is a clear link between lack of representation and bad governance leading to failures that range from the embarrassing and costly through to major corporate catastrophes.

In this chapter, we began by setting the context by discussing the broad parameters in which inclusion sits and by understanding the serious consequences of getting inclusion wrong. The relationship between inclusion and ESG helped us to navigate the three generations of Diversity, Equity and Inclusion. This context is good, but it is of little value if we can't find a methodology or framework to make change and embed good practice, so, the 10-step process and the review of case studies and practical examples provided an explanation of what it means to be well governed. Finally, the three-step equity process embodied by the ACT acronym can be used to test, challenge, monitor and act to make the changes that are necessary.

Key takeaways

There is a generational model of inclusive governance, akin to the inclusion maturity model used throughout this book and situated within the wider ESG debate. The most mature organizations will realize good governance is much more than legal compliance and will have developed an infrastructure for inclusion governance including Board, Executives, employees and new infrastructure such as an Inclusion Council.

Use the 10-step framework, identified in this chapter, as a diagnostic and self-assessment to kickstart work on embedding your inclusion strategy.

To ensure action on good governance, reflect on three questions:

1 Is your inclusion strategy simple enough to be understood and acted upon?

2 Is the inclusion strategy owned by the Board and embraced by the organization?

3 Have you integrated and embedded the inclusion strategy for your staff and other external stakeholders?

Further reading

Greenbiz.com (2021) Global sustainable investing assets surged to $30 trillion in 2018 | Greenbiz www.greenbiz.com/article/global-sustainable-investing-assets-surged-30-trillion-2018 (archived at https://perma.cc/89RZ-6W7L)

Kell, G (2021) The Remarkable Rise Of ESG, Forbes www.forbes.com/sites/georgkell/2018/07/11/the-remarkable-rise-of-esg/?sh=551751861695 (archived at https://perma.cc/6FY3-PNTX)

Sdgs.un.org (2021) THE 17 GOALS | Sustainable Development. sdgs.un.org/goals (archived at https://perma.cc/J2EP-PK6Z)

Unglobalcompact.org (2021) The Ten Principles | UN Global Compact www.
    unglobalcompact.org/what-is-gc/mission/principles (archived at https://perma.
    cc/UWM7-MGDB)
United Nations (2015) Transforming our world: The 2030 Agenda for Sustainable
    Development sdgs.un.org/2030agenda (archived at https://perma.cc/5N5Y-L6J2)
World Economic Forum (2021) Toward Common Metrics and Consistent
    Reporting of Sustainable Value Creation www.weforum.org/whitepapers/
    toward-common-metrics-and-consistent-reporting-of-sustainable-value-creation
    (archived at https://perma.cc/K7ZJ-HWUM)

References

1   Simmons, D (2021) Rio Tinto shareholders vote in protest against remuneration
    of former CEO Business News Australia www.businessnewsaustralia.com/
    articles/rio-tinto-shareholders-vote-in-protest-against-remuneration-of-former-
    ceo.html (archived at https://perma.cc/S4RQ-YMAC)

2   GOV.UK (2021) Ethnic diversity of UK boards: the Parker review www.gov.uk/
    government/publications/ethnic-diversity-of-uk-boards-the-parker-review
    (archived at https://perma.cc/3PWZ-C43A)

3   BBC News (2021) L&G demands non-white board members at FTSE firms
    www.bbc.co.uk/news/business-54421844 (archived at https://perma.cc/P4MF-
    VB9G)

4   Global Reporting, (2021) GRI – Standards www.globalreporting.org/standards/
    (archived at https://perma.cc/2565-A4R2)

5   World Economic Forum (2021) Over 50 global companies adopt new ESG
    reporting metrics www.weforum.org/our-impact/stakeholder-capitalism-50-
    companies-adopt-esg-reporting-metrics/ (archived at https://perma.cc/
    S6WX-TZBX)

6   World-nuclear.org (2021) Chernobyl | Chernobyl Accident | Chernobyl
    Disaster - World Nuclear Association www.world-nuclear.org/information-
    library/safety-and-security/safety-of-plants/chernobyl-accident.aspx (archived at
    https://perma.cc/FMG7-HDAR)

7   US EPA (2021) Deepwater Horizon – BP Gulf of Mexico Oil Spill | US EPA
    www.epa.gov/enforcement/deepwater-horizon-bp-gulf-mexico-oil-spill (archived
    at https://perma.cc/93Y8-FBV5)

8   BBC News (2021) Beirut explosion: What we know so far www.bbc.co.uk/
    news/world-middle-east-53668493 (archived at https://perma.cc/2P56-7XNM)

9   GOV.UK (2021) Biffa fined £1.5 million for 'reckless' export breach www.gov.
    uk/government/news/biffa-fined-15-million-for-reckless-export-breach (archived
    at https://perma.cc/4F86-WRMU)

10 GOV.UK (2021) Record £90m fine for Southern Water following EA prosecution www.gov.uk/government/news/record-90m-fine-for-southern-water-following-ea-prosecution (archived at https://perma.cc/39JB-FPFA)

11 GOV.UK (2021) Rogue employers named and shamed for failing to pay minimum wage www.gov.uk/government/news/rogue-employers-named-and-shamed-for-failing-to-pay-minimum-wage (archived at https://perma.cc/E86E-Y55S)

12 GOV.UK (2020) National Minimum Wage Naming Scheme Round 16, December 2020: education bulletin assets.publishing.service.gov.uk/government/uploads/system/uploads/attachment_data/file/948356/nmw-naming-scheme-round-16-educational-bulletin.pdf (archived at https://perma.cc/52KC-DRBY)

13 O'Connor, P, Harris, l and Gosling, T (2021) www.pwc.com/gx/en/issues/reinventing-the-future/take-on-tomorrow/download/Linking-exec-pay-ESG.pdf (archived at https://perma.cc/7W2S-KM7Y)

14 FTSE Women Leaders (2021). 2011 – 2015 The Davies Review - FTSE Women Leaders ftsewomenleaders.com/2011-2015-the-davies-review/ (archived at https://perma.cc/DG38-DF9L)

10

Leadership

STEPHEN FROST AND DEIRDRE GOLDEN

Consider two worlds. One world is a university campus, composed of free thinking, highly intelligent, sensitive and articulate students exploring new thinking and ideas. Critics and sceptics, however, might suggest a politically biased atmosphere, extreme sensitivity to inequities, and threats to free speech.

The other world is a commercial pharmaceutical company. Here, similarly intelligent, numerate and dedicated researchers operate in a scientific environment that prioritizes evidenced based research above all else. Critics and skeptics might point to the mixed reputation of 'big pharma' and the fact its commercial culture might be in stark contrast to left wing campus politics.

These two worlds are, in some ways, a million miles apart. Yet both entities worked in collaboration to develop a break-through vaccine against the COVID-19 virus. The vaccine would not have come about without the collaboration of both these entities. They need each other. The pharmaceutical company needs smart, new talent that could bring a fresh perspective and add to its research culture. The university needs funding and sponsorship and jobs for its soon to be graduates.

The two worlds are Oxford University and AstraZeneca. They are not imaginary worlds, they are very real. What brought them together and enabled them to work effectively with each other was leadership. Leaders at each organization thought bigger than themselves, and seized the opportunity to do something that had not been done before and go on to save millions of lives.

What is leadership?

Leadership is activating a group of people to work together towards a shared goal. While management is about executing within defined parameters, leadership can often be about changing the parameters to achieve more, as was the case in the development of the Oxford-AstraZeneca vaccine.

We are influenced greatly by the work of[1] on adaptive leadership. Adaptive leadership is a group process that helps individuals and organizations face up to changed realities. We are similarly influenced by our colleagues and clients on inclusive leadership. Inclusive leadership is convening a group of often very different people towards a common goal, usually by adapting to others, rather than expecting them to adapt to you.

This chapter shares the principles and qualities of inclusive leadership that are necessary to positively support organizations to effect the changes they seek and to maximize individual and team performance.

Think of it this way.

One ship drives east and another drives west

With the self-same winds that blow

'Tis the set of the sails

And not the gales

That tells them the way to go.

These words are an excerpt from a poem by Ella Wheeler Wilcox.[2] It can be seen as an allegory where setting the sails is setting out the vision of where you want to get to, and guiding others (in this case the ship) on the journey despite the many obstacles, or indeed prevailing winds, that may get in the way.

Effective leadership is having a vision about where you want to get to, and the emotional intelligence and empathy to understand those you are leading. It's about persuading or inspiring people to align with the vision and bringing them along with you, even when the journey is seen as difficult.

Ineffective leadership, on the other hand, is more about ego, often with personal ambition at its core. The inability or lack of clarity in the vision makes buy-in difficult for followers, and reliance is more on compulsion rather than persuasion.

What's missing from this latter form of leadership is the ability to sustain it over time. Where leadership is only accepted through compulsion or fear, such as in autocratic leadership, people may start to resist when they have the opportunity.

While leadership is a quality we recognize when we meet it, we may find it hard to describe. While some of it may be innate and intuitive, it is also a skill that can be learnt. As a result, we cannot say for certain, if you do things in a particular way, you will be an effective leader but we can say, if your leadership style includes certain qualities you will have a greater chance of succeeding and sustaining your leadership over time.

Why is leadership important?

Leadership is important because leaders transform the vision into reality. It's about getting things done, often in ambiguous circumstances. Going back to our analogy, the leader sets the sails and unites everyone behind the vision. Leadership is not the same as management, which focuses on the allocation and control of resources to achieve objectives. Leadership is the emotional response, and management is the operational response.

Inclusive leadership has never been more important. As our world, and our workplaces, become ever more diverse and polarized, we need leaders to bring us together to get work done. Examples of difference and polarization abound. Take the Transgender debate for example, it has brought many university campuses to seeming paralysis. The language and protocols that have developed on some campuses are a million miles away from some workplaces, as outlined in our introduction. Or take politics, where populist positioning is easier, and often transcends reasoned debate.

But this is not just a theoretical debate playing out, this is deeply personal. Take our own cognitive dissonance, for example. How often do our actions and behaviours match our words and our rhetoric? How big is the gap? How willing are we to adapt, or do we expect others to adapt to us?

So much of the current challenges organizations face won't be solved through management alone. Every day, clients ask us what words and language they should use. They ask us how to manage a multi-generational workforce. They ask us how to deal with conflict. They ask us what are reasonable adaptations to 'accommodate' differences. These are not straight-forward management operational asks, they are questions that require leadership to answer them.

A model of inclusive leadership

There are numerous models of leadership that exist. Most tend to focus on the added value (above and beyond competent management) that leaders bring. This includes attributes such as confidence, people-centricity, long-term vision, good communication and empathy. When it comes to inclusive leadership, there is a lot of overlap. This reinforces the point that good leadership is often inclusive leadership and vice versa. However, there are elements of leadership that are especially important for inclusion, and increasingly important for managing diverse teams navigating complex realities.

Catalyst, the gender equality nonprofit, includes accountability, ownership, allyship, curiosity, humility, and courage in its definition of leadership. Deloitte, a professional services firm, includes commitment, courage, bias awareness, curiosity, cultural intelligence and collaboration. At *Included*, we have reviewed decades of academic work on leadership and our own practice over the last decade and distilled a model that we detail below. It's based on our theory of change and how people learn leadership.

Included Theory of Change

For over 10 years we have built on our academic and practitioner research and have developed a simple framework that correlates to our established theory of change: Understand, Lead and Deliver

Understand is about leaders creating their own personal *why?* This is critical to leaders recognizing that true inclusion stems from personal understanding of DEI and self-awareness.

Lead is about leaders taking personal responsibility for their behaviours and understanding their own impact.

Deliver is about taking concrete action to effect sustainable change. Culture in an organization is made up of behaviours and processes that hopefully contribute to inclusion, but more often than not, detract from inclusion. Deliver, focuses on targeted interventions to change the specific aspects of an organization that needs focus and re-aligning.

To operationalize leadership training following this theory of change, *Included*'s Inclusive Leadership Programme starts with using organizational and personal data as a diagnostic tool to identify key areas for development. This is followed with a group session on the theory of change. By then conducting one-to-one coaching we can explore the cognitive dissonance between what people might say in public or a group versus what they really believe or how they behave in private. This gap is critical to explore because it is the main focus for leaders to work on – to close the gap. Finally, group sessions reiterate the theory of change with emphasis on *deliver*, where personal actions are developed that will be sustainable. By making this process personal, experiential and iterative, we have the best chance of developing behavioural change and actions that will endure.

Our behavioural framework, shown in Figure 10.1, identifies the core skills needed to understand, lead and deliver inclusive leadership. We'll explore and detail the ABC behavioural framework, starting with Appreciating Differences (Understand), followed by Building trust (Lead) and finishing with Cultivating innovation (Deliver).

FIGURE 10.1 Core skills of inclusive leadership

Competency		Example actions
APPRECIATING DIFFERENCES	A1) Aware of, and working to mitigate their biases	• Take the Implicit Association Test
	A2) Able to empathize with others experiences and perspectives	• Participate in reverse mentoring • Engage in diverse media and read stories of others
	A3) Actively seeks out diversity of thought	• Ensure there are diverse panels when making decisions
BUILDING TRUST	B1) Maintains a consistent approach across different aspects of their work	• Conduct a review to debias processes and systems • Uses the same processes for talent management across different teams
	B2) Embeds transparency and objectivity into decision making	• Communicate decision making processes to your team
	B3) Integrates trust into interpersonal relationships	• Build psychological safety into collaborative settings
CULTIVATING INNOVATION	C1) Displays cultural and emotional intelligence	• Use inclusive language for all communications
	C2) Drives transformation through commitment and collaboration	• Makes a visible commitment to inclusive leadership • Track progress through organizational/departmental KPIs
	C3) Inspires others to thrive with authenticity	• Share personal experience of inclusive leadership

Appreciating differences (Understand)

Diversity is a reality. That doesn't always mean people appreciate the differences in their midst. To do so, we need to build self-awareness, develop greater empathy and actively seek out diversity.

A1 – SELF-AWARENESS, ESPECIALLY AROUND BIASES

In 2014, not long after he took over as CEO of Microsoft, Satya Nadella was interviewed at a conference celebrating women in computing. He was asked to give his advice to women who felt uncomfortable requesting a raise. 'It's not really about asking for the raise, but knowing and having faith that the system will actually give you the right raises as you go along,' he answered. Not asking for raise, he added, was 'good karma' that would help a boss realize the employee could be trusted and should have more responsibility'.[3]

His response met with near disbelief. A male CEO, in a male dominated industry, actively seeking to address their gender bias, telling a conference of women to wait their turn for a raise and hope they would be noticed for their work. He completely misjudged the situation angered women, and undermined efforts Microsoft were making in diversifying their employee base. Later, in an email to all Microsoft employees, he acknowledged he had answered the question completely wrong. He was clear he had made a mistake, he didn't try to cover up the mistake and blame it on his words being taken out of context, being misquoted, or misunderstood, he chose to be humble about the error he had made and quickly sought to rectify it.

A2 – EMPATHY

Being empathetic is no longer seen as being a sign of weakness, but rather as a sign of strength. Showing empathy allows a leader to listen to others, understand their perspective and take it into consideration. Crucially it's about adapting to others, rather than expecting them to adapt to you.

Jacinda Adern, Prime Minister of New Zealand is often held up as example of an empathetic leader. She has been praised for her honesty, trustworthiness and empathy, steering her country through national crises including responding to the Christchurch Mosque shootings and leading the country through the COVID 19 pandemic.

A3 – ACTIVELY SEEK OUT DIVERSITY (OF THOUGHT)

Former Hewlett-Packard chairman and CEO, Carly Fiorina, the first woman to lead a Fortune Top-20 company, said, 'To be successful, we must harness diversity of thought. Yes, diversity of people, diversity of background, diversity of experience, diversity of skills. But most important, diversity of ideas. This is about a new definition of diversity that has to do with more than national origin or race or creed – it has to do with keeping the market in motion by feeding it new models, new ideas, new approaches.'[4]

Often we cultivate or unconsciously sponsor subordinates who 'get it' which often means they agree with us and think like us. This might provide more comfort and facilitate easier management, but it also means an absence of challenge and fresh thinking. We need to consciously seek out and hear different perspectives.

Building trust (Lead)

Trust not only makes for more psychologically safe, happier workplaces, it's also incredibly efficient facilitating devolved decision making closer to the action. To build trust we need to strive for behavioural consistency, be transparent in our decision making and make trust central to our interactions.

B1 – CONSISTENT BEHAVIOUR IN ALL RELATIONSHIPS
Consistency in behaviour is often a tall order because we experience a range of emotions and events throughout the day, let alone week or month. However, a lack of consistency from leaders can create a challenging environment for colleagues as they may feel less certain in sharing ideas.

We've all been there with trying to catch the boss, in the right mood, in order to land our point most effectively. With bad bosses, catch them at the wrong time and your hard work and proposed solution could be in vain.

Consistency creates psychologically safe environments for others. Sometimes, as a leader, you have to sacrifice your own feelings in the moment in order to create the space for others to be themselves. It is an art. Yes, be yourself, but try and be consistent, even if it means biting your tongue on occasion.

B2 – TRANSPARENT, OBJECTIVE, DECISION MAKING
Along with thoughtful behaviour, transparency in decision making is one of the biggest contributors to an inclusive culture. There are times when confidentiality is of course important, or even essential, however often it's the default without good reason. If employees know as much as possible, it levels the information inequality in an organization.

Take pay, for example. One of the reasons most organizations have a gender and ethnicity pay gap is because women and ethnic minorities know less about the pay culture and expected level than others do. When organizations focused on decreasing the pay gaps, they often defaulted to bonus. Bonus discussions are less objective, more opaque, and linked to substantially higher gender and ethnicity pay gaps. So if you can be as transparent as possible that helps everyone.

B3 – INTEGRATES TRUST INTO ALL INTERPERSONAL SKILLS

Trust is perhaps the most valuable free currency there is. It's the firm belief that what someone is saying to you is true. Not only does that create happier, safer workplaces, it's also incredibly efficient.

Being trusted is empowering. In fact trust, can not only be efficient, it can be value adding. If someone is trusted with money, a new position, a deliberate task etc, they are likely to deploy discretionary effort on it because they know your relationship is the currency that is permitting that action.

Conversely, a lack of trust can have a damaging effect on the relationship and reduce it to merely transactional with a lot of paperwork needed to detail the audit trail.

Cultivating innovation (Deliver)

If we can appreciate difference and build trust, we can cultivate innovative delivery. This is essential for us to grow as leaders and organizations.

C1 - CULTURAL AND EMOTIONAL INTELLIGENCE

In Chapter 3 we discussed cultural intelligence (CQ) in depth. It's taking emotional intelligence to the next level and deploying curiosity to genuinely increase our skill in adaptation. It's about adapting to others so that they need to adapt less to us. This is incredibly powerful for someone in a position or power or authority to deploy.

Conventionally, a subordinate would adapt to a superior. If the boss is able also to adapt to their employees not only do they grow as a professional and as a human being, they create the space for those around them to grow also.

C2 – DRIVES TRANSFORMATION THROUGH COMMITMENT AND COLLABORATION

The opposite to commitment and collaboration is micromanaging. This not only draws leaders into the weeds, but can also lead to exhaustion, not just for the leader but for those who are being micromanaged. Commitment and collaboration are easier to achieve when people are not in fear of being accused of doing the wrong thing. Leadership is about trusting people and bringing them along with you.

C3 – INSPIRES OTHERS TO THRIVE WITH AUTHENTICITY

An authentic leader is someone who shows others their true selves, they are seen as genuine and do not seek to hide their imperfections or vulnerabilities. An authentic leader is self-aware, recognizing their own strengths and weaknesses, and understanding of impact on others. To be authentic takes courage not least because it is contrary to how leaders have traditionally positioned themselves (infallible).

In 2011 the newly appointed CEO of Lloyds Banking Group António Horta-Osório took a leave of absence because he was suffering from fatigue. Mr Horta-Osório had taken up his role in the immediate aftermath of the 2010 financial crisis when Lloyds was in a very difficult financial position, the pressure of the situation started to affect his mental and general health.

However rather than trying to soldier on, he acted in what only can be described as a courageous way and took the action necessary to return himself to health and took a leave of absence. He has since talked openly of what happened. His personal story and ability to share the experience has led him to re-evaluate the importance of mental health for all of the bank's 65,000 employees, and elicited appreciation from his employees of his efforts to destigmatize mental health.[5]

Measurement

We've discussed definitions, importance and models of inclusive leadership, but how do we know if we are being successful? Ultimately, we might simply feel it. Others might feel it also and hopefully give us feedback, spurring further development. However, we have also developed a measurement framework for evaluating how we are performing as inclusive leaders to allow us to benchmark ourselves and also situate our behaviour in the context of others

Our framework takes into consideration the four levels of Kirkpatrick's evaluation model.[6] The model measures:

- The Reaction of the student (you). E.g. Self-review of how you are leading, perhaps through keeping a journal.

- The resulting increase in knowledge or capability (learning). E.g. a personal diagnostic, competency assessment, or feedback from colleagues and manager.
- The extent of behavior and capability improvement and implementation/ application. E.g. feedback from a coach, feedback from peers/cohort, 360 feedback.
- The effects on the business or environment.

We can look for examples in each area and adopt a positive record of evidence. For example, if we changed the time of a team meeting to accommodate a team member with caring responsibilities that might be a clear example of appreciating differences. If we empowered a colleague with enhanced budget responsibility that might clearly indicate building trust. By keeping our own log of improvements and even more importantly by soliciting feedback from others, we can track our progress towards becoming more of an inclusive leader.

Leadership in action - individuals

Historically, far more is written about male leaders, but we can learn much from extraordinary women leaders such as Indra Nooyi, the former chairman and CEO of PepsiCo, Dame Carolyn Julia McCall, CEO of ITV, Emma Walmsley at the global pharmaceutical company GSK, and Mary T Barra, CEO of General Motors Company. There are also many examples in the world of politics, being the first in anything is to act as a trailblazer, but particularly so in the world of politics which institutionalizes the cut and thrust of power:

- Ellen Johnson Sirleaf, who served as President of Liberia for 12 years, was the first woman to hold the position in that country, and the first woman elected head of state of an African country, a phenomenal achievement. Among her many accomplishments, she won the Nobel peace prize in 2011 for helping secure peace after civil wars from 1989-2003 and went onto establish a Truth and Reconciliation Committee to probe corruption and heal ethnic tensions. In June 2016, she was elected as the Chair of the Economic Community the Community of West African States, making her the first woman to hold the position since it was created. She is still regarded by many today as the country's most successful leader.
- Angela Merkel was the first female chancellor of Germany and became one of its longest serving leaders. In 2014 she also became the longest-serving incumbent head of government in the European Union. Her style of leadership was modest, consensual and emphasized international

cooperation. Her decision in 2015 to welcome over one million refugees from the Middle East was not appreciated by everyone, but she showed leadership in the face of an extraordinary situation.[7]

Leaders are not without flaws. They can and do make mistakes and take decisions, or say things that they realize afterward was wrong. However, the difference between an effective leader and an ineffective leader is the former have the humility to acknowledge mistakes and to correct them quickly, and in that way, from learning comes growth.

Mahatma Ghandi, Dr Martin Luther King Jr and Nelson Mandela, were all considered great leaders, and they led in situations where they had limited positional power. They did not have a high office of state behind them, and as such were constrained by their personal circumstances, but despite that, they inspired people to follow them and achieve their vision.

What all these leaders had in common was a vision which wasn't just a personal vision based on ego and ambition, but an inclusive vision for greater good. They had the ability to share their vision in a way that people understood and wanted to be a part of, and in doing so they connected emotionally to their followers, and this enabled them to bring people along with them.

Inclusive leadership is active, not passive

As our world becomes ever more diverse, we need courageous leadership deployed by individuals who are willing to lean into discomfort, and actively bridge divides.

Leadership doesn't just happen, management can happen reasonably efficiently and automatically, within pre-agreed parameters. However, leadership requires extra effort.

When Ofcom, the UK's communications regulator, wanted to raise the bar on broadcaster diversity, it decided to convene the organizations it regulates. With the willing participation of its regulated entities, it gained buy-in to collect data on their diversity. It produced an annual Diversity in broadcasting report for each of the last five years and catalysed progress in the sector. This progress, these new opportunities for thousands of people, would not have happened if it had stuck to its pre-determined remit. By leading the sector, getting buy-in for change, Ofcom has engineered additional benefit for all that would otherwise not have happened.

At the London 2012 Olympics and Paralympics, there were multiple examples of leadership, from the most senior to the most junior of staff. Mohammed, a junior volunteer in the event services team, came up with the idea of

Ramadan packs. These were takeaway picnics that Muslims could purchase at any point during the busy working day and use at the break of fast in the evening. Anyone could buy them – they became an additional revenue line as well as creating a more inclusive catering experience for spectators and staff. Others used the prayer rooms for people of various faiths as well as people on the autistic spectrum who needed to get away from crowds for a while. There are many more examples detailed in The Inclusion Imperative,[8] not least the visit of Desmond Tutu, who inspired many to lead ever more inclusively.

When the online fashion company, Zalando, wanted to kick start its DEI programme, it decided to open up the event to all like-minded organizations in Germany. This vulnerability and generosity was reciprocated by hundreds of others attending the event learning about DEI, and who would otherwise have missed out.

The charity formerly known as the Sir John Cass Foundation was wrestling with its history, and the endowment that had originated in the founder's involvement in the transatlantic slave trade. After discussion with multiple stakeholders, the Board decided to rename the organization to the Portal Trust. They are very open about the origins of their endowment and use it explicitly to tackle race-based and poverty-based injustice in central London.

The tiny charity, Music Masters, is committed to providing access to classical music and instruments for poorer schoolchildren in the UK who are far less likely to end up playing a musical instrument. Despite their size and lack of resources, they were able to partner with Included to develop the 'I'm In' index for the classical music sector. It convened other small organizations in the sector as well as the largest most famous orchestras to commit to a programme of change.

Reconciling different worlds

Adaptation to others is at the core of inclusive leadership. Steve remembers working with the team at Stonewall that helped secure equal treatment for LGBT+ people in service provision. No more could a hotel turn away a same sex couple. Yet, after the law changed, many gay men complained to Stonewall about straight people in 'their' gay clubs, however, equality is a two-way street.

Evelyn Beatrice Hall, who wrote under the pseudonym Stephen G. Tallentyre, was an English writer who wrote the phrase often attributed to Voltaire, 'I disapprove of what you say, but I will defend to the death your right to say it'.[9] This is often used in defence of free speech. Free speech has limits. Words that are deliberately incendiary, racist or dangerous are not OK. However, within the realms of legality and civility, we need to run towards different viewpoints. How can we possibly grow as leaders without subjecting our views to challenge and refinement? How can you possibly make the best decision without understanding where the other (affected) side is coming from?

The platinum rule will help. Adapt to others, rather than expecting them to adapt to you. Raafi-Karim Alidina (co-author of Building an Inclusive Organization) and Steve have an ongoing joke that one is the evil businessman and one is the ivory tower academic (we'll leave you to assume who is who). But the seriousness behind this discussion is that universities aren't always good proxies for organizations. Academics and students need appreciate that a commercial environment with other variables at stake requires empathy for the people who are trying to make it work. Similarly, organizations ploughing forward with non-evidence based DEI initiatives won't succeed either.

Critical thinking requires us to disagree. It's the facilitation of that disagreement, in a respectful, civil, manner that is the practice of good leadership. Safe spaces need to be productive spaces. Gracious spaces, if you will, allow for respectful disagreement, which is core to furthering learning. Psychological safety is critical for people to bring their talents to the table, but this is not to be confused with so called, cancel culture, where people with different views are not allowed to speak. We need to be empathetic with people who get language wrong, rather than castigate them.

Leaders need to avoid backlash, so they need to walk the line in order to bring the group with them. It's often helpful to focus on the goal. If the goal is greater inclusion, we need to candidly challenge ourselves and each other, are you actually contributing to that? Or are you part of the problem?

Key takeaways

1 Leadership is about challenging parameters and conventions, as opposed to management which is working within them. Inclusion can't happen without inclusive leadership, bringing different people together, in order to get work done.

2 We offer a simple ABC behavioural framework, overlaid on our Understand, Lead, Deliver theory of change. This can guide you in your leadership style, as well as offering ways of measuring progress.

3 Adapting to difference, bringing different people together and challenging segregation are critical workstreams today. You can exercise leadership and make a difference, independent of your role, seniority or power.

Further reading

Ramalingam, B, Nabarro, D, Oqubay, A, Carnall, R, and Wild, L (2020) 5 Principles Guide to Adaptive Leadership. Harvard Business Review hbr. org/2020/09/5-principles-to-guide-adaptive-leadership (archived at https:// perma.cc/4S9Q-F852)

Reynolds, A and Lewis, D (2017) Teams Solve Problems Faster When They're More Cognitively Diverse, Harvard Business Review hbr.org/2017/03/teams-solve-problems-faster-when-theyre-more-cognitively-diverse (archived at https:// perma.cc/P26Z-A6ZX)

Tulsiani, R (2013) Understanding the business benefits of cognitive diversity, HR Magazine www.hrmagazine.co.uk/content/features/understanding-the-business-benefits-of-cognitive-diversity (archived at https://perma.cc/GBG9-MFDR)

References

1 Heifetz, R A, Linksy, M, Grashow, A (2009) The Practice of Adaptive Leadership: Tools and Tactics for Changing Your Organization and the World. Harvard Business Press, Brighton

2 Wilcox, E W (1916) The Winds of Fate. Hearst's International Library Company, New York

3 Rhodan, M (2014) Microsoft CEO says he was inarticulate when arguing women shouldn't ask for raises TIME time.com/3489858/microsoft-ceo-women-raises/ (archived at https://perma.cc/BFW8-ASAR)

4 Fiorina, C (2001) Technology, business and our way of life: What's next, HP www.hp.com/hpinfo/execteam/speeches/fiorina/minnesota01.html (archived at https://perma.cc/3SJ7-N9HS)

5 Treanor, J (2011) Lloyds chief Horta-Osório takes time off with fatigue, The Guardian www.theguardian.com/business/2011/nov/02/lloyds-chief-leave-absence-stress (archived at https://perma.cc/N3HM-2UHA)

6 Kirkpatrick, D L (2010) Evaluating Human Relations Programs for Industrial Foremen and Supervisors, Createspace Independent Publishing Platform, Scotts Valley

7 Alexander, R, Huth, P, Poschardt, U (2017) Angela Merkel Interview, Welt am Sonntag www.welt.de/politik/deutschland/plus168025776/Frau-Merkel-haben-Sie-in-der-Fluechtlingsfrage-Fehler-gemacht.html (archived at https://perma.cc/ MJ6A-89QU)

8 Frost (2014) The Inclusion Imperative

9 Hall, E B (1903) The Life of Voltaire. Smith, Elder & Co, London

11

Systems and processes

HELEN CORBISHLEY

Introduction

Included facilitated a focus group for a FTSE 100 leisure company at one of their Central European offices. The objective was to explore ways that systemic interventions could further inclusion in the organization. The conversation quickly turned to flexible working, and the notion that, in one participant's words, it would be a 'game changer'.

During the conversation, it became apparent that flexible working had never been formally considered at this office, despite the fact all local child-care facilities closed a full half hour before the office did. This left those with care giving responsibilities in an often impossible and stressful situation. It was women who were disproportionately impacted, and when one woman did feel empowered to speak up, the mention of childcare caused her argument to be dismissed as a 'women's issue'.

Was there a reason flex working had never been mooted or implemented? The answer is no. Working hours were simply a systems and process legacy from when this particular office opened. As for the idea this was a 'women's issue', when it was proffered that everyone could benefit from flexible hours, whether it be staggering commute times, carrying out personal admin, or going to the gym, all of a sudden the impetus was there to make this happen. It turns out, adjusting core start and finish times was relatively easy to implement too, with just a few tweaks to existing processes. Flexible core hours became the default, and the impact on equity and inclusion was profound.

Defining and designing systems

Small tweaks to systems and processes, specifically people processes, can disproportionately support equity and inclusion. However, inclusion cannot happen by default, it has to happen by design.

Consider Global Charitable Foundation The Wellcome Trust. Tackling potential inequalities by measuring inclusion, they discovered engagement scores for disabled staff were 26 per cent lower than for non-disabled staff. This was in part due to disabled staff feeling unable to take full advantage of flexible working arrangements. People who were most likely to need flexible working arrangements felt least able to request it, for fear of it negatively impacting their career.

Acting upon this, Wellcome made flexible working the default. This turnaround, or reframe, meant that on measuring inclusion a year later, the gap between disabled and non-disabled employees had been eliminated. In a similar way to our leisure company, they proactively put interventions in place that resulted in demonstrably better outcomes.

When we talk about systems and processes, we reference those interrelated structures or principles through which an organization operates. They are literally the infrastructure of an organization. So, for example, think of the procedures that enable recruitment and retention to happen, such as recruitment methodologies, career development practices or indeed work scheduling. Let's not forget systems outside of HR, such as procurement, product design and marketing. These are the building blocks through which an organization operates, and DEI must be firmly embedded in order to make inclusion a part of the culture.

Systems and processes are often seen as immovable. They are not, as we will show in this chapter. By scrutinizing these systems and processes, as with the above illustrations, we can identify potential gaps or biases. We can then establish interventions or nudges to help mitigate these biases. This will lead to a more equitable, diverse and inclusive environment for all, as well as contributing to organizational efficiency and performance. Many of the systems improvements we can make do not require training. They can be low cost or no cost, even saving time and money.

Nudges

Nudge theory is a behavioural economics term popularized by Thaler and Sunstein in their 2008 book, (perhaps unsurprisingly), called Nudge.[1] They build on the premise that decision making can be influenced by positive reinforcement, or suggestion, and that this is preferable to other mandated methods of influencing behaviour, such as education or enforcement. Moreover, these nudges are frequently small, easy and inexpensive to administer, and yet can have a disproportionate effect on outcomes.

Kepinski and Nielsen have taken this a step further. As DEI professionals, they have collated hundreds of practical examples of nudges that perpetuate inclusion. *Included* has contributed several more to their growing volume. Moreover, they talk not just about inclusion, but how nudge theory can create a more equitable climate. Systems, or 'process design inclusion nudges'[2] are highlighted as a key part of this.

One often cited example of a successful nudge, and a particular favourite, is the case of the Schiphol urinal.[3] In an effort to reduce bathroom cleaning costs, Amsterdam's Schiphol airport painted an image of a housefly by the drain in the men's urinals. The idea was to give users something to aim at, in the hope this would reduce 'spillage'. It worked! The airport reported an 80 per cent reduction in said spillage, (though one may question exactly how they measured this), and an 8 per cent reduction in cleaning costs.

The Schiphol urinal is an example of choice architecture, or a different way in which choices can be presented. If these are systemic, and embedded in procedure, it follows they will be both more effective, and more readily adopted.

Belief in nudges is such, that in 2010 the UK Government set up their Behavioural Insights Team, known informally as the *nudge unit*. In 2020, nudge theory was cited as a strategy with which to help them tackle the coronavirus pandemic, to help reach so called herd immunity.

The benefits of nudges are multifarious. They are often low, or no, cost. They don't rely on training or *buy-in*, and can easily be incorporated in existing systems and processes. In addition to making flexible working the default, or the Schiphol urinal, there are literally thousands of ideas we have implemented in organizations all over the world.

It stands to reason that taking a close look at systems and processes, and implementing nudges, seems not only pragmatic, but a pre-requisite when it comes to truly delivering on DEI. We are seeing a proliferation of organizations recognizing the benefits of debiasing systems, and requests for support and advice in this domain have escalated. Organizations are opening up to the notion that this is a pragmatic method of implementing sustainable and meaningful change. Moreover, it provides a way to create Inclusion 4.0.

What follows is a run through of the most common systems and processes you are likely to want to influence, in order to create a more inclusive culture.

The employee lifecycle

Talent acquisition

As well as increasing the diversity of interview panels, and utilizing technology to re-examine job specifications, global healthcare company Novartis have been vocal in their endeavours to lessen the potential for bias in talent selection. In an attempt to address a lack of women in research and development roles, they now include childcare options and information as an intrinsic part of the interview process.

This serves not only to inform potential candidates' decision making, but is testimony to the fact the company care enough to recognize this as a potential barrier, and to address it. While we cannot say conclusively that this has directly impacted the gender mix at Novartis, they have reported an increase in women in management roles. Novartis are also included in the Bloomberg Gender-Equality Index, a list of companies achieving the highest standards in inclusion metrics, many relating to gender parity.

Recent discussions with a highly successful, mixed race, openly gay employee from a pharmaceutical company were insightful. When asked why they had applied for a position at the organization, they were explicit that it was the overt commitment to DEI that had 'sealed the deal'. The employee had seen DEI was a part of the firm's core values, and this had been highlighted at each stage of the recruitment process.

For example, a clear and overt commitment to employee diversity and wellbeing featured as part of the organization's careers site. This translated to the communications received during the application process, such as testimonials and imagery featuring current employees from under-represented groups. These are simple nudges, yet can create a distinct competitive advantage. The employee had choices, but decided upon this particular firm because as they disclosed; *I wanted to feel wanted, I wanted to belong*.

Debiasing recruitment systems

Recognizing their hiring process was not as diverse or inclusive as it could be, and that their staff base was not representative of their stakeholders and wider community, a well-known academic institution wanted to carry out a thorough examination of their recruitment practices. In order to do this, *Included* enacted a three-step process.

Firstly, a series of stakeholder interviews were carried out with HR, hiring managers, agencies and new hires, in order to establish what actually happens throughout the process, from end-to-end. Examining everything from reaching out to potential employees, application, shortlisting, interview and offer, *Included* were able to build a picture of their lived experiences, and the mechanisms in place at grassroots level.

Simultaneously, a documentation review was initiated, considering policies, job descriptions, interview and shortlisting grids, monitoring data, and any other documentation pertinent to the recruitment process. Having looked at the component parts, a thorough SWOT analysis was conducted. In breaking down the end-to-end recruitment process into its micro components, we were able to identify areas of bias, debias them and/or suggest nudges to counter the effect of the bias.

The aggregated outcomes were presented as a list of over 100 bespoke recommendations. These accounted for impact versus effort in order to prioritize. Many of these nudges could be implemented immediately, for example switching and increasing the number of job boards positions were advertised on, a regulated shortlisting process, using gender decoding tools on job advertisements, or making paired interviews standard. Others required escalation for approval or resourcing, such as developing a strategic workforce plan or partnering with agencies. This allowed the organization to sequence and prioritize impactful changes.

Talent retention

We've discussed talent acquisition systems, but just as important in fostering equity, inclusion, and belonging are retention practices. Performance management forms a big part of this, and specifically transparency in decision making surrounding both salary and promotions. If these systems are not transparent, there is more potential for bias in decision making. Consider the furore in recent years around the gender pay gap, for example. While there are countless reasons for a pay gap, many of which could incidentally be tackled using nudge theory, a lack of openness around decision making with reference to both pay and promotion contributed.

A number of organizations have uncovered this as one of the most contentious issues influencing equity and inclusion. The good news is, there are nudges which can be implemented to ensure these systems are less ambiguous. Simply publishing salary bandings and promotional protocols, and ensuring these are adhered to, can go a long way to instilling trust. Similarly, utilizing performance management tools such as a 9-box grid allows for a more objective assessment of performance and potential. The 9-box grid refers to the talent management tool developed by McKinsey, whereby employees are divided into 9 segments based on their performance and potential. The 9-box grid, and related frameworks, allow for consistency and clarity when making decisions, and are a valuable tool in informing further areas for development.

Included recently partnered with a well know luxury fashion brand in examining employee engagement and inclusion. The objective was to listen to staff and unearth practical interventions that would be most impactful in improving psychological safety and belonging. The company were somewhat confounded to discover it was their promotion systems that were the primary cause for concern with a vast number of employees. Development decisions were neither formalized or transparent, leading to feelings of confusion and mistrust among staff. What's more, this could be directly linked to job satisfaction and higher staff turnover.

The company are now working to make their promotions more transparent and robust by developing a transparent framework and guidelines. They are coupling this with training for people managers in order that the framework will be properly and fairly administered. In doing this, the organization can go a long way to helping alleviate these feelings of exclusion.

Systemic attraction and retention

We can develop our thinking even further here, not only looking at systemic interventions that attract and support staff, but looking at those which simultaneously work as retention tool, as well as a pull factor to draw potential employees in.

Sporting goods brand Reebok have been particularly efficacious here. Their ground-breaking *Passports* Employee Resource Group (ERG) has been praised for its ability to make new employees from diverse backgrounds and locations feel included. Recognizing that employees who move for a role can have a difficult time in assimilating themselves into the organization, something that is overlooked by many organizations, Reebok decided to establish a group to help. Staff are supported with everything from practical immigration assistance or finding a local hairdresser, to understanding cultural references, or just being a conduit through which to voice concerns and share experiences. In many cases, the group has acted as a surrogate family, broken down barriers, and enabled these staff members a more equitable experience. This has been particularly germane during the coronavirus pandemic. Furthermore, membership of this ERG is embedded into the onboarding process, so employees feel welcomed and valued from the outset. As Co-Chair Emma Varsanyi states, 'We are building a welcoming, safe, respectful and inclusive environment for employees from all over the world to thrive in. Employees that are thriving are more productive, spread motivation, and are less likely to leave.'

Off-boarding

From attraction to retention, there are distinct examples of how we can make our people systems and processes more equitable and inclusive. We can round this off, appraising the entire employee lifecycle, by considering offboarding.

For example, the often overlooked, but hugely informative stay interview is an opportunity to examine any gaps or further opportunities in procedures. A considered stay interview, by which we mean one that asks the right questions and acts upon the feedback, enables an organization to adjust systems and processes accordingly.

One educational establishment spent a great deal of time theorizing the reasons they were hemorrhaging staff in a specific department. Only through informal stay interviews did they discover that organizations in the locality were actively poaching staff with higher wages and development opportunities as soon as they had been trained. This not only led to an overhaul of the department's salary and promotional processes, there is now a recognized and communicated promotional path, but it also highlighted the value of stay interviews, which at the time of writing are subsequently becoming a standard mechanism for evaluating equity, inclusion, affiliation and belonging.

Systems and processes outside of HR

Procurement and supply chain

While people processes are pivotal to an organization, we are increasingly seeing DEI become an influential part of the procurement process. CIPS (The Chartered Institute of Procurement and Supply) have been particularly vocal in their commitment to, and support of, DEI. They openly acknowledge its importance to internal teams, but markedly to the supply base too. After all, procurement both connects with, and shapes a wide range of stakeholders, so it stands that inclusive design can exert a huge influence here.

Take HS2, the new high-speed rail network in the UK, a multi-billion pound project considered the biggest transport investment programme in a century. Inevitably this means a colossal supply chain, and extensive procurement process. In light of this, and recognizing the far-reaching consequences of a successful DEI programme, the company embedded DEI in its systems from the get go. Ongoing DEI training and awareness is in place for all staff working on behalf of HS2 for example, and for suppliers, they must be able to demonstrate a commitment to DEI by submitting monthly or six-monthly data reports to ensure this is followed through. Furthermore, the organization provides assistance with demographic tools to ensure all suppliers are readily able to capture this information. A supply chain information hub has also been set up offering advice and information by way of case studies, best practice, looking at current suppliers, business/network event information and DEI policy.

HS2 have been applauded for meeting and exceeding industry benchmarks on gender, disability and race. 22 per cent of their supply chain are women, for example, compared to a construction sector average of just 13 per cent.

Product design

Second to people, products are often considered the nucleus of an organization. Let's therefore consider what we traditionally think of as product, tangible commodities which have to be built or created. In particular, let's examine running shoes (or trainers, sneakers or techies, depending on where you're from).

Opinions differ slightly, but the first performance trainers as we know them today were developed in the late 19th century. Back then, and for many years to follow, these trainers consisted of an upper to cover the top part of the foot, and a specially designed sole geared towards running. While a variety of updates and developments were applied to these shoes, for over 70 years they were designed with men in mind. Little, if any thought was given to the fact that women might want to use these shoes, and may also have different wants and needs.

In the 1970's women's training shoes were released onto the mass market. While this was touted as a step forward, to use industry lexicon, a women's shoe was simply a 'shrink it and pink it' version of what already existed. In other words, it hadn't really been designed or tested on women's feet. It was typically just smaller, and with 'girly' colours applied.

Systems and processes surrounding product development have changed exponentially in the last 20 years or so. Brands are now developing, seeking feedback on, and testing these products on as many women as men. They employ interventions to examine women's feet and the way in which women move their bodies in detail. They continue to innovate, for example using materials that adapt to a woman's body, improving comfort and responsiveness. The result? Women's running has never been more popular, the female market is more profitable than ever, creativity and innovation has snowballed, and women continue to break down barriers and experience unmitigated success as runners.

Embedding DEI in tech processes too is vital. Consider the example of eminent tech company Cloudflare, who, in 2021, found that their new internet filtering product was blocking LGBTQ content. The idea was to limit access to adult content, which inadvertently also blocked sites and services supporting gay and trans groups, and sex education sites. There was no check in place to assess any anomalies or unintended consequences. Cloudflare acted quickly to acknowledge and address the issue, and immediately carried out a review of their product development systems and processes. As part of this, checks and balances now ensure a full analysis of information filtration upfront.

Google and Twitter have also been heavily criticized for bias, specifically racial bias, in their search and crop algorithms. Twitter for example were called out for focusing on white faces over Black faces in image cropping. This resulted in them employing what is described as 'open source analysis' as part of their design process, opening up the review and testing of their product to as diverse an audience as possible.

What's clear, is that many of us need to reconsider our approach to product design. Introducing disruptors to enable inclusivity is no doubt lucrative, yet we cannot always include everyone in this choice architecture. In creating training shoes for women, we may not be catering for women with wide feet, or those with disabilities for example. We need to ensure we are cognizant of the decisions we do make however. Our decisions should be inherently active and not passive, hence DEI should always be top of mind. In this way we can both benefit, and likely avoid the pitfalls associated with getting it wrong.

Marketing and communications

As the external face of an organization, marketing systems are increasingly being considered for de-biasing. The World Federation of Advertisers (WFA) have created a 12-point guide whereby areas for potential bias in the creative process can be called out. These range from 'business and brand challenge', or gaining stakeholder buy in, to 'evaluation and analysis', harnessing that all important data. The WFA also talk to nudges, and what questions we can ask when reviewing our marketing and communications. For example, they ask whether there is a supply chain of diverse partners, highlighting that different systems such as procurement and marketing follow the same protocols and are inextricably linked.

There are a number of examples of communications cited as great examples of DEI. There is a danger, however, that these are not the product of robust, inclusive de-biased systems or processes, but simply what's hailed as vanity marketing, or marketing that is inauthentic, and doesn't move the needle when it comes to DEI progression. Fundamentally, we want to see true equity and inclusivity throughout, which leads to better decision making.

The Institute of Practitioners in Advertising (IPA) in the UK have been working to champion diversity and inclusion in the industry for some time. At the time of writing, they are developing this remit with their Future of Fairness initiative, designed to support advertisers not just with DEI as it relates to their own workforce, but as it relates to their external messaging as well. In particular, they provide information on how to understand minority group audiences more authentically, and showcase diverse advertising best practice.

Although we have taken examples from a select number of business areas, the DEI theory, its application, and impact, applies to all functions, and indeed it should. Accounting, legal, operations, customer service, payroll, all can, and will, undoubtedly benefit from inclusive design.

Conclusion

In previous chapters we examined the four pillars of strategy, data, governance and leadership, all of which are key to building an inclusive culture. The essential catch-all, however, is systems. After all, if we get this right, individuals, business, and indeed society can benefit. We don't even necessarily need to create buy-in or train people, if systems and processes are de-biased, it will happen intuitively.

That said, this is not always an easy undertaking. Although nudge theory provides us with some compelling tools, embedding DEI in systems and processes requires focus, adaptability and resource. Systems can be intrinsically complex, and are constantly evolving. This is therefore an iterative process, and DEI a perpetual journey.

The consequences of not embedding DEI into our structures and processes could in fact be detrimental. We have seen clear evidence of the consequences of this in product design for example, where the ramifications of DEI oversights were far-reaching.

The business case for creating a truly inclusive culture that promotes equity and belonging is increasingly robust. As we gather more data, we can see that debiasing systems has an impact not only on inclusion, or on that one functional business area being considered, but influences the entire ecosystem in which an organization operates. Equity diversity and inclusion is no longer a *nice to have* based solely on empirical or theoretical assumptions. Whereas it was once considered discretionary effort, particularly with regard to systems and processes, it is now imperative. If we get this right, the rewards as we have seen can be limitless.

Key takeaways

1 Systems and processes are critical enablers in helping organizations create authentic, inclusive cultures.

2 A review of the end-to-end process is the best method of identifying areas to debias. Behavioural nudges emerging from this provide effective mechanisms to embed DEI into organizational systems. Often high impact and low effort, they can reduce implicit bias and improve decision making.

3 While not without challenges, failure to address systemic issues could be damaging to an organization. If businesses get this right however, the benefits are incontrovertible.

Further reading

Bateman, A Barrington, A Date, K (2020) Why You Need a Supplier Diversity Programme Harvard Business Review, 17 August hbr.org/2020/08/why-you-need-a-supplier-diversity-program (archived at https://perma.cc/7MEW-R6VP)

Froio, C (2019) Reebok's Chris Froio on learning to talk about diversity and inclusion www.gameplan-a.com/2019/12/reeboks-chris-froio-on-learning-to-talk-about-diversity-and-inclusion/ (archived at https://perma.cc/59CE-FLZE)

Hern, A (2021) Student proves Twitter algorithm 'bias' toward lighter, slimmer, younger faces, 10 August www.theguardian.com/technology/2021/aug/10/twitters-image-cropping-algorithm-prefers-younger-slimmer-faces-with-lighter-skin-analysis (archived at https://perma.cc/47XK-AFYN)

Hootology (2021) About hootology.com/about (archived at https://perma.cc/TRP5-FGVZ)

HS2 (2021) Suppliers and businesses www.hs2.org.uk/building-hs2/suppliers-and-businesses/ (archived at https://perma.cc/7YT4-LHHV)

HS2 (2021) HS2 first to secure Platinum Standard for equality and diversity mediacentre.hs2.org.uk/news/hs2-first-to-secure-platinum-standard-for-equality-and-diversity (archived at https://perma.cc/6U2J-HHDB)

HS2 (2021) HS2 Webinar: Leading from the front – How HS2 is embedding inclusive practices www.youtube.com/watch?v=qWyYzW05jQw (archived at https://perma.cc/S6J3-2X6V)

IPA (2021) Initiatives: Diversity ipa.co.uk/initiatives/diversity/ (archived at https://perma.cc/8GQB-SBS3)

Merryweather, E (2021) Diversity and Inclusion in Product: Why it Matters Productschool.com, 20 April productschool.com/blog/product-management-2/diversity-inclusion-product/ (archived at https://perma.cc/9XQT-83SB)

Mildon, T (2021) Inclusive Procurement at HS2 mildon.co.uk/inclusive-procurement-at-hs2/ (archived at https://perma.cc/GV3H-EAFR)

Novartis (2021) www.novartis.co.uk (archived at https://perma.cc/T9YZ-N45H)

Wfanet (2021) WFA publishes final DEI Census wfanet.org (archived at https://perma.cc/57R5-UJUR)

With thanks to Emma Varsanyi at Reebok

References

1 Thaler, R H & Sunstein, C R (2008) Nudge: Improving Decisions about Health, Wealth and Happiness, Penguin Random House, London

2 Inclusion Nudges (2021) inclusion-nudges.org/ (archived at https://perma.cc/S6YR-Z7TZ)

3 Ingraham, C (2017) What's a urinal fly, and what does it have to with winning a Nobel Prize? Washington Post, 9 October www.washingtonpost.com/news/wonk/wp/2017/10/09/whats-a-urinal-fly-and-what-does-it-have-to-with-winning-a-nobel-prize/ (archived at https://perma.cc/ZGH4-2T2J)

PART FOUR

Unlocking the Future

Introduction

STEPHEN FROST

At a recent team retreat, using client work in a variety of organizations, *Included* colleagues explored what the future might look like from an inclusion perspective. On the one hand, it was bleak. The scale of change and discombobulation was overwhelming to many. Fear of change, fear of the other, fear in general, had taken over and people were retrenching. They were sticking to who they knew (affinity bias) and what they knew (confirmation bias). System 1 was in the ascendancy and polarization was accelerating.

When you stop and contemplate this reality, and this future, it's not one that most of us actually want.

One the other hand, the future was exciting. The change was so overwhelming, from political to social, to technological, economic and environmental, that we had to change the system. This didn't mean escape to a campfire and start singing songs waiting for the apocalypse to arrive. It meant very intentionally redesigning the processes we rely on in our work. Rather than trying to reduce car emissions, drive an electric one instead. Rather than flying to a meeting, using zoom instead. Rather than hiring people to fill a succession plan, changing the succession plan instead. The realization that we are empowered, we have talent in abundance, all we lack is time and the ability to stop and plan.

We've now covered the essential keys to inclusion; you, your team, and your organization. We want to finish with where this is all going. What does the future of work, the future of inclusion, the future of our own careers actually look and feel like? We'll take what we have learnt so far and apply it in various scenarios to paint this picture and make it as clear, vivid and tangible as possible.

We'll start with the future of work itself. What is work? What is 'a job'? Only when we have answers to these questions, can we postulate, 'what skills do I and my team need?' The reality is that the skills you've learnt in your life to date, whether at school, at university or college, or on the job, are increasingly out of date. Learning has shifted from content (knowing things) to ideation (creating things). What we know has an increasingly short life span so it's only by applying it, and creating new things (ideally in diverse teams) that we can remain relevant and succeed.

Skills such as empathy, creativity, ideation are going to be increasingly in demand. I recall a conversation with a colleague who was worried he was, 'a jack of all trades, a master of none'. This is a frequent retort I hear from many successful professionals. In fact being 'a master' of anything right now is at best short lived, and at worst, downright delusional. I have been practicing DEI for over 20 years but the field has changed immeasurably during this time. Without working in a team I would never stay abreast of knowledge or skills essential to create new solutions.

It's in the imagination age that we will explore how inclusion has impact. We'll talk about what impact means, beyond the hyperbole of so many organizations who are now convinced they have impact. What kind of impact are we talking about and how does this manifest? In particular, we'll look at those sectors that are changing the rules of the game – technology, financial services and broadcast media. While a deep dive into these sectors will recap many of the tools we have introduced throughout this book, from strategy to data and governance to leadership, it will also demonstrate that there are important nuances. To be successful in different contexts, we need to adapt. While design thinking is critical to the future of inclusive technology, the evidence suggests to effect change in banking, we need to strongly link incentives to pay and compensation. In other words what works for tech might not work for banking and vice versa.

So we end with all the tools at our disposal deployed, but with important context that will guide you as the specific buttons you want to press, the particular incentives you want to build in your own context to truly unlock the power of inclusion.

12

Welcome to the imagination age: Inclusion in the future of work

NICK BASANNAVAR

Introduction

In a 1929 interview for the *Saturday Evening Post,* Albert Einstein stated his belief that 'imagination is more important than knowledge. For knowledge is limited, whereas imagination encircles the world'.[1]

78 years later, the philosopher Rita J King wrote an essay for the British Council, a soft power organization promoting international connections on matters of art, culture and education. In it, she heralded the beginning of what she termed the 'Imagination Age'.[2] This would be a period, charged by the latest digital technologies and global citizens' immersion in and utilization of them, that would usher in new standards for human interaction.

In King's words, digital advancements had 'irrevocably changed the nature of our cultural perspectives', and a grand prize was at stake: greater 'collaborative sophistication', 'social change', and a transformation of the global economy.[3] The Imagination Age would succeed the Industrial Age (mid-18th century until mid-20th century) and the Information Age (mid-20th century to early-21st century), serving as a bridge to the highly advanced Intelligence Age.[4] It would mark a shift from the tangible world of industry to the intangible, virtual world of digital lives, code and analytics. Elsewhere, this has been defined as a shift from the 'knowledge economy' to the 'skills economy'.[5]

It is now something of a truism that the accumulation of information – or Einstein's 'knowledge' – alone is no longer a signifier of organizational progress. The academics and business thinkers Julian Birkinshaw and Jonas Ridderstråle pointed in 2017 to the stifling ubiquity of 'big data' and the 'limits of 1s and 0s' as competitive advantages.[6] Since then, the global COVID-19 pandemic has accelerated the vast digital changes which we already knew were coming, and which were outlined in Chapter 6. In place of task-based roles and lifelong vocational skills, a new consensus formed around the need of the organization to strengthen its emphasis on other 'human skills from emotional empathy to cognitive judgement and decision-making', in the words of the futurist Lynda Gratton.[7]

We are experiencing a moment in which 'creativity and imagination become the central drivers of economic value'.[8] One could argue that the insights behind King's bold vision are transhistorical; humankind has always managed to mark itself out from other species and propel itself forward through relentless imagination, finding solutions to seemingly unmanageable issues. But Einstein's maxim and King's theories seem ever more prescient today, given seismic events in recent years and the extreme disruption that large parts of the world are experiencing politically, economically, socially, technologically, legally and environmentally (see Chapter 7). In short, given the disorder we find ourselves in, fundamental human qualities – with imagination at the centre – have never been more important.

The problem is that imagination has not always been, and is not currently, equally accepted or distributed. This chapter argues that inclusion needs to be at the centre of the imaginative working world of the future. Creativity and imagination will have a limited effect if they come from the same sources that have owned the conversation until now. The significant challenges that we face as a species need King's 'collaborative sophistication' and the input of different voices. Inclusion is the nexus at the intersections of Industry 4.0, the Imagination Age, and the Skills Economy. It is the necessary response to demographic, digital and pandemic-induced challenges.

The chapter starts with an overview of key trends in the future of work, spotlighting the themes that are driving the need for a skills and empathy-based approach. It sets out the challenges and opportunities for inclusion that the new world of work brings. It then dives into what the key skills of an inclusive future are, with reference to practical tips, case studies and extant best practice.

A history of the future

As far back as 2011, Lynda Gratton believed that 'the future of work is already here'.[9] She argued that a combination of drivers, centring around technological change, demographic shifts, globalization, and socio-cultural movements would create a 'fundamentally transformed' world of work.[10] Many scholars, business thinkers and practitioners since have agreed.[11] In 2021 Gratton reflected on her predictions of 10 years prior, feeling that she was right about demographic change and globalization, but that she had not foreseen the increases in inequality which would unfold, nor a global pandemic which would significantly accelerate the impacts she had identified.[12]

The future of work is a largely (and necessarily) nebulous, intangible series of concepts, always mutating from one year to the next, at once visible and opaque. Here we look at the main features of this new world of work, through the lenses of technology, demography and pandemic-accelerated change.

Technological change

Many of the key technological changes and features of Industry 4.0 were covered in Chapter 6, with a particular focus on automation and AI. The key driver for rethinking the future of skills is indeed the significant impact of automation, which is replacing – or otherwise fundamentally redefining – large numbers of jobs. The Word Economic Forum predicted in 2020 that by 2025, 85 million jobs will be displaced as a result of advances in automation and AI – a shift becoming manifest, as they put it, in 'the division of labour between humans and machines'.[13] However, they note that a higher number of jobs – 97 million – will be created in order to manage the shifting interplay of human, machine, and algorithm-based work.[14] This in turn was due to have a large impact on skill requirements as people essentially shift from completing tasks themselves to strategizing and writing algorithms for machines to do so.

Demographic change

Demographic shifts are also widely identified as a significant driver for skills changes. To take the UK as an example, mortality has dropped consistently over time since the mid-19th century. A life expectancy of 40.2 for men and

42.3 for women for babies born in 1841 became 56 and 59 by 1920. By 2019, thanks to ongoing and significant advances in medicine, awareness of health risks, and universal health care, this was 79.8 and 83.4 years.[15] While COVID-19 interrupted this trend,[16] the long-term curve is still clear and material. And longer life expectancy currently means longer working lives. This increase in longevity has been termed the '100-Year Life'.[17]

Global migration is another major influence on demographic change; the International Organization for Migration (IOM) estimated in 2019 that there were 272 million international migrants – 3.5 per cent of the world's population. This was up from 192 million in 2000, with the U.S. the foremost destination. Political catastrophes, conflict, and climate change are key drivers, and this is expected to intensify as polarization, economic disruption and environmental damage worsen.[18]

This combination of demographic factors is having profound individual and collective implications for statecraft, for organizational change, and for work more broadly drawn – not least the ways that individual people organize their lives and careers. This is particularly so when demography is multiplied by rapid technological changes which are making traditional skills obsolete. People are changing jobs and reskilling much more regularly than in prior decades and centuries, with up to five different careers in a lifetime given as an estimate by the Social Market Foundation – often running concurrently in a side-hustle, gig economy.[19]

COVID-19

The wildcard entry to this landscape is, of course, the global COVID-19 pandemic. This brought both an acceleration of extant transformations, and a surfacing of new or dormant issues.[20] Digital adoption took a quantum leap as corporate organizations the world over reorganized themselves: towards digital services; towards digital supply-chain engagement; towards home working; towards virtual teaming.[21] This has meant a corresponding accentuation of agile learning and digital skills. The pandemic has also created and entrenched inequalities within and between communities and skills markets. The disruption on workers has been remarkable; in a global survey of 16,000 workers, EY found in March 2021 that more than half (54 per cent) were willing to quit their jobs – a sign of the Great Resignation – with desired flexibility being a key factor.[22] This in turn has sparked much corporate soul-searching about culture, particularly how to create more than purely transactional employee relations. Pandemic-fuelled disruption has 'changed the pace and magnitude of all forms of transformation'.[23]

The inclusion/skills challenge

As a 2018 Deloitte study put it, there have been significant changes in *how* work gets done, thanks to new digital technologies; in *who* does the work, particularly given demographic change, developments in the gig economy and increasing use of AI; and even in *what* work looks like, with fundamental changes to business models (see Chapter 5) and rapid digitization.[24] To this thesis we should also add and acknowledge that the *why*, as we established in Chapter 7, is shifting as organizations reconsider their purpose and mission in light of new technological, demographic, global, economic, and socio-cultural realities and imperatives. The pandemic has only accelerated these shifts.

In among these features of the current (and future) world of work, there are profound implications for humans that centre around the skills they will need to serve and thrive within organizations. And inclusion is central to this process.

As we saw in Chapter 6, the rapid scaling of advanced technologies including automation and AI could end up entrenching inequalities, rather than solving them. The world of Industry 4.0 is likely to generate a hierarchy of skills. There is a strong risk that this will positively bias those from elites with highly tuned, adaptable skillsets and social networks, and negatively bias those without. 'Highly skilled' workers benefit from a virtuous cycle in which they continuously receive training to learn new skills, either from their employer or via their private networks. However, according to the UK skills agency Nesta, half of adults from poorer backgrounds 'have had no training since leaving full-time education'.[25] We also know that there is a strong demographic connection between skills deficits and those from the most precarious and vulnerable communities, for example older workers and marginalized ethnic, racial and socioeconomic groups.[26]

As a result of the pandemic, remote and hybrid working are now firmly established realities. Who should be in the office and who not? How do we equalize experiences of our workers when some are fielding calls from a shared kitchen table in a small loft conversion, while others are zooming in from their private office in the east wing of their country estate or seaside pad?

The remote working narrative also heavily biases those in white collar, corporate roles. A huge number of workers *can't* work from home. Indeed, the workers who kept countries running during lockdown did so from hospitals, streets, plants and factories. The same workers in the highest risk, most precarious jobs. All this has significant implications for skills.

With so many moving parts, we face a mighty challenge to even understand the skills that currently exist in our organizations, let alone to set and execute an iterative, inclusive skills strategy that envisions and provides the skills that we need in the future. But doing so is a commercial, moral and social imperative.

The inclusion/skills opportunity

If we don't get on top of these issues and consciously choose inclusion, then exclusion will grow. Technological, demographic and economic change will stifle us, rather than empower us. Polarization will continue; inequality will entrench. As King said back in 2007, 'the challenge now, for those of us focusing on making a meaningful contribution towards collective creativity and organized action, is to apply the technology towards the inclusion of as many people as possible'.[27]

In other words, imagination will be at the centre of the future. And imagination is inextricably bound to inclusion. Human imagination and inclusion, combined, make up the toolkit of the new world of work. Technological advances can free us to seek out and imaginatively deploy difference to solve problems: different strategies, skills, perspectives, ideas. Demographic upheaval can be reframed positively by embedding inclusion, building a thriving intergenerational workforce, and nurturing imaginative and multi-skilled teams.

Then King's vision of the Imagination Age – and the skills that are necessary within it – becomes more urgent and significant. What is clear is that we are now far advanced beyond what we might term the 'legacy' skills bases of the industrial and information ages. We would also do well – if the future of work is already here – not to complacently lean on recommended skills that have surfaced in recent analyses of the future of work. Instead, it is time to grasp the new, inclusive age of skills.

Towards an inclusive skills framework

In October 2020, the World Economic Forum published results from its Future of Jobs survey, revealing its respondents' view on what the top 10 skills of 2025 would be. Tellingly, human skills such as creativity, ideation, innovation, and problem-solving featured prominently.[28] We might pool these, loosely, as skills of the *imagination*.

However, inclusion did not feature – a critical omission. It is both imagination and inclusion that will be central to work of the future – and these are closely bound together. Conceptually, the three major challenges for the future of work (Industry 4.0, demographic change, and the impact of the pandemic) reveal to us three major necessary approaches to skills:

- Technology
- Leadership
- Problem-solving

Here, we apply an inclusion lens to these three areas and give a flavour of what an inclusive skills framework of the future entails, illustrated with some case studies. These skillsets may be read on both an individual (personal) and a collective (organizational) level.

Feature 1: Inclusive technology skills

As Industry 4.0 speeds up, weaving inclusion deeply into all our digitally led work will become more critical if we want to create positive impact, as we have seen throughout this book. Doing so will help to mitigate bias in design algorithms, and to debias and de-racialize products and services. It will help to enfranchise individuals and communities who to date have not benefitted from the digital revolution. It will help to ensure that everyone ultimately benefits from more accessible, better products and services, rather than just a privileged proportion of the global community.

Technology should not be viewed as an end in itself. Rather, it is a set of tools that can enable humans to pool skills and solve critical global issues. Inclusive technological skills, collectively, constitute the expertise that will help to achieve those outcomes. But we need diversity at the table. There are, for example, an estimated one billion disabled people on this planet, spanning a wide variety of conditions and degrees of severity. It is an imperative that disabled people are included in technology design processes.[29]

Perhaps recognizing this, Microsoft – the world's largest software company – launched a global skills initiative in 2020 to broaden and equalize access to digital skills.[30] By 2021, it had reached 30 million people.[31] The initiative, in partnership with some of Microsoft's key subsidiaries, brought free e-learning content across LinkedIn Learning, Microsoft Learn, and the GitHub Learning Lab. This included more than 500 online courses 'and hundreds of free demonstration modules that teach technology and coding'.[32]

The Vice-Chairman and President of Microsoft Brad Smith has said that 'the good news is that most people everywhere want to learn new digital skills'.[33] But marrying intention and practical action is often a tricky balance within organizations. Cloudflare, one of the world's major Internet performance and security firms, has a mission to make the Internet a better place.[34] Cloudflare has consciously been closing the intention-action gap in recent years, working on embedding inclusion throughout their strategy, behaviours, and processes. In 2021 they conducted an exercise, led by Director of Product Management Patrick Donahue, to challenge, reconsider, and rebuild aspects of their product design. Working with *Included,* Donahue and his team went back to the drawing board on many of their Internet security products. They threw an inclusion lens across every process step, seeking to uncover blind spots, challenge inherent bias, and ensure the final product worked for everyone. There are very few major organizations which are not now either tech-enabled or transitioning to digital product. They might consider some of the same approaches as Cloudflare.

Feature 2: Inclusive leadership skills

Late on the night of 11 July 2021, in a corner of North-West London, Bukayo Saka stood up to take a penalty kick in an international football match. Saka was just 19 years old. Born in London to Nigerian parents, he had spent a large part of his young life flitting between West and North London, between his family and Arsenal Football Club's academy.

Saka's penalty was saved by goalkeeper Gianluigi Donnarumma to hand Italy the Euro 2020 title.[35] Within minutes, it started: the sadly predictable, deathly drip of racist emojis and racist language, emanating from the UK and abroad. It was directed towards Saka, Marcus Rashford and Jadon Sancho, three young, Black, brilliant English attackers who had all missed their penalties. What could have been England's finest footballing hour since 1966 turned into horrible and sobering national introspection. For anyone who believed that overt racism was a thing of the past, here was the counterevidence, plastered across social media.

Sadly, not everyone feels that Black sportspeople are worthy of their places in the world. Many thousands of supporters have continued to boo players who take the knee in solidarity for people of colour (colleagues and non-colleagues) who suffer from racial inequality.[36]

In among all the individual and collective trauma this caused in England and elsewhere was a glimpse of hope: the quiet leadership of Saka's England manager, Gareth Southgate, and his coaching staff including Chris Powell, a Black former England international.[37] As a player himself, Powell had been the subject of racist abuse from English terraces in the 1980s and 1990s, which led to his parents feeling unable to watch his matches in person.[38]

National football teams have historically been an interesting barometer of demographic and social progress.[39] England has one of the most diverse top-level teams in the world of football. For English football, diversity is a reality. But although Southgate and his team showed us what inclusive leadership could look like, inclusion is sadly not always a choice that many within the game are willing to make.

Southgate wrote a moving letter for the *Player's Tribune*, 'Dear England', in which he said:

> *'I know my voice carries weight, not because of who I am but because of the position that I hold... I have a responsibility to the wider community to use my voice... Unfortunately for those people that engage in that kind of [racist] behaviour, I have some bad news. You're on the losing side. It's clear to me that we are heading for a much more tolerant and understanding society, and I know our lads will be a big part of that. It might not feel like it at times, but it's true.'*[40]

As we saw in Chapter 10, inclusive leadership in business is about so much more than simply leaving the overburdened Head of DEI, HRD, or someone else to do the work. It's about being visible and taking accountability for measurable progress. Anyone wondering what the skills needed are should look no further than Southgate, Powell and their team: visible and active anti-racism; allyship; absorption of criticism; elevation of marginalized colleagues; emotional intelligence; public humility and vulnerability. This is inclusive leadership.

Feature 3: Inclusive problem-solving skills

One of the central tenets of inclusive problem-solving is the active disintegration of the barriers between art and business. Use of the right-hand side of the brain – the artistic and the creative – will become more and more relevant in a working world that previously more highly valued the left-hand side's cold analytical method.[41]

To some, this is as instinctively uncomfortable as an AI-written novel. As the entrepreneur Nir Hindi puts it, 'there is a deep-rooted belief that artists and business fundamentally don't mix'.[42] The Boardroom 2030 movement, an innovation by the impact collective B Lab, argues differently. It states that the creative process should become a more prominent feature of executive teams and boardrooms, whether through playing music during breaks or key moments in meetings, starting or closing sessions with spoken poetry, or utilizing visual art in storytelling.[43]

Catherine Wallwork is the Head of Innovation Engagement and Mindset at professional services giant Deloitte UK. Her role is to help the firm build a perpetual culture of innovation, marrying creative processes such as story-telling to psychological concepts to help colleagues frame, discuss and solve difficult problems.

For Wallwork, innovation is constantly in the service of inclusion – and vice versa. Heads of innovation who think only about economic benefit have 'hit the mark, but missed the point'. Wallwork knows that diversity of thinking helps you build better cultures, products and solutions: 'so, we set up specific forums and spaces where people could come alive with ideas in a productive way, and disagreement is encouraged. You can't create that without inclusion'.[44]

One such space is Innovation Forums, an open-invite event running since 2018 within Deloitte UK. Innovation Forums was designed to encourage engagement with big human issues such as AI, workplace culture, drones, the blockchain and more. Free to colleagues, clients and others, the open nature of the event is rare and generative. Wallwork says that 'there's no inbox to register or anything. You have the power to invite somebody else. It's not concentrated power where there's a mailbox and authority to invite. That process creates a neighbourhood effect'.[45]

The methods used in those events – from posing philosophical questions at the start, to breaking down problem statements to their constituent parts, to the use of music to lift senses – has now been replicated in senior settings in the firm, client discussions, and elsewhere. The key has been that people 'are getting used to going into a meeting and not having a deterministic view of the outcome'.[46] In this way, inclusion has helped to bring different perspectives powerfully to the fore.

The creative process is a critical part of human life. Why wouldn't we draw on artistic skill and expression – things that inspire us, things that make us human – to solve big human problems? The blocking out of emotion and imagination in business has been unproductive and short-sighted.

There have been many other examples of organizations bringing imagination to solve problems, for example to attract a more diverse pool of talent and build more inclusive organizations. In 2012, IKEA Australia put job descriptions (labelled 'career instructions') into some of their flat-pack delivery packages that went direct to customers. They received 4,285 applications and made 280 new hires from a pool of people they hadn't considered before: customers already deeply engaged with the brand.[47]

In 2013, the British intelligence agency GCHQ launched an open competition via a website; anyone who could crack the code would be offered a job.[48] The campaign attracted 400,000 applicants with the code being cracked by just one per cent of those who attempted it.[49] This evoked memories of a creative Second World War campaign, where Alan Turing set a crossword puzzle in the Daily Telegraph in an attempt to attract 'a team of crack cryptologists and code breakers'.[50]

Such campaigns make for salutary examples in a discussion about inclusive, creative problem-solving. They sound deceptively simple as ideas, but organizations have been getting this wrong for centuries. Of course, such approaches are not perfect – those who are digitally excluded already may be less likely to have the skillsets needed to detect hidden code in a website. Yet the ads demonstrate creativity in their hiring approaches. Critically, they also value requisite skills over backgrounds or identities. In this way, they are at least theoretically meritocratic.

The inclusive skills framework

The Table 12.1 provides a summary of these concepts, showing the key features of the inclusive technology skills, inclusive leadership skills, and inclusive problem-solving skills that will be required in the future world of work.

TABLE 12.1 Key features of the inclusive skills framework

Future of work challenge	Inclusive skills category	Features (examples)
Industry 4.0 requires...	**...inclusive technology skills** (technical, digital)	• Understands and mitigates the impact of uninclusive/biased tech • Expertly draws on all kinds of diversity to cover technological blind spots and build better code and products/services • Places accessible design at the heart of all work • Deploys technology not simply to drive growth, but to free up humans to solve strategic and social issues and increase their wellbeing • Actively advances digital inclusion for communities and countries that are excluded from digital benefits
Demographic shifts require...	**...inclusive leadership skills** (relational, interpersonal)	• Treats colleagues as *they* would like to be treated, rather than how *I* would like to be treated • Gives colleagues an active role in building their own working environment and policies • Truly listens • Learns little and often • Understands one's own impact • Prioritizes psychological safety and safe challenge • Constant allyship for and sponsorship of marginalized colleagues • Elevates others rather than dictating • Shows vulnerability • Actively anti-racist • Considers circumstances of team members when decision making
Pandemic-driven work shifts require...	**...inclusive problem-solving skills** (systemic, contextual, physical)	• Imagination, artistry, creativity at the heart of problem-solving • Looks in new places for talent • Emotional insight • Recognizes and acts on the need to include widest possible mix of viewpoints to assess problems and create ideas • Draws on diverse methodologies and techniques to solve problems (philosophy, art, culture, external views)

Conclusion

To close where we started, with the words of Rita J. King:

'The only hope of clashing cultures is to find a common ground beyond the shackles of time and place to which each human is bound. This place is the imagination, where ideas are born. Increasingly, the delicate glass bulb of the future will be lit by a tangled filament of intertwined ideas. People from all over the globe, having been left out of the dialogue for so long, will add vital new dimensions to global unity.'[51]

It is not possible for one person, one group of people, or one culture to have all the answers. The great novelist Kazuo Ishiguro once claimed that 'I discovered that my imagination came alive when I moved away from the immediate world around me'.[52] Looking in places we wouldn't normally look can lead to brilliant things. By surrounding ourselves with difference, we open up perpetual learning and successful futures. The future of work needs leaders who are going to listen, be humble, be empathetic, and learn from others to fuel the imagination.

Key takeaways

1 In recent years, world events have catapulted us into what Rita J. King termed the Imagination Age.

2 The future of work is here already, with technological and demographic changes occurring at a rapid rate, exacerbated by the global COVID-19 pandemic. These changes bring huge challenges for skills, and in turn for diversity and inclusion.

3 By tying inclusion to imaginative approaches, we can build a better working world. Inclusive technology skills, inclusive leadership skills, and inclusive problem-solving skills need to be at the centre of the new, imaginative world of work.

References

1   Viereck, G S (1929) What Life Means to Einstein: An Interview, *The Saturday Evening Post,* 26 October. www.saturdayeveningpost.com/wp-content/uploads/satevepost/what_life_means_to_einstein.pdf (archived at https://perma.cc/K6VU-WR7W)

2, 3, 27, 51 King, R J (2007) The Emergence of a New Global Culture in the Imagination Age, *British Council* [Preprint] archive.md/bcUT (archived at https://perma.cc/X4MX-S8X2)

4   King, R J (2016) The Origin of the Imagination Age, *LinkedIn,* 22 June www.linkedin.com/pulse/origin-imagination-age-rita-j-king/ (archived at https://perma.cc/76VY-NR5L)

5, 23 de Sousa, R (2021) Reinventing Today's Workforce: Welcome to the Skills Economy, LHH www.lhh.com/us/en/organizations/our-insights/reinventing-the-workforce-welcome-to-the-skills-economy (archived at https://pcrma.cc/2DQN-E4GV)

6   Birkinshaw, J and Ridderstråle, J (2017) *Fast/Forward: Make Your Company Fit for the Future,* Stanford University Press

7, 17 Gratton, L and Scott, A (2020) *The 100-Year Life: Living and Working in an Age of Longevity,* London: Bloomsbury Publishing

8   Willis, K S and Aurigi, A (2020) *The Routledge Companion to Smart Cities.* London: Routledge

9, 10 Gratton, L (2011) *The Shift: The Future of Work Is Already Here.* London: HarperCollins UK

11   Perkin, N. and Abraham, P (2017) *Building the Agile Business through Digital Transformation.* London: Kogan Page Publishers

13, 14, 28 Whiting, K (2020) These are the top 10 job skills of tomorrow – and how long it takes to learn them, *World Economic Forum,* 21 October www.weforum.org/agenda/2020/10/top-10-work-skills-of-tomorrow-how-long-it-takes-to-learn-them/ (archived at https://perma.cc/Y2KT-RKL5)

15   Raleigh, (2021)

16   ONS (2021) *National life tables – life expectancy in the UK.* Office for National Statistics. www.ons.gov.uk/peoplepopulationandcommunity/birthsdeathsandmarriages/lifeexpectancies/bulletins/nationallifetablesunitedkingdom/2018to2020 (archived at https://perma.cc/ZJ2F-Q9LN)

18   IOM (2019) *World Migration Report 2020,* International Organization for Migration publications.iom.int/books/world-migration-report-2020 (archived at https://perma.cc/A3YP-NNJN)

19   Petrie, K (2020) Work, education, skills and the 100-year life: How can policymakers ensure the workforce is ready for extreme longevity? *Social Market Foundation,* 2 March www.smf.co.uk/publications/work-education-skills-100-year-life/ (archived at https://perma.cc/9RSZ-AAYA)

12, 20 Gratton, L (2021) The future of work came faster than we thought, *think at London Business School,* 26 February www.london.edu/think/wcn-the-future-of-work-came-faster-than-we-thought (archived at https://perma.cc/B8G2-N7NQ)

21 McKinsey & Company (2020) COVID-19 digital transformation and technology, 5 October www.mckinsey.com/business-functions/strategy-and-corporate-finance/our-insights/how-covid-19-has-pushed-companies-over-the-technology-tipping-point-and-transformed-business-forever (archived at https://perma.cc/TQ6P-GXYH)

22 EY Global (2021) More than half of employees globally would quit their jobs if not provided post-pandemic flexibility, EY survey finds, 12 May www.ey.com/en_gl/news/2021/05/more-than-half-of-employees-globally-would-quit-their-jobs-if-not-provided-post-pandemic-flexibility-ey-survey-finds (archived at https://perma.cc/MM75-KX2E)

24 Stockton, H, Filipova, M and Monahan, K (2018) The evolution of work, *Deloitte Insights,* 30 January www2.deloitte.com/us/en/insights/focus/technology-and-the-future-of-work/evolution-of-work-seven-new-realities.html (archived at https://perma.cc/S9NQ-9FY6)

25 Nesta (2019) *Precarious to Prepared: A manifesto for supporting the six million most at risk of losing their jobs in the next decade.* Nesta www.nesta.org.uk/report/precarious-to-prepared/ (archived at https://perma.cc/FUY8-RA9H)

26 Blundell, R et al *(2021) Inequalities in education, skills, and incomes in the UK: The implications of the COVID-19 pandemic, Institute for Fiscal Studies* ifs.org.uk/inequality/inequalities-in-education-skills-and-incomes-in-the-uk-the-implications-of-the-covid-19-pandemic/ (archived at https://perma.cc/E5GA-FV5F)

29 Stern, J (2020) How can your organisation become digitally inclusive? *Management Today,* 1 April www.managementtoday.co.uk/article/1678830?utm_source=website&utm_medium=social (archived at https://perma.cc/J7JZ-3C8B)

30 Smith, B (2020) Microsoft launches initiative to help 25 million people worldwide acquire the digital skills needed in a COVID-19 economy, *The Official Microsoft Blog,* 30 June blogs.microsoft.com/blog/2020/06/30/microsoft-launches-initiative-to-help-25-million-people-worldwide-acquire-the-digital-skills-needed-in-a-covid-19-economy/ (archived at https://perma.cc/6RWD-NSMF)

31, 32, 33 Smith, B (2021) Building a more inclusive skills-based economy: The next steps for our global skills initiative, *The Official Microsoft Blog,* 30 March blogs.microsoft.com/blog/2021/03/30/building-a-more-inclusive-skills-based-economy-the-next-steps-for-our-global-skills-initiative/ (archived at https://perma.cc/5PXP-UGMV)

34 Cloudflare (no date) *Cloudflare: about us, Cloudflare* www.cloudflare.com/about-overview/ (archived at https://perma.cc/D3E7-JDP7)

35 Hytner, D (2021) Italy crush England's dreams after winning Euro 2020 on penalties, *The Guardian,* 11 July www.theguardian.com/football/2021/jul/11/italy-crush-england-dreams-after-winning-euro-2020-on-penalties (archived at https://perma.cc/RV7Z-BBWA)

36 Rushden, M (2021) We all need to be braver and create space for people in football to speak out, *The Guardian,* 27 August www.theguardian.com/football/2021/aug/27/football-taking-knee-create-space-for-people-to-speak-out (archived at https://perma.cc/4WRD-G8J9)

37 A (2021) The Black role models inspiring a generation, *BBC Sport,* 19 October www.bbc.co.uk/sport/football/58909087 (archived at https://perma.cc/HG6W-CUKU)

38 Cross, J (2019) Chris Powell recalls racist abuse which stopped mum and dad from watching him, *Daily Mirror,* 15 November www.mirror.co.uk/sport/football/news/chris-powell-recalls-racist-abuse-20890059 (archived at https://perma.cc/F96P-8RKW)

39 Goldblatt, D (2019) *The Age of Football: The Global Game in the Twenty-first Century.* London: Pan Macmillan

40 Southgate, G (2021) Dear England, *The Players' Tribune,* 8 June www.theplayerstribune.com/posts/dear-england-gareth-southgate-euros-soccer (archived at https://perma.cc/42Q5-PC37)

41 White, L and Newall, E (2014) Which side of the brain is most important for a business leader? *The Guardian,* 29 May www.theguardian.com/sustainable-business/psychology-right-side-brain-business-leader (archived at https://perma.cc/N85X-86JC)

42 Hindi, N (2020) The Imagination Age, *The Artian,* 8 December www.theartian.com/the-imagination-age/ (archived at https://perma.cc/H8L4-PT38)

43 B Lab (2021) *Boardroom 2030 Activation Kit,* B Lab United Kingdom

44, 45, 46 Wallwork, C (2022) Author interview with Catherine Wallwork, Deloitte UK

47 TrendHunter (2012) Flat-Pack Job Postings, *TrendHunter,* 4 January www.trendhunter.com/trends/ikea-career-instructions (archived at https://perma.cc/MT76-YUXU)

48 BBC Newsbeat (2013) GCHQ launches online code breaking competition for jobs, *BBC News,* 12 September www.bbc.com/news/newsbeat-24061568 (archived at https://perma.cc/WX2B-TJQ5)

49, 50 Slater, B (no date) The 17 Most Creative Recruitment Campaigns, *Beamery* beamery.com/resources/blogs/the-17-most-creative-recruitment-campaigns (archived at https://perma.cc/CBE5-V7LD)

52 Hunnewell, S (2008) Kazuo Ishiguro, The Art of Fiction No. 196 www.theparisreview.org/interviews/5829/the-art-of-fiction-no-196-kazuo-ishiguro (archived at https://perma.cc/4D69-MEHU)

13

Beyond greenwashing: Approaches to creating real impact

NICK BASANNAVAR

London is a vibrant bric-a-brac of a city. 43 per cent of the population comes from minority ethnic communities. More than one-third of Londoners were born outside of the UK. 19 per cent of Londoners self-identify as being disabled. The total population is expected to grow to as much as 10.4 million by 2041.[1] Within this assemblage of voices, ideas, colours and enterprises, Transport for London (TfL) facilitates the economic activity of the city, with five million passenger journeys every day on the London Underground.[2]

Each year, TfL reports on the inclusive impact it creates in its responses to 'inequalities in our city, our transport network and our workforce'.[3] By placing itself self-reflexively within the highly complex urban context it inhabits, and creating the space to think hard about how to create more equal outcomes, TfL makes a contribution to improving the lives of London's millions of citizens. In 2021 it reported on – among other impact – a new campaign to support women into cycling; creating the 79th step-free underground station, introducing a £25 million cash scheme to support disabled car owners; reaching 95 per cent of accessible (step-free) bus stops; and rolling out mental health support for all of its workers.[4]

Impact like this matters. It shows the potential for public good that lies within every organization. In her 1999 book *Reason for Hope,* the celebrated primatologist Jane Goodall posed a question: 'we cannot live through a day without impacting the world around us – and we have a choice: what sort of impact do we want to make?'[5]

In Chapter 7 we set out our view of Inclusion 4.0 and the Inclusive Purpose Organization (IPO). One of the major features of the IPO is that performance metrics ought to be impact-led, rather than purely commercial (driven by revenue and profitability).

But what do we mean by *impact*? It can be a nebulous concept, devoid of concrete proof points. Impact reporting often constitutes a collection of abstract figures that together purport to tell a story about that organization's activity. Increasingly, this is connected to social and environmental impact, for example Coca-Cola's ambition to reduce its carbon footprint by 25 per cent by 2030.[6]

Cynics may argue that impact statistics are often rolled out by wily Corporate Social Responsibility (CSR) departments, in prominent positions on company homepages, to appease critical observers and mask less altruistic (or more purely commercial) corporate activity. This may be tagged as 'greenwashing' (the overstating or masking effect of climate advocacy, or the understating of a product's climate impact), 'pinkwashing' (the overstating or masking effect of LGBT or gender advocacy), or 'bluewashing' (the overstating or masking effect of responsible social practices).

This chapter considers these debates and introduces the concept of 'inclusive impact': what it looks like, how to measure it, and practical examples. It argues that no matter our sector, size, or purpose, inclusive impact should be at the core of what we do. This moves beyond window-dressing, 'colourwashing', and marketing-led approaches and truly places impact at the centre of organizational activities.

Ann Mei Chang, CEO of Candid, a New York-based data charity, has written that 'it's time for us to reinvent our approach to social good for the twenty-first century'.[8] This means focusing on radical social good, rather than 'just releasing another app or making more bucks'.[9] The multifaceted challenges that we face as a planet, laid out in Chapter 7, require a change of organizational perspective: the IPO, with inclusion at the centre, and systematic and imaginative approaches to impact.

Corporate conscience and *kyosei*

There are many different approaches to impact. The Oxford English Dictionary points to its active quality; something coming into contact with something else, creating an influence of some kind. Notably inherent in this definition is the quality of neutrality. Impact can be either positive or negative, but either way it is noticeable and significant (forcible and marked).

In the context of a terrifying climate catastrophe, many organizations are thinking about how they can move beyond being a net *drain* on the planet towards contributing a net positive *impact*. This can be seen in the case of the B Corporation movement which seeks to benefit people, communities and planet.

The concept of organizational conscience is certainly not new. The Greek Platonist philosopher Plutarch (c.46-119AD) noted the deeply social properties of human life and the importance of good moral behaviour. In his work, Parallel Lives, he called on the need for strong role models, using salutary examples such as Cicero, Caesar and Alexander the Great. Rufus (c.25-95AD), the Roman Stoic philosopher, beseeched his students to act ethically and to track and measure behaviour through journal entries – perhaps an early iteration of the dreaded key performance indicator (KPI).[10]

In 1997 Ryuzaburo Kaku, then-Chairman of Japanese global electronics firm Canon, wrote a piece for the Harvard Business Review. In it he pointed out that 'global corporations rely on educated workers, consumers with money to spend, a healthy natural environment, and peaceful coexistence between nations and ethnic groups'.[11] Channelling the idea of 'kyosei', or a 'spirit of cooperation' which was at the centre of Canon's purpose, Kaku wrote of the importance of cooperating outside of the company.[12] He stated that 'global activism' was necessary to advocate for positive reforms and to address economic, social and environmental imbalances.[13] Conscience and activism can point the way to impact, both within and beyond organizational contexts.

Towards inclusive impact

Kaku and Canon's theories, now decades-old, remind us that diversity and inclusion are not merely recent or fashionable concepts. We have simply failed to apply them for too long. Practical action and measurement have been sorely lacking. In many areas we have gone backwards since the 1990s. The years leading up to 2022 have seen tremendous division and upheaval. Recent data suggests that gender pay gaps in major UK firms may be widening.[14] There are still many locations where basic human rights for gay people are a distant hope.

Progress that has occurred (for example, on gender and LGBT equality) has been hard-won, and often despite mainstream government and organization priorities. In the UK, public bodies have habitually adopted Equality Impact Assessments (EQIAs), tagged to the 2010 Equality Act, to ensure that no individual or group is discriminated against because of their characteristics. While important, EQIAs have often been treated as a tick-box compliance exercise, representative of a deficit model of impact (Diversity 101) when what is needed is a forward-thinking, inclusive design approach.

Elsewhere, organizations have focused on the pursuit of commercial gain, with results including widening inequality gaps socially, economically, geographically, and technologically. Many have taken a zero-sum approach to impact, assuming (incorrectly, in the view of business theorist Alex Edmans) that an increase in social outputs must mean a reduction in profits. Edmans argues that this is a false dichotomy and that responsible capitalist organizations should instead focus on growing the pie to deliver both profit and purposeful impact.[15] Critics of this approach argue that 'green growth' is oxymoronic, given that growth can only come from the extraction of planetary resources; in their view shuffling metrics around within a capitalistic system is a waste of time given that said system has brought us to the brink of environmental collapse.[16]

A PESTLE analysis (see Chapter 7) reveals broken structures politically, economically, socially, technologically, legally and environmentally. If we adopt Inclusion 4.0 and the IPO – which states that organizations need to rethink themselves with inclusion at their heart – we can think about how to make genuine improvement (impact).

The PESTLE view of the world suggests that it is time to take an inclusive impact-led approach: truly purpose-driven, positive change, through the creation of mutually reinforcing equalizing effects. Inclusive impact involves closing global inequality gaps, widening access, tackling privilege, and deconstructing and reconstructing racist, sexist, homophobic, and inaccessible structures. It involves broadening our gaze and activities beyond the narrow walls of our own organization, departments, and shareholders. It involves accepting Jane Goodall's proposition: that what we do matters, and that we have an impact on the world around us every day. It involves accepting that if we truly want to create positive impact, inclusion has to be at the centre of our thinking.

Spaces and scope

Impact as an organizational concept has (notwithstanding a growing number of for-profit social enterprises) often been the preserve of the non-profit/third sector, for example in international developmental agencies. In these settings, programmes as defined by the International Initiative for Impact Evaluation are 'about improving outcomes: boosting incomes, increasing productivity, encouraging learning, improving health and protecting the environment'.[17] It is through impact measurement and evaluation that we can know how successful any given intervention is.

The United Nations Sustainable Development Goals (UNSDG) Impact group has pointed out that alongside development bodies, 'investors and enterprises are increasingly aligning their activities with the SDGs'.[18] Some of this is window-dressing. Some of it creates genuine change. However, even in private organizations that are thinking about impact, the scope has either been limited in breadth (restricted to key areas around sustainability, environment, and education), or in depth (with impact measurement tools still rather disconnected and anecdotal). We argue here that inclusive impact needs to have a broader and deeper scope than it does currently.

In our work at *Included*, we think about six impact areas that we define as SECMED. This is adapted from a classic PESTLE model. If PESTLE explains to us past and current challenges, SECMED is reframing those challenges to think proactively about the potential impact we can make. If PESTLE helps us to react to the past and the present, SECMED helps us to think about the future. It moves beyond structural pillars such as politics and law which are a key part of PESTLE, to instead think about the impact that such structures are *driving*: social, environmental, cultural, medical, economic, digital. Here we introduce each one, along with examples of what organizations are doing – either directly, in partnership, or through other bodies – to create positive impact:

Socially inclusive impact

This relates to improving the ways in which every person can socially participate in their communities. Interventions by organizations (for example, governmental or public sphere bodies) focus on positively changing the experiences of marginalized groups (who may be disadvantaged due to gender, ethnicity, disability, sexual orientation, religion or other characteristics) who have historically been excluded from important social features such as political franchise, legal frameworks, equal human rights, or access to key services such as health and utilities or the Internet.[20]

Ofcom is the UK's communications regulator. It is embedding inclusion in its strategic thinking to help greater numbers of the population access key communications services, including online access. They have done this by convening key thinkers from within and without the regulator to pool their collective expertise, and think hard about how to create more equitable outcomes for all UK citizens.

The Pensions Regulator (TPR) is exploring pension deficits across the UK population with a long-term goal of mitigating the impact of pensions inequality.[21] Women aged 50 have saved, on average, half the amount of men the same age, and minority ethnic groups have worse savings outcomes. TPR's CEO Charles Counsell and his leadership team have been clear on the need to intervene now to improve long-term prospects, 'potentially changing retirement outcomes for the better for millions'. This has included starting an industry-wide working group to explore the future of inclusion in the sector.[22]

There are more than 10 million people in the UK with a criminal conviction. The employment prospects of those individuals have historically been diminished. Timpson, a provider of retail services (including repair services for shoes, watches, and mobile phones, plus engraving, dry cleaning and photography services), has deliberately pursued a compassionate recruitment strategy that seeks out marginalized groups. 10 per cent of its workforce is now made up of people with criminal convictions, with a retention rate for those workers of 75 per cent. By giving ex-offenders a second chance, Timpson has empathetically worked to solve a long-standing issue, creating positive social impact and finding that 'recruiting ex-offenders has been great for our business'.[23]

Environmentally inclusive impact

As many prominent climate activists have pointed out, the global impact of climate change is profoundly unequal, with communities of colour, and poorer nations of the Global South, suffering disproportionately.[24] Within individual nations, too, there are large environmental inequalities, with those from (typically urban) lower socio-economic groups generally having far less access to green spaces. Data from the US has shown that minorities 'spend less time in the outdoors than white people do'.[25]

Organizations working to create inclusive impact in this sphere include the environmental consultancy SYSTEMIQ, spun out of McKinsey & Company in 2016, which adopts a systems-based approach to solving environmental challenges. In collaboration with partners including Borealis, SYSTEMIQ launched Project STOP in Indonesia to build more effective circular waste management systems.[26] By 2020, Project STOP's impact includes 133,500 people in waste management services (most of them for the first time), providing increased dignity and access that had been previously lacking; by 2022 this will be 450,000 people, with 45,400 tonnes of waste predicted to be kept out of the environment.[27]

Culturally inclusive impact

Many marginalized groups are currently shut out of cultural participation, whether that be the one billion disabled people on the planet who struggle to access arts spaces physically or otherwise, or those from lower socio-economic groups who cannot afford the high cost of cultural products and performances.[28] Cultural inclusion and cultural capital are important concepts in sociology and urban policy. Cultural participation matters because it adds dignity, wellbeing, expression and enjoyment to people's lives.

In the UK, the work of Music Masters has created broad and deep impact by widening access to classical music for underprivileged children. They have also created, launched and now facilitate a sector-wide approach to tackling racism and measuring inclusion.[29] I'M IN, which launched in 2021, is a landmark moment for inclusive impact in music. In its approach to measuring diversity inclusion and driving governance, it is designed to 'dismantle racism, encourage organizational accountability and drive systemic change within the sector'.[30]

Medically inclusive impact

There are gross inequalities in medical care on a global level. Look at the impact of COVID-19 on marginalized ethnic groups throughout the world, as the pandemic compounded suffering on those who were already economically, socially or medically vulnerable.[31] By 9 August 2021, only 12.6 million of the 4.46 billion COVID-19 vaccine doses had been administered in low-income countries.[32] Or take the fact that cardiovascular disease is the biggest killer of women worldwide, yet women remain vastly underrepresented in cardiovascular trials.[33]

Inclusive impact here looks like the work of Loughborough University and the Healthcare Safety Investigation Branch (HSIB) in using artificial intelligence to reduce health risks to pregnant Black women.[34] Research has shown that women from Black ethnic groups are four times more likely to die in pregnancy than white women.[35] The AI research intervention will utilize machine learning to understand what factors contribute to risk, and how those factors interact with each other; this will then enable more effective care approaches. Elsewhere, Macmillan Cancer Support in the UK has made ending cancer care inequalities one of the key aspects of its strategy. They state that 'if we focus on tackling inequality and understanding its root causes we can achieve outstanding cancer care services for all, not just for some'.[36] They approach inclusion not simply from an internal organizational perspective, but through a UK-wide patient impact lens. Wellcome has broadened its gaze even further, realizing that the key to managing the COVID-19 pandemic is by taking an inclusive, global view rather than a narrow nation-by-nation approach to vaccination.[37]

Economically inclusive impact

In 2018, research showed that almost 25 per cent of the global population were 'unbanked', meaning they did not have a bank account. In the UK, unbanked adults were estimated to number two million. As the innovative UK challenger bank Monzo pointed out, 'not having access to financial services today puts you at a significant disadvantage in society and often means you pay more, save less and can't access basic services needed to live. This is unacceptable'.[38] Fintech company Pockit have calculated an unbanked premium of up to £485 for vital utilities; being unbanked also adversely affects credit scores (Flavius, 2021).[39]

Monzo and other challenger banks like Starling, N26 and Tide have heavily disrupted traditional banking paradigms. Monzo has focused on tech-enabled economic inclusive impact. More than 80 per cent of the world's population owns a smartphone.[40] Monzo and others have seized upon this, heralding a direct, accessible route to banking distinct from red-tape-laden traditional banks. Monzo's approach has also had highly successful commercial results, with the bank valued at $4.5 billion by December 2021.[41] Elsewhere Triodos Bank, founded in 1980 in the Netherlands, only finances companies that focus on creating a positive impact via 'people, the environment, or culture'.[42] This has led to £8.2 billion worth of 'impact investment' loans made across Europe that benefit 'people and planet'[43]

Digitally inclusive impact

The rapid, historic shift to digital services and employer models, acceler-ated by the pandemic, has exposed an uncomfortable reality: a huge number of people remain digitally excluded. This means losing out on access to basic financial management, education, social interactivity, and more. Digital inclusion is about two things: 1) access to digital and 2) ability to use digital.[44] The Office for National Statistics (ONS) calculated in 2020 that 6.3 per cent of UK adults had still never used the Internet, down from 14 per cent in 2013.[45]

In 2018, as many as 11 million of the UK's population lacked the 'basic digital skills they need to participate fully in our digital economy'.[46] People need help in safely navigating quickly changing digital spaces at a time when online discourse is polarized, and 'fake news' and online harms are multiply-ing. COVID-19 revealed the fault lines of digital inequality with, for example, children from poorer groups unable to access education as they did not necessarily have Wi-Fi access or an Internet-enabled digital device.[47]

The positive impacts of digital inclusion include minimizing loneliness, reducing overall social exclusion, increasing digital skills, and helping those with disabilities to interact socially. The World Benchmarking Alliance (WBA) publishes a report spotlighting organizations which display commitment and tangible achievements on digital inclusion.[48] In 2020 the Korean mobile manufacturing giant Samsung was praised for its AI ethics principles, its Creative C-Lab programme which incubates solutions to social problems, and its open-source 'ecosystem' approach to innovation which yielded more than 130 projects by early 2021.[49]

In each of the SECMED examples above, the organizations in question look *beyond* their own organizational environment and aim to create inclu-sive impact for the populations of the countries they operate in, their customer bases, or marginalized groups that they had not typically engaged with. The impact is about more than just window-dressing or publishing a feelgood report once a year; it is coordinated, systemic and meaningful – like the Inclusion 4.0 approach set out in Chapter 7. In the chapters that follow this one, we dive into three of these impact areas through case studies on finance, the arts, and tech. How people participate in the world econom-ically, culturally, and digitally will determine a large part of our individual and collective experiences as we move into an uncertain future.

Purpose-led impact: why measure?

The business thinker Simon Sinek has pointed out that 'genius is in the idea. Impact, however, comes from action'.[50] It is measurement – an impact proof point – that distinguishes theory or rhetoric from genuine positive change. Intrinsic motivation to create impact is derived from the personal desires, passions and commitments of people and teams to create change, whether that's hiring more diverse talent, improving the experiences of minority colleagues, or improving accessibility to products and services. Intrinsic motivation is the platform for extrinsic motivational tools such as goal-focused measurement. In turn, this commitment to tell an outward-facing story drives motivation and makes organizations accountable; you can't hide behind rhetoric or passion if the results tell a conflicting story.

There is an enormous array of approaches to impact measurement. This is both encouraging (in that it reflects manifest improvements in the number of organizations thinking about impact) and bewildering (with a confusing multitude of different standards, definitions, measurement criteria, and reporting methodologies).[51]

Amidst all the noise, how can we pick a way through to effective measurement? Research to Action, an impact think tank, has defined this issue quite neatly. The statistical approach to impact measurement looks for counterfactuals: measurement of a result with and *without* the intervention in question. The OECD, on the other hand, simply looks for 'any long-term effect, whether intended, unintended, positive, negative, direct or indirect' as a means of measuring impact.[52] As Rick Davies puts it, the former looks for 'causes of an effect' (a more purely causal approach) whereas the latter looks for 'effects of a cause' (correlational)[53] The distinction between causation and correlation is important because it is causal metrics that help us understand the direct impact we make. Correlational evidence may be explained by impact from our own interventions, but it might also be down to other factors.

Theories of change

There are three major approaches to inclusive impact measurement. The first is around the building of theories of change, or logic models. A typical logic model might take the following form shown in Table 13.1; let's imagine this in the context of a mid-sized tech company thinking about its diversity and inclusion work, internally and externally:

There are many sophisticated approaches to theories of change, including cross-geographical, cross-functional groups working to set best practice and devise global standards such as the Impact Management Project, SoPact and the University of Pennsylvania's Center for Social Impact Strategy.[54, 55, 56]

Impact coalitions

The second major development is that of impact coalitions forming around the world. One of the most prominent is B Corporation, a community of more than 4,000 certified organizations in 77 countries that looks to better balance 'profit' and 'purpose'. It does this by mandating its member organizations to report their impact on their own workers, communities, customers and environment.[57] This coalitional approach seeks to accelerate a 'global culture shift' to build a more 'inclusive and sustainable economy'.

Impact goals

Thirdly, we have groups that amplify the goal-based approach to impact. The most widely referenced example here is the United Nations' 17 Sustainable

TABLE 13.1 An example of change steps

Theory of change steps	Features
Inputs	resources needed, e.g. diversity and inclusion strategies and gathering of data
Activities	key actions to drive impact, e.g. behavioural training, active debiased recruitment, programmes to embed inclusion in product design
Outputs	evaluation metrics, e.g. 100 inclusive leadership training sessions run, 10 new debiased recruitment programmes run, 5,000 project hours on debiased products
Outcomes	positive changes as a result of the work, e.g. improved behavioural metrics, a more diverse workforce, better retention figures, higher sales, improved commercials
Impact	long-term key changes, e.g. changed lives: happier people within the organization, improved products that better include customers and drive social good

Development Goals. This has inspired a raft of social, environmental and diversity indices including the Tortoise Responsibility 100 Index in the UK. Hard targets pertaining to climate change and environmental damage are also influential, including the Science Based Targets group (SBTi) which encourages its members to work towards net zero carbon emissions.[58] The thinking of these groups is that clear red-line targets are what will drive behavioural change, action, and ultimately positive impact.

Inclusive impact measurement: success factors

There is a lot to think about, and to do. The following steps aim to help organization leaders seeking to effectively activate and measure inclusive impact.

1. CLEARLY DEFINE YOUR INCLUSIVE IMPACT

- Think hard about why DEI matters to your organization, and what impact you want to make. Don't restrict your thinking to the four walls of your organization; throw open your thoughts to your interaction with the world.

- Think about *internal* impact metrics, including the diversity of your people and how included people feel in your organization. Look at the approach of organizations like Monzo, which has taken an extremely thorough approach to its internal diversity challenges, spanning DEI data capture (across a very broad set of characteristics), inclusive training, allyship, inclusive language, toolkits, blind recruitment and more.[59]

- Clearly define *external* change metrics, including your spaces of impact (whether social, environmental, cultural, medical, economic, or digital inclusion) the diversity of your stakeholders, customers, and beneficiaries, and what change you want to make in the world.

- Aim for coordinated, structured, embedded impact frameworks and logic models, rather than merely tokenistic soundbites or marketing-friendly numbers that look good in an annual impact report.

2. BROADEN YOUR DATA CAPTURE

- Move beyond unconnected, purely indicative raw numbers and towards a broader and deeper scope of impact.

- Diversity is only one part of the puzzle; real impact comes through *including* diverse sets of people. Shift your gaze on impact measurement from diversity to diversity *and* inclusion. As we saw in Chapter 8, it is possible to measure inclusion using tools such as *Included's* unique Inclusion Diagnostic.[60]

- Look at both quantitative (change over time on the diversity and inclusion of your workers and beneficiaries) and qualitative (through conducting focus groups, listening groups and interviews that help you to unlock the textured, previously unvoiced stories of your people and stakeholders) impact datasets.

- Measure the past, the present, and the future. Understand your 'to date' and 'as is' on diversity and inclusion through annual diversity statistics capture, and an annual inclusion diagnostic. Model the future diversity of your organization by conducting diversity projection modelling exercises, as global pharmaceutical company UCB has done.

3. MOVE TOWARDS CAUSAL METRICS

- Causal evidence bases for DEI are still patchy.

- However, to better understand the impact of our interventions, we need to move away from the purely correlational.

- If lacking truly causal impact measurement tools through counterfactual statistical models, step back and take a more human approach: ask people.

- Ask your stakeholders, clients, and people (through pulse surveys, interviews and other interactions) what *they* think the impact (if any) of your interventions has been. This will give you a baseline on causality.

- Of course, continue to track as much correlative evidence as you can: the 'effect of your cause', in Davies' words.

4. REPORT: DISRUPT YOUR RHETORICAL NORMS

- Change the way you tell stories and talk about success in your organization, taking an 'impact first' approach.

- As we saw at the beginning of this chapter, TfL produces an annual impact report on diversity and inclusion. Ofcom, the UK's communications regulator, produced a five-year impact report in 2021 looking at changes in diversity across the entire television and radio sectors in the UK.[61] This is a great way to tell stories, celebrate and hold ourselves accountable.

- Stop beginning team meetings with commercial results at the front and centre. In inclusive impact-led organizations, commercials represent an output, not the end goal.

- At *Included*, we report on impact first at every major team meeting, retreat, management team meeting and board meeting.

5. ITERATE

- Think about progress as cyclical, rather than linear.
- Don't stand still once you've reported your successes.
- Go back to the beginning and think again about what impact it is you want to achieve (definition and strategy). Repeat and iterate the process which has been set out here.
- Don't rely only on yourself to measure your progress; benchmark yourself against peers, canvas your beneficiaries and ask for expert support to help you be better.
- Act on your insights, but don't assume that what worked before will work again. What can we do better next time?

Conclusion

Inclusive impact needs deep thought and hard work. In this chapter we have explored why it matters and how we might get it right. We saw that 'conscience' has been an organizational concept for most of human history, although we may have forgotten how to display it somewhere along the way. We looked at spheres of impact (social, environmental, cultural, medical, economic, digital) and examples of inclusive impact from regulatory work, to medical research, to financial equity. We looked at some of the theoretical ways that organizations approach impact measurement, and at practical steps to get started. We are left with a reminder that Jane Goodall's question is a useful one to regularly ask ourselves: what sort of impact do we want to make?

Key takeaways

1 The roots of inclusive impact can be seen in Greek and Roman philosophical ideas about moral behaviour and role modelling. Today, the role of the organization continues to be critical in creating inclusive impact in social, environmental, cultural, medical, environmental, and digital spheres, demonstrated through some compelling recent examples.

2 Without measuring impact, efforts risk being redundant. We need to move beyond window-dressing. There is a huge array of different approaches to impact measurement to draw on.

3 By following some simple success factors, we can start to create a powerful, broad baseline for inclusive impact measurement and impetus for change: define, measure, think causally, report, iterate.

References

1, 3, 4 TfL (2021a) *Annual Diversity and Inclusion impact report 2019/20*, Transport for London content.tfl.gov.uk/tfl-diversity-and-inclusion-impact-report-2019-20.pdf (archived at https://perma.cc/2RC5-7XFK)

2 TfL (2021b) *What we do, Transport for London*, www.tfl.gov.uk/corporate/about-tfl/what-we-do (archived at https://perma.cc/6DKS-T3R3)

5 Goodall and Berman (1999)

6 Coca-Cola (2021) *Sustainable Business, The Coca-Cola Company* www.coca-colacompany.com/sustainable-business (archived at https://perma.cc/3AQ9-SEGN)

7 Wallwork, C (2022) Author interview with Catherine Wallwork, Deloitte UK

8, 9 Chang, A M (2019) *Lean Impact: How to Innovate for Radically Greater Social Good*, New Jersey: John Wiley & Sons.

10 Evans, J (2012) What can business leaders learn from ancient Greek philosophers? *The Guardian*, 4 May www.theguardian.com/sustainable-business/business-learn-from-ancient-philosophers (archived at https://perma.cc/GT3G-CD99)

11, 12, 13 Kaku, R (1997) The Path of Kyosei, *Harvard Business Review*, 1 July hbr.org/1997/07/the-path-of-kyosei (archived at https://perma.cc/AJN6-Y4NX)

14 Topping, A, Thomas, T and Duncan, P (2021) Gender pay gap at UK's biggest firms is growing, data suggests, *The Guardian*, 29 December www.theguardian.com/world/2021/dec/29/gender-pay-gap-at-uks-biggest-firms-is-growing-data-suggests (archived at https://perma.cc/QDX7-JX6W)

15 Edmans, A (2020) *Grow the Pie: How Great Companies Deliver Both Purpose and Profit,* Cambridge University Press

16 Hickel, J (2020) *Less is More: How Degrowth Will Save the World*, London: Random House

17 3ie (2021) *Impact evaluation | 3ie, International Initiative for Impact Evaluation* www.3ieimpact.org/What-we-offer/impact-evaluation (archived at https://perma.cc/M82T-AANV)

18 UNDP (2021) *SDG Impact | United Nations Development Programme (UNDP), SDG Impact | United Nations Development Programme (UNDP)* sdgimpact.undp.org (archived at https://perma.cc/W9QG-PSRP)

19 World Bank (2021) *Social Inclusion, World Bank* www.worldbank.org/en/topic/social-inclusion (archived at https://perma.cc/3CZV-XBUN)

21 Counsell, C (2021) *Equality, Diversity and Inclusion Strategy,* The Pensions Regulator www.thepensionsregulator.gov.uk/en/document-library/corporate-information/equality-diversity-and-inclusion-strategy (archived at https://perma.cc/8BCU-BWLS)

22 Counsell, C (2020) An industry to be proud of, *The Pensions Regulator Blog,* 27 July blog.thepensionsregulator.gov.uk/2020/07/27/an-industry-to-be-proud-of/ (archived at https://perma.cc/L5QM-4V4Q)

23 Timpson Group (2021) *The Timpson Foundation, Timpson* www.timpson-group.co.uk/timpson-foundation/ex-offenders/ (archived at https://perma.cc/66Z4-4TUZ)

24 Quintero, A (2020) The Importance of Inclusion in the Environmental Movement, *Journal of International Affairs SIPA* [Preprint] jia.sipa.columbia.edu/importance-inclusion-environmental-movement (archived at https://perma.cc/MNL4-ESNL)

25 Dolšak, N and Prakash, A (2016) Environmental Inclusion: A Moral Imperative and Political Necessity, *Stanford Social Innovation Review* [Preprint] ssir.org/articles/entry/environmental_inclusion_a_moral_imperative_and_political_necessity (archived at https://perma.cc/M4R3-XUKD)

26 SYSTEMIQ (2021) Project STOP - SYSTEMIQ, *SYSTEMIQ* www.systemiq.earth/portfolio/project-stop/ (archived at https://perma.cc/QY3N-D383)

27 Project STOP (2021) Project STOP 2020 impact, *Project STOP*, 29 March www.stopoceanplastics.com/en_gb/project-stop-shows-positive-2020-impact-in-circular-waste-management-in-indonesia/ (archived at https://perma.cc/KZ8B-RCX6)

28 Halder, S and Assaf, L C (2017) *Inclusion, Disability and Culture: An Ethnographic Perspective Traversing Abilities and Challenges, Springer*

29 Music Masters (2021) I'M IN: Main Page | Music Masters, *Music Masters* musicmasters.org.uk/im-in/ (archived at https://perma.cc/W3VF-S9NR)

30 Included (2021b) Music Masters: Driving systemic change within the music sector, *Included Impact Bulletin*, December www.included.com/wp-content/uploads/2021/12/Included_ImpactBulletin_2021_SinglePages-1-1.pdf (archived at https://perma.cc/7SAT-B8F7)

31 The Lancet Public Health (2021) COVID-19—break the cycle of inequality, *The Lancet Public Health*, 6 (2), p e82

32 The Lancet Infectious Diseases (2021) COVID-19 vaccine equity and booster doses, *The Lancet Infectious Diseases*, 21 (9), p 1193

33 Jin, X. et al (2020) Women's Participation in Cardiovascular Clinical Trials From 2010 to 2017, *Circulation*, 141 (7), pp. 540–548.

34 BBC News (2021) Artificial Intelligence plan to reduce harm to pregnant Black women, *BBC News*, 17 November www.bbc.com/news/uk-england-leicestershire-59306908 (archived at https://perma.cc/7PJ4-9PZG)

35 MBRRACE-UK (2021) *Saving Lives, Improving Mothers' Care*. NPEU, Oxford University www.npeu.ox.ac.uk/assets/downloads/mbrrace-uk/reports/maternal-report-2021/MBRRACE-UK_Maternal_Report_2021_-_Lay_Summary_v10.pdf (archived at https://perma.cc/NY86-PFG8)

36 Macmillan Cancer Support (2021) *Inequalities and cancer* www.macmillan.org.uk/about-us/what-we-do/how-we-work/inclusion/inequalities-and-cancer.html (archived at https://perma.cc/LQF6-F8RC)

37 Farrar, J and Ahuja, A (2021) *Spike: The Virus vs The People - the Inside Story*, London: Profile Books

38 Thomas, T (2018) Financial Inclusion: Helping everyone access the financial world, *Monzo*, 29 May monzo.com/blog/2018/05/29/financial-inclusion (archived at https://perma.cc/RY89-C6UE)

39 Flavius, S (2021) The unbanked: What it's like not to have a bank account, 14 June www.money.co.uk/guides/unbanked-what-its-like-not-to-have-a-bank-account (archived at https://perma.cc/R9CA-K29S)

40 Turner, A (2021) How Many People Have Smartphones Worldwide (Oct 2021) www.bankmycell.com/blog/how-many-phones-are-in-the-world (archived at https://perma.cc/3W2B-NJ3T)

41 Venkataramakrishnan, S and Morris, S (2021) Monzo valuation hits $4.5bn on back of drawing thousands of new customers, *Financial Times*, 8 December www.ft.com/content/9e9bbe27-2dac-447b-a015-b2cd3bc9c868 (archived at https://perma.cc/PLJ2-V4TH)

42, 43 Triodos Bank (2021) *Triodos Bank* www.triodos.co.uk/ (archived at https://perma.cc/4WRR-ARU8)

44 Citizens Online (2021) *Digital Inclusion • Citizens Online, Citizens Online* www.citizensonline.org.uk/digital-inclusion/ (archived at https://perma.cc/G44P-ZZU6)

45 Prescott, C (2021) *Internet users - Office for National Statistics* Office for National Statistics www.ons.gov.uk/businessindustryandtrade/itandinternetindustry/datasets/internetusers (archived at https://perma.cc/P829-68HQ)

46 Good Things Foundation (2018) *The economic impact of digital inclusion in the UK*, Good Things Foundation www.goodthingsfoundation.org/insights/economic-impact-digital-inclusion/ (archived at https://perma.cc/WF89-UVSF)

47 UNICEF (2021) *Closing the Childhood Digital Divide: an end to digital exclusion for children and young people in the UK*, UNICEF UK www.unicef.org.uk/policy/closing-the-digital-divide-uk/ (archived at https://perma.cc/QA4X-PLGT)

48 World Benchmarking Alliance (2020) *Digital Inclusion Benchmark, World Benchmarking Alliance* www.worldbenchmarkingalliance.org/publication/digital-inclusion/ (archived at https://perma.cc/8C6D-NUB8)

49 Samsung (2021) Samsung's Noteworthy Quest to Advance Digital Responsibility, *Samsung*, 5 January news.samsung.com/global/samsungs-noteworthy-quest-to-advance-digital-responsibility (archived at https://perma.cc/V99U-6BHR)

50 Sinek, S (2014) *Genius is in the idea, Twitter* twitter.com/simonsinek/status/486857437266190337 (archived at https://perma.cc/8H7K-A4Q9)

51 Hall, F (2021) A global ESG reporting standard: where are we, and where are we heading? | Global Counsel, *Global Counsel*, 8 July www.global-counsel.com/insights/report/global-esg-reporting-standard-where-are-we-and-where-are-we-heading (archived at https://perma.cc/KKU8-WBV8)

52, 53 Hearn, S (2016) What do we mean by 'impact'? *Research to Action*, 18 February www.researchtoaction.org/2016/02/what-do-we-mean-by-impact/ (archived at https://perma.cc/9FVP-EGLP)

54 IMP (2021) *Impact Management Project, Impact Management Project* impactmanagementproject.com/ (archived at https://perma.cc/54BF-RQW9)

55 CSIS (2021) The Center for Social Impact Strategy, *The Center for Social Impact Strategy* csis.upenn.edu/about/ (archived at https://perma.cc/JB93-3N7J)

56 SoPact (2021) *About SoPact, SoPact* www.sopact.com/company/about-us (archived at https://perma.cc/S7TP-FDHV)

57 B Corp (2021) *Certification, Certified B Corporation* bcorporation.uk/certification (archived at https://perma.cc/5X48-S626)

58 SBTi (2021) SBTi launches world-first net-zero corporate standard, *Science Based Targets*, 28 October sciencebasedtargets.org/news/sbti-launches-world-first-net-zero-corporate-standard (archived at https://perma.cc/6NST-4JF9)

59 Atcheson, S (2020) Our 2020 diversity and inclusion report, *Monzo*, 15 April monzo.com/blog/our-2020-diversity-and-inclusion-report (archived at https://perma.cc/VS6G-FXZ2)

60 Included (2021a) Included Services: Data, *Included* www.included.com/service/data/ (archived at https://perma.cc/7Z35-5T39)

61 Ofcom (2021) Diversity and equal opportunities in TV and radio, *Ofcom*, 4 October www.ofcom.org.uk/tv-radio-and-on-demand/information-for-industry/guidance/diversity/diversity-equal-opportunities-tv-and-radio (archived at https://perma.cc/KGF4-SAD3)

14

The key to inclusion in tech

SINEAD DALY AND ELANI BUCHAN

The 'Ketchup Question' is a thought experiment that exists among different tech communities. The premise is simple – where do you keep your ketchup? In some parts of the US people keep their ketchup in the cupboard, while others in the refrigerator.

Say you are out of ketchup, and need to reach for an alternative. If you keep your ketchup in the fridge, you might reach for mayo, whereas if you kept it in the cupboard, you might reach for vinegar or salt.

This gets to the essence of why we need diversity in startups. Startups are solving new and complex problems. We need a diversity of experiences and perspectives to develop these solutions. If we only engage the people who keep their ketchup in the fridge, we're going to get mayo every time.

Following the murder of George Floyd and the Black Lives Matter movement in 2020, awareness of DEI has increased significantly. However, DEI terms serve different purposes, and are often conflated. Catalina Coleman, Director of HR and Inclusion, wrote a concise summary of the differences;

> Diversity is the presence of differences within a given setting. Equity is the
> process of ensuring that processes and programs are impartial, fair and provide
> equal possible outcomes for every individual. Inclusion is the practice of
> ensuring that people feel a sense of belonging in the workplace.[1]

Startups often lump these terms together, usually measuring progress against 'diversity' without accounting for these other aspects. This hinders progress, and increases box ticking.

This chapter will explore the negative societal impacts of tech, the dangers of groupthink and accumulation of diversity debt. It will then dig deep into representation, the facets of an inclusive culture, and the role holistic strategies, leadership mindset and employee voice have to play in building psychologically safe environments. Finally, this chapter will look at ways tools and resources can be leveraged to accelerate efforts - and ultimately help leaders to stay accountable.

If we don't build diverse companies, their products will exclude pockets of society.

The tech ecosystem has an opportunity to build products that make a long-lasting impact not only on the financial returns of its stakeholders, but on the very fabric of society. Venture capitalists, and the companies they fund, have a huge opportunity to determine how inclusion manifests – if they build diverse, non-homogeneous teams from the start, they will go on to crack new markets, and build truly new and innovative solutions.

A company's lack of diversity can be felt by users, once its product hits the market.

When Kodak based decades of photography developments on the 'Shirley Card' – a photo of a white woman – they built bias against Black people and people with darker skin tones into their products.[2] In the 60's, Kodak eventually looked into capturing darker tones more accurately, but only to better photograph mahogany furniture.[3]

In 2015, a Black software developer used Google's Photo tool, and found that photos of him and another Black friend were labelled as 'gorillas' by the product.[4] Two years later the company was still unable to find a fix, and it is unclear if they succeeded.

Computer Science Professor, Vicente Ordóñez, noticed that the image recognition software he was building frequently associated an image of a woman with a kitchen.[5] This built-in gender bias can also be found in two of the world's most prominent research image collections; one supported by Microsoft and the other Meta – associating activities like shopping and cooking with women and sports with men.[6]

Researchers from Boston University and Microsoft identified that software trained to collect text from Google News also displayed gender biases.[7] When asked to complete the statement 'Man is to programmer as woman is to X' the software replied 'homemaker'.

In 2021, the impact of poor visual and gender recognition goes beyond exclusion, and has potentially deadly consequences.

In the US, discriminatory law enforcement practices led to a disproportionate amount of Black Americans being arrested and incarcerated for minor crimes.[8] As a result, they are overrepresented in mugshot databases, which use facial recognition in predictions. This creates a vicious cycle, where Black Americans are subject to biased police practices, rooted in racism.[9]

By 2040, there will be an estimated 33 million autonomous driving cars on the road.[10] The technology is unable to identify Black people, or wheelchair users with the same accuracy as white faces, or those who are able-bodied.[11] Researchers at Georgia Tech found that algorithm accuracy decreased by five per cent when identifying people with darker skin tones.[12]

2021 saw a flurry of interest in decentralized technology, aimed at democratizing access. On its launch, the average cryptocurrency owner was a 38-year-old male, earning $111,000.[13] Seventy-four per cent of cryptocurrency holders identified as male and 71 per cent white.

The startup world of Silicon Valley can feel lightyears away, yet everyone feels the impact of these companies. You don't have to be an employee or product user. Embedding DEI initiatives at the beginning will not only ensure better solutions, but also serve to safeguard against building products that directly or indirectly perpetuate biases in society.

Groupthink is the biggest barrier to long-term growth

Tech companies (and the people that fund them) are most often born of like-minded individuals coming together to solve problems they understand deeply. While this means teams can build trust and scale quickly, it also means that a lack of broader perspectives can hinder growth in the long-term. This is called 'diversity debt', similar to technical debt – the cost of decisions made earlier on that prioritize quick wins.

We all think differently. We all have different experiences to bring to the table. Right now, the tech sector is most often built to accommodate a particular perspective and experience; the white straight man. The problem? Together, these leaders can struggle with the notion of inclusion, and fall into the trap of hiring people that look and sound exactly like them. They blindly look for 'culture fit', dismissing anyone who doesn't fit this mould.

Social psychologist Irving Janis, coined the phrase Groupthink,[14] in 1972. It's a term that the likes of Google, Facebook and Uber are all too familiar with, and this 'psychological drive for consensus at any cost' has proven a huge risk to effective decision making – with lone voices and challengers less likely to speak up and share their perspective.

Representation: whose voice is, or isn't, in the room?

To avoid this phenomenon, we must build more representative, non-homogenous teams. Tech communities are renowned for processing complex data, yet when it comes to measuring DEI, the use of data is surface level, and at best, tokenistic. One specific DEI consideration is the difference between diversity and representation. Audrey Blanche, notable DEI author, wrote in a 2017 piece in Wired,

> 'The issue of diversity and inclusion in tech is what designers call a wicked problem. It's a cluster of systemic and individual biases, compounded by years of denial, complicated by changing socioeconomic forces. Still, that's no excuse – especially since Silicon Valley prides itself on solving impossible problems, and given its exceptional influence in the business community and around the world.'

The standard for measuring diversity within an organization looks at the company as whole, which instead captures diversity instead of representation. To move the needle you have to look at the diverse makeup of each individual team (marketing, engineering, sales etc.). Aggregates provide an overall picture, but are unable to show nuance – a company may have a diverse overall composition to shout about, without needing to share that women mostly occupy administrative roles, that women are barely present in engineering, or that there are no Black leaders or decision makers at the top of the organization.

Diverse teams thrive, only in inclusive environments

For non-homogeneous teams to thrive, they must be able to navigate their surroundings with as few barriers as possible. This can be one of the biggest challenges in fast-paced, unregulated environments, where there is often a false (and subjective) impression of meritocracy. Regardless of whether it's a VC firm, startup or scaleup, individuals are operating in unpredictable environments; where there are no set processes, inexperienced managers and never-ending opportunities for personal bias to creep in.

In the absence of guardrails and consistency, businesses risk their people being mistreated based on their identity. This is damaging to business growth (as turnover starts to affect knowledge retention), and to the individuals reaping the repercussions and trauma of the ways they've had to operate – a theme reflected in Minda Harts' book, *Right Within: How to Heal from Racial Trauma in the Workplace.*[15]

Tech leaders are focused on building competitive cultures that boost retention and their ability to win the war on talent. There is often a disparity between ways companies talk about culture, and the experience of their people. In recent years countless articles and books have been released by former tech workers for instance, *Disrupted: My Misadventure in the Start-Up Bubble* (Lyons, 2016)[16] and *Brotopia: Breaking Up the Boys' Club of Silicon Valley.*[17]

Tech startup Fair HQ measures inclusion through five different pillars; fairness, openness, psychological safety, belonging and voice. Of these, fairness and openness are the building blocks. When centering decision making around these two areas, diversity and inclusion will become second-nature, and positively impact outcomes when it comes to hiring and firing patterns, career progression, equal pay and wellbeing.

Meaningful inclusion is further unlocked through the three remaining facets of Fair HQ's inclusion measure; psychological safety, belonging and voice. Psychological safety leads to a sense of trust and therefore belonging, which in turn leads people to feel they can speak up. If these three are true, it increases a company's ability for people to take risks, and be comfortable with making mistakes – which in environments when you need to move quickly, become of paramount importance.

Think long-term, think impact

Fast-growth businesses come with different constraints and challenges at different stages, but for the most part, time (need to move quickly) and money (investment in deepening activities) are often the biggest blockers. That's why a holistic and embedded approach is needed, from day one. Equitable and inclusive practices must be a priority, and woven into company values, rituals, meetings and the way companies operate day to day, or else these constraints become hard stops in the road to DEI.

Often, it is tempting to tackle the 'low hanging fruit' but these short-term fixes won't help. They are simply band-aids. Companies that set up employee resource groups with no budget, launch compliance training with no manager buy-in, hire 'diverse talent' with no support mechanisms, or release external statements with no internal buy-in erode trust and will fail to build belonging.

Leadership needs to engage, proactively

Tech companies pride themselves on the vision and values they live by. Founding teams should clarify how inclusion and collaboration can be placed at the heart of their values and frameworks. These can then be woven into ways of working; growth frameworks, interview questions, moments for recognition, reward, events, reporting and more.

Alongside alignment on approach, it's important that leaders (and by leaders, this is anyone who manages people) take on active and visible responsibility for DEI. That means, taking on individual objectives and goals, taking on training and then speaking up and acting as a visible ally and role modelling that training. It means weaving inclusive practices into communication and management styles, and ensuring teams have role models that look like them represented in higher up positions and reporting on both personal, and team success.

Leaders see outsized impact when they adapt not only their management style, but approach to communication. In 2019, fintech startup Revolut faced scrutiny over leaked Slack messages from its founder,[18] and in 2021, Better.com's CEO faced backlash by announcing hundreds of layoffs over zoom.[19] In contrast, Uber's CEO drew praise, after displaying emotional intelligence when communicating plummeting stocks to staff,[20] and, Airbnb's founders were praised for their human approach to announcing layoffs in the middle of the 2020 pandemic.[21]

Ultimately, it's all about taking on a role of empathetic leadership. Engaging in forums, taking feedback on and being cognizant of their experience gap. It's time to move away from the beer and pizza, and start being comfortable with being *uncomfortable* everyday.

Employees need to feel seen

Companies can acknowledge individuality, by prioritizing choice. Instead of unpicking 'one-size-fits-all' strategies, baking flexibility in before programmes go live. This can start small, and specific. Take Paddle, a SaaS startup, who in 2021, acknowledged the ever changing need for new ways to recharge, and launched their Navigate benefit,[22] enabling their team to work outside their country of employment, complete with Airbnb credits. Meanwhile HR scaleup Beamery, noticed blanket wellness activations were no longer fit for purpose, so launched a monthly budget,[23] enabling their team to unlock access to wellbeing and growth in ways that suited them.

These little interactions send big signals, however they must translate into more significant policies. In 2020, when the world was suddenly thrown into new ways of working, it gave the power back to a wider distribution of employees, who might typically have been left behind,[24] enabling them to take control of running their day, their way. More companies are waking up to the competitive advantage flexible policies can provide, and the dominance of brands like Flexa, who in 2021 announced for the first time a list of the most flexible companies,[25] shows this approach is here to stay.

Employees need to feel heard

In 2020 and 2021, Basecamp[26] and Coinbase[27] felt the repercussions of attempts to curtail societal and political discussions in the workplace, a move heavily scrutinized not just within their businesses, but by global press. It exemplified more than ever, the need for employees to be given an active voice.

On a simplistic level, this means defining a surveying methodology that suits the working patterns of a business, this could be a weekly pulse, a quarterly check in, or an intensive bi-annual or annual questionnaire. It could mean taking a deeper dive with a platform like InChorus, a startup pioneering research into the micro-behaviours shaping workplace cultures. Irrespective of approach, the way an organization, or community communicates its interpretation of its data, and plan of action is key. When it comes to approaching those communications, leaders should share using language levels their team understands, taking into account the implications of cultural, ability and gender bias.

Hard data doesn't always lead to effective action, yet coupled with anecdotal feedback via Employee Resource Groups, they can do. Regardless of a company's growth stage, these can be challenging to get off the ground. Culture Amp believes that employee interest, group mission and leadership and organizational support are the ingredients for success.[28] Another approach to kick off is to create a more holistic forum. At HR scaleup Beamery, this group is called the Inclusion Collective, creating space for constructive conversations that build a global sense of belonging.

Leverage tools and technology

There are several playbooks and tools that support tech companies to build inclusively. In 2021, the Tech Talent Charter (TTC) launched its annual Hackathon, with a winning entry focused on Reward and Retention strategies.[29] In the same year, Tech Nation released its Diversity & Inclusion Toolkit,[30] following the release of its Diversity in Tech Report in 2018. There are several accreditations like BCorp,[31] the newly released 'All In' Promise,[32] or commitments like the 'FinTech for All' Charter.[33] Tools like Fair HQ, InChorus or recently launched Tigim, who are looking to revolutionize the value we place on language and accessible communications, can also be great starting points.

In the world of Venture Capital, Diversity VC's pioneering Toolkit for Venture Capitalists[34] shook up the industry and made way for programmes like OneTech and Included VC to disrupt, through education. Alongside these, organizations supporting underrepresented founders, like YSYS, Foundervine, or Tech Nation's most recent scaling programme Libra, are well placed to help high-potential future leaders.

There is however, another side to consider when leveraging resources. These tools should serve as guidance, and always be reviewed with a human context in mind. For instance, language is constantly evolving, and tools that originally assessed gender bias in communications, and subsequent algorithms, were built in the early 1960s/70s, with little changes adapting to the present day, yet are still used in tooling today.[35]

In addition to these playbooks and tools specific to solving for DEI, it's also important to explore ways to bake inclusion into pre-existing tools. In 2020, HR scaleup Beamery updated their pronouns across their HRIS system, Slack, Zoom and Email Signatures,[36] with guidance baked into onboarding. Other tools, such as Temporall, which is changing the way organizations measure communication, can also support leaders in understanding where exclusion exists.

Sharing openly leads to accountability

When focusing on the long-term, it is useful to understand how you are going to measure success, through regular reporting cadences. Indicators of how equitable a company truly is will come out in lagging metrics; how people from underrepresented groups in a business are being promoted, or leaving in the first year? What's equal pay, or gender pay gap – and how is this closing year-on-year?

Metrics are just one approach to drive accountability. It is equally important to openly talk, even without hard numbers, about where a company is at, and what action it is taking to manage its way to success.

Each year, Monzo, a FinTech challenger bank, publicly publishes a yearly report on the progress they've made when it comes to DEI. Additionally, recently they've talked about the developments in the accessibility of their product ensuring those with needs, like the ability to use sign language when signing up to use the product are able to.[37] Monzo's report, and broader commitments are a great demonstration of looking beyond the glossy headlines of the new hires metrics.

Legaltech platform Valla, enables individuals to self-represent in civil court. With 80 per cent of individuals unable to afford legal services, the founders, Danae Shell and Dr. Kate Ho, knew they needed to build a product that served a large cross-section of the population. They deeply considered DEI at different strategic points in their business. The makeup of their investor pool is 75 per cent women, 25 per cent people of colour, 12 per cent disabled and 12 per cent LGBTQIA+. Even as a tiny startup, they have taken big adjustments, including sharing their code of conduct in job ads, proactively offering adjustments for interviewees and working with content strategists to boost accessibility across all content. Putting inclusion at the forefront.

These are two great examples of companies stepping into the limelight to share where they are at. For many tech companies, DEI doesn't make it into internal, let alone external narratives. Taking everyone on a journey, each day is important. For tech companies and VCs, the 'sprint' nature of working patterns and All Hands meetings, provide great forums to share, plan and reflect. If companies aren't talking about diversity, equality or inclusion in the spaces – they should be. To make these topics a ritual, it's as simple, in the first instance, as adding an agenda prompt.

Making a lasting impact

If venture capitalists, founders and employees work together to build more diverse, equitable and inclusive organizations, technology will be able to have a long-lasting impact on the very fabric of society. It is both economically and socially advantageous for tech leaders to consciously think and act differently about the way they operate.

As seen throughout recent history, the bias that has previously been built into the products and services that we use every day has been extensive – because we are funding and building companies that fall into the pitfalls of groupthink. This is having damaging effects on employees, and the customers who are engaging with these products and services.

It's time to wake up to the benefits of non-homogeneous teams that truly represent the world around us. For these teams to thrive, we need new ways of thinking and managing the way tech businesses scale. Rather than rudderless, organic growth, there is a need for very deliberate culture building, underpinned by equitable processes and an inclusion-first mindset. 2020 proved to be a disruptive year for all businesses, and it challenged the world of tech to think more consciously about bias and accessibility, for the first time.

As business leaders, it's important that the urgency and importance of building a competitive culture is linked heavily to inclusivity, equity and diverse teams. For teams to thrive a holistic, authentic and long-term commitment must be woven into the fabric of the way things are done.

Key takeaways

1 Representation matters. You can't be who you can't see, and you can't build for perspectives you don't understand. Don't fall into the pitfalls of Kodak, Google or Web3. Understand who's building your product, and where you have glaring experience gaps – where will you keep your ketchup?

2 Bake equity into your foundations. Prioritize choice and flexibility, show people they are seen, and heard. Create processes, policies and programmes that are futureproofed and ready to scale as you grow – without the risk of a mess that you'll have to clean up later.

3 Be loud, and be proud. Talk to every mistake, misstep or failure. Be clear on how you will be accountable, and then communicate your progress as an individual, as a team and as a company.

Further reading

Kahzan, O (2021) What Slack Does for Women, *The Atlantic*, 8 October amp-theatlantic-com.cdn.ampproject.org/c/s/amp.theatlantic.com/amp/artic le/620325/ (archived at https://perma.cc/4V5H-NTTX)

Tech Nation (2018) Diversity and inclusion in UK tech companies. technation.io/
   insights/diversity-and-inclusion-in-uk-tech-companies/ (archived at https://
   perma.cc/Z35U-VQ4K)

References

1   Coleman, C (2021) What Does Diversity, Equity and Inclusion (DEI) Mean in
    the Workplace? *BuiltIn*, 13 December builtin.com/diversity-inclusion/what-
    does-dei-mean-in-the-workplace (archived at https://perma.cc/RX6W-KNTU)
2   Roth, L (2009) Looking at Shirley the Ultimate Norm: Colour Balance, Image
    Technologies, and Cognitive Equity, *Canadian Journal of Communication,* 34,
    pp. 111–136
3   Huang, S (2021) Time for a new lens: The hidden racism behind photography,
    Calgary Journal, 28 February calgaryjournal.ca/2021/02/28/time-for-a-new-
    lens-the-hidden-racism-behind-photography/ (archived at https://perma.cc/
    U2DM-HR2T)
4   Simonite, T (2018) When It Comes to Gorillas, Google Photos Remains Blind,
    Wired, 11 January www.wired.com/story/when-it-comes-to-gorillas-google-
    photos-remains-blind/ (archived at https://perma.cc/UK9Q-8ZFY)
5   Simonite, T (2017) Machines Taught by Photos Learn a Sexist View of Women,
    Wired, 21 August www.wired.com/story/machines-taught-by-photos-learn-a-
    sexist-view-of-women/ (archived at https://perma.cc/9RVH-EZ5W)
6   Zhao, J et al (2017) Men Also Like Shopping: Reducing Gender Bias
    Amplification using Corpus-level Constraints, *Proceedings of the 2017
    Conference on Empirical Methods in Natural Language Processing,*
    doi:10.18653/v1/D17-1323
7   Bolukbasi, T et al (2016) Man is to Computer Programmer as Woman is to
    Homemaker? Debiasing Word Embeddings, *CoRR,* abs/1607.06520
8   Najibi, A (2020) Racial Discrimination in Face Recognition Technology,
    Harvard University: The Graduate School of Arts and Sciences, 24 October
    sitn.hms.harvard.edu/flash/2020/racial-discrimination-in-face-recognition-
    technology/ (archived at https://perma.cc/F5LJ-JB98)
9   Crockford, K (2020) How is Face Recognition Surveillance Technology Racist?
    ACLU, 16 June www.aclu.org/news/privacy-technology/how-is-face-
    recognition-surveillance-technology-racist/ (archived at https://perma.cc/
    MJ39-HUKX)
10 Kopestinsky, A (2021) 25 Astonishing Self-Driving Car Statistics for 2021,
    Policy Advice, 29 April policyadvice.net/insurance/insights/self-driving-car-
    statistics/ (archived at https://perma.cc/6562-KAHT)

11   Lawcom (2021) Automated Vehicles www.lawcom.gov.uk/project/automated-vehicles/#related (archived at https://perma.cc/WY8R-RL6F)

12   Wilson, B, Hoffman, J and Morgenstern, J (2019) Predictive Inequity in Object Detection, *ArXiv*, abs/1902.11097

13   Shah, K (2021) Building an Inclusive World of Crypto, *FWB*, 14 November www.fwb.help/wip/building-an-inclusive-world-of-crypto (archived at https://perma.cc/ZJ4S-MCNH)

14   Janis, I L (1972) *Victims of groupthink; a psychological study of foreign-policy decisions and fiascoes*, Boston: Houglin, Miflin

15   Harts, M (2021) *Right Within: How to Heal from Racial Trauma in the Workplace,* New York: Seal Press

16   Lyons, D (2016) *Disrupted: My Misadventure in the Start-Up Bubble.* Atlantic Books, London

17   Chang, E (2018*) Brotopia: Breaking Up the Boys' Club of Silicon Valley.* Portfolio, New York

18   Mellino, E (2019) Revolut insiders reveal the human cost of a fintech unicorn's wild rise, Wired, 28 February www.wired.co.uk/article/revolut-trade-unions-labour-fintech-politics-storonsky (archived at https://perma.cc/7RZ8-2RXP)

19   Gupta, G (2022) Adapting Corporate Culture – Before It's Too Late: Lessons From Better.com Forbes, 4 January www.forbes.com/sites/johnkotter/2022/01/04/adapting-corporate-culture--before-its-too-late-lessons-from-bettercom/ (archived at https://perma.cc/29QP-EFCG)

20   Bariso, J (2019) Uber's CEO Sent an Extraordinary Email to Employees After the Company's Stock Plunged, Inc.com www.inc.com/justin-bariso/ubers-ceo-sent-an-extraordinary-email-to-employees-after-companys-stock-crashed.html (archived at https://perma.cc/A582-AWZH)

21   Parikh, A (2021) Airbnb's Layoff Process Shows You The Right Way To Do It, Grey Journal, 9 January 2021 greyjournal.net/hustle/inspire/airbnbs-layoff-process-shows-you-the-right-way-to-do-it/ (archived at https://perma.cc/A3KS-5NK8)

22   Bindley, K (2021) Working Vacations Have Never Felt This Good, *Wall Street Journal*, 10 December www.wsj.com/articles/working-vacations-have-never-felt-this-good-11639151975 (archived at https://perma.cc/99X3-U527)

23   Beamery (2021) How we're helping our people BE AMazing, thanks to Ben! 28 July careers.beamery.com/blog/our-culture/how-we-re-helping-our-people-be-amazing-thanks-to-ben/ (archived at https://perma.cc/XX3T-NW7X)

24   Hunt, S (2021) How Hybrid Remote Work Improves Diversity And Inclusion, *Forbes*, 12 May www.forbes.com/sites/sap/2021/05/12/how-hybrid-remote-work-improves-diversity-and-inclusion/?sh=52b146ad321f (archived at https://perma.cc/TN6K-9LCP)

25 Flexa (2021) Most flexible companies to work for 2021 flexa.careers/top-50 (archived at https://perma.cc/K82G-6ZYN)

26 Newton, C (2021) Breaking Camp, The Verge, 27 April www.theverge.com/2021/4/27/22406673/basecamp-political-speech-policy-controversy (archived at https://perma.cc/6CE2-UTB7)

27 Newton, C (2020) Why Coinbase will struggle to ban politics from the workplace, The Verge, 30 September www.theverge.com/interface/2020/9/30/21493906/brian-armstrong-coinbase-blog-post-politics-workplace-activism (archived at https://perma.cc/6AFU-2H7M)

28 Culture Amp (2021) How to start an employee resource group at your company www.cultureamp.com/blog/start-employee-resource-group (archived at https://perma.cc/C6TL-REHC)

29 Tech Talent Charter (2021) Open Playbook www.techtalentcharter.co.uk/open-playbook (archived at https://perma.cc/P8DG-RAHD)

30 Tech Nation (2021) Diversity and Inclusion Toolkit technation.io/diversity-and-inclusion/ (archived at https://perma.cc/U2WW-3Z4R)

31 B Corporation (2021) B Corp Certification bcorporation.uk/b-corp-certification/ (archived at https://perma.cc/GQS4-ZXC3)

32 All In (2021) All In Purpose/Mission www.allin.works/about#purposemission (archived at https://perma.cc/3MNL-N8UF)

33 InChorus (2021) Fintech for All inchorus.org/fintech (archived at https://perma.cc/XEJ2-M4YK)

34 Diversity V C (2018) Diversity & Inclusion in Tech www.inclusionintech.com/wp-content/uploads/2018/12/Diversity_Inclusion_in_Tech_Guide_2018.pdf (archived at https://perma.cc/KQN8-7CR5)

35 Harrigan, J A, Lucic, K S Attitudes about gender bias in language: A reevaluation. Sex Roles 19, 129–140 (1988) doi.org/10.1007/BF00290150 (archived at https://perma.cc/AD9T-KEB7)

36 Beamery (2021) Beamery: Pride Month, and Always, 30 June careers.beamery.com/blog/diversity-equity-inclusion/beamery-pride-month-and-always/ (archived at https://perma.cc/39UU-T6YY)

37 Monzo (2021) Monzo Accessibility monzo.com/i/accessibility (archived at https://perma.cc/2EUZ-83GE)

15

The key to inclusion in the TV and film sector

ANJANI PATEL

On 5 October, 2017 in an article published by The New York Times, Hollywood moghul and producer Harvey Weinstein was accused by several women, including the actresses Rose McGowan and Ashley Judd, of sexual harassment and misconduct spanning three decades.[1] Three days later, Weinstein was sacked by the board of the Weinstein Company.[2] A total of 87 women came forward with allegations of sexual misconduct and in 2020 Weinstein, 69, was sentenced to 23 years in prison.

The Harvey Weinstein case sent shockwaves through the entertainment industries across the globe. As allegations against more and more men in entertainment began to surface, the impact was felt far and wide. In Hollywood and in the UK, the case led to industry action to change working environments in production. The Weinstein fallout also intensified the wider debate on equality in the film and TV industries on the lack of recognition or equal pay for female directors and on the need to make film and TV sets more diverse and inclusive.

In 2020 the murder of George Floyd and campaigns of the Black Lives Matter movement brought into sharp focus issues of racial bias in society and reignited the calls for change in the content production sector. Hundreds of programme makers, freelancers, actors, presenters, unions, production company bosses and campaigners signed open letters in the UK and in response, many industry organizations made public commitments to action on anti-racism.

Now the hashtags #MeToo, #Timesup, #OscarsSoWhite, #BaftasSoWhite, often lead press reports on diversity and inclusion in Film and TV, but what isn't visible to the wider public is that behind the headlines there is an acknowledgement of the problems and a different and more urgent engagement with inclusion. Across the sector, there is work taking place to try to correct the imbalances, to improve diversity both on and off screen and to create cultures on set where everyone feels they belong and can speak out.

This chapter focuses on some of the cross sectoral work that has made an impact. It also analyses at the approaches to inclusion within independent production businesses who make a large proportion of the UK's film and TV content. These production businesses, often SME's, are members of Pact, the Producers association for Cinema and Television in the UK. In line with Pact's remit to support production businesses, Anjani works with these production companies to create practical strategies that deliver real inclusion. Before we explore more about this work, it is important to understand the context and structure of the sector and its specific challenges.

The Business Case – reaching a wide range of audiences across the globe is key

The UK has created some of the most influential and loved cinema and television in the world. Its reputation in filmmaking, TV production, animation, and special effects is recognized globally. The film and television sector is also a major contributor to the UK creative industries economy. A report commissioned by the British Film Institute shows that UK tax reliefs power unprecedented boom in UK screen industries. The report finds that record levels of production in the UK have resulted in £13.48 billion to UK economy and created 219,000 jobs.

Successes include the imaginative fantasies of *Harry Potter and Doctor Who,* the compelling TV series *Game of Thrones, Line of Duty, The Crown, Broadchurch* and *Peaky Blinders,* nature documentaries including *Planet Earth* and *Blue Planet,* and action movie franchises including the *Bond* series, *Star Wars,* and *Avengers: Infinity War.* The independent television sector produces some of the most iconic and ground-breaking television seen around the world, from dramas like Michaela Cole's acclaimed *I May Destroy You* to formatted shows with international sales like *The X-Factor, Strictly Come Dancing/Dancing with the Stars,* and *Who Wants to be a Millionaire?*

But to maintain this success and place on the world stage, the UK's TV and Film content makers need to appeal to a wide range of audiences. In a rapidly changing media landscape, with the growing popularity of the global streamers like Netflix, Amazon Prime Video and Disney+ the UK's Public service broadcasters and its content makers are facing tough competition.

The UK's public service broadcasters are also struggling to reach audiences from specific demographic backgrounds. The OFCOM (Office of Communications responsible for regulating the UK's broadcasters) report on the BBC's performance from 2020–2021 found that the broadcaster needed to do much more to connect with a wide range of audiences particularly young people, or it would risk losing a generation of potential license-fee payers.[4] The report stated that viewing time among young adults and children fell while Netflix's reach grew. It also found that the BBC was struggling to reach audiences from ethnic minority backgrounds and those from the nations and regions. Some audiences reported being unhappy with how they are portrayed on the BBC and that news offerings represented a white, middle class and London-centric point of view that was not relevant to their lives.

In order to reach wider audiences across the UK and globally, the sector needs to employ diverse talent with diverse voices from a wide range of perspectives and backgrounds, so that in turn the content created authentically represents a variety of audiences.

The Business case is clear – attracting and retain a diverse talent pool ensures you get the best people for your workforce. Diverse teams with different life experiences lead to a broader number of ideas which connect with wider numbers of the public. Research shows us that diverse teams make better, more efficient decisions, and can be more creative in their thinking. Attracting higher ratings through appealing to a broader audience, ultimately leads to greater profitability through more commissions.

Structural barriers and challenges

The TV and film sector has a complex structure which makes achieving equity a complex challenge. This creates unique issues and barriers from talent from under-represented backgrounds.

BARRIER 1 *PROJECT BASED STRUCTURE WITH FREELANCE TEAMS*

TV and film production companies work on a project-based system, hiring freelance teams for specific productions, then shrinking back to a skeletal staff structure until the next production comes along. Most job opportunities in the sector are for freelance contracts of between one and six months. This makes offering stable, long-term career paths challenging for companies. For the workforce, this system creates an issue for people who have less capacity to take career risks due to socio-economic factors.

BARRIER 2 *INFORMAL PROCESSES*
Due to the project-based nature of the sector and the reliance on freelancers, the sector uses informal hiring processes with a reliance on informal networks. This allows bias to creep in. Heads of department, Lighting, Photography and Costume will hire their own teams for the project. Tight-knit, interdependent networks dominate the landscape. For the workforce, informal networks are often formed outside of work through social and industry events where 'being seen' and fostering relationships with potential employers is important.

An audit of the film industry conducted by BFI also found that there is a sense among many that the industry is a 'closed shop' with producers wanting to use the same crews over and again. The issue is amplified at the highest levels of TV and Film, where decisions makers and commissioners are often from the same social class and educational background, further reinforcing bias and homophily through the shows and producers they choose to commission and fund.

BARRIER 3 *FRAGMENTED DECISION MAKING AND ACCOUNTABILITY*
Film and TV content is most often commissioned by broadcasters, streamers and the BFI and made by production companies, many of these are independent production companies who classify as SME's. This structure means that decision making and accountability on a project is fragmented, the broadcasters or buyers of content are often heavily involved in decision making.

BARRIER 4 *TIGHT TIME FRAMES*
broadcasters tend to commission projects with tight turn around schedules, allowing very little time for formal recruitment and other HR processes to be implemented. Often a production company will have just a few weeks to hire a large crew for a particular project, consequently there is little time for formal recruitment processes and an increased reliance on closed informal networks, The 'little black book' of contacts. These tight time frames also have an impact on other processes vital for Inclusive culture.

Resulting barriers for talent

In 2016, Channel 4 published the first ever study of social mobility in the UK's television industry.[5] The study, by Professor Sam Friedman from Kings College London found that television is one of the most exclusive industries in the UK, with people from privileged backgrounds over-represented at both C4 and in independent production companies.

- 66 per cent of people working in television were from professional or managerial backgrounds compared with 44 per cent among other professions.
- 10 per cent of C4 staff and just 2.5 of management-grade staff were from a working-class background.
- 79 per cent of those working in commissioning are from professional or managerial backgrounds whereas in HR, Finance and Estates the figure is 54 per cent.

How does the 'class ceiling' in TV and Film work?

Interviews with C4 staff from all backgrounds pinpointed a number of barriers to social inclusion in television:

- Those from middle-class backgrounds can rely on 'the bank of mum and dad' to help them negotiate the creative financial 'tightrope'. By contrast, poorer candidates often decide not to follow the 'creative' pathway in television due to economic risk and uncertainty, or make sideways or downward moves out of the creative route, mid-career. This in turn restricts the supply of those from low socio-economic backgrounds entering the pool for commissioning roles.
- The culture of 'forced intimacy' found in TV production ensures that mentor-mentee relationships often emerge informally. Intangible qualities such as trust and reliability play an invisible yet powerful role when hiring, especially for senior roles, so recruiters often focus on candidates with a similar social background. This culture of sponsorship in television, especially in production and commissioning, tends to reward those from high socio-economic backgrounds.
- 'Studied informality', a 'knowing' mode of informality in dress codes, humour, and interpersonal familiarity is more prevalent in television than in other professions. Studied informality is weakly correlated to intelligence or one's ability to be a good television professional yet is an important

aspect of perceived 'fit' within the industry. However, those from low socio-economic backgrounds disproportionately struggle to adopt this code.

- The ability to namecheck highbrow culture in creative discussions is highly prized, whether or not it is necessary in a discussion about the programme in question. Those from low socio-economic backgrounds find this cultural norm alienating and intimidating.

Solutions

A cross sectoral data collection solution

In response to the barriers in the sector listed above, this chapter will tackle some of the solutions, both cross sectoral and at individual company level.

A cross sectoral data collection solution

Data and analytics should play a key role in creating greater diversity and inclusion, as it provides the ability to identify gaps, to prioritize areas for action, and enables ongoing measurement of progress. But data collection is one of the biggest challenges for this sector with project-based work and a predominantly freelance workforce. Whilst a large or even a small business or organisation with a sitting staff base can monitor the workforce through traditional methods, this is just not possible in the TV and film sector.

In 2016, the TV sector launched its own data collection system – Diamond. Diamond (acronym for Diversity Analysis Monitoring Data) is an end-to-end process for collecting and reporting diversity data, across all the main UK broadcasters, and allows the industry to answer the key questions 'Who's on TV?' and 'Who makes TV?'.

The Diamond system, collects data (both on- and off-screen) from all the TV programmes commissioned by the BBC, Channel 4, ITV, Sky, Channel 5 and UKTV. The system allows the broadcasters and the Creative Diversity Network (CDN) who run Diamond to produce reports.

Diamond Reports then pose two key questions:

1 Does the workforce on UK productions, both on- and off-screen, reflect the diversity of the UK population?

2 Are audiences seeing themselves reflected on-screen?

Since Diamond began, over two million programme contributions have been analysed to highlight important issues for the industry to address. The Diamond 5th cut report, published in 2022, highlights the following:

- Disabled people are under-represented across UK programmes. Off-screen, disabled people make just 6 per cent of contributions, and on-screen, 8.3 per cent (18 per cent of people in the UK population identifying as disabled).

- Those who identify as Black, Asian or minority ethnic are better represented on-screen (20.9 per cent) compared to off-screen (12.9 per cent). Whilst representation is on a par with national population figures (12.8 per cent), those identifying as Black, Asian and minority ethnic groups are also less well represented in senior roles.

- Craft and technical roles continue to be highly gendered, with females dominating hair, make-up, costume and wardrobe positions, and males dominating others such as lighting, camera and sound.

- While there has been some good progress in some areas of on-screen representation, off-screen crews and senior roles still don't reflect workforce stats or the audiences of the UK.

Diamond data is published every year, allowing the TV sector to better understand the gaps and to pinpoint its work to increase diversity and to embed inclusion. (More information can be found at https://creative diversitynetwork.com/diamond/.)

Cross sectoral levers – diversity targets

The UK's main broadcasters started to set diversity targets for the content they commission in 2016. Channel 4, the BBC, Channel 5, ITV and Sky now all require suppliers of TV content to hit on and off-screen targets to improve representation with a focus on race, disability, LGBTQI and gender, social class and region. The focus is on ensuring that production teams and the case are from diverse backgrounds and that content is authentic in representation and voice. The British Film Institute (BFI) who fund a proportion of British film production have diversity standards in place for the films they fund and any Films and TV shows nominated for British Academy of Film and Television Awards (BAFTA) are also required to meet the BFI's diversity standards.[7]

I believe that in part these targets and the impact of gender pay gap reporting, the #MeToo, Times up and the Black Lives Matters movements have been important levers in creating a tangible shift towards greater engagement in the sector, to improving representation on and off screen and creating inclusive workplace cultures.

It is also important to acknowledge the impact of the unions and individual campaigners in the sector. To name a few, actor and writer Lenny Henry and news editor Marcus Ryder, who have highlighted the lack of senior Black, Asian and minority ethnic talent in the sector; Adeel Amini, who led the Coalition For Change agenda to improve freelancer working conditions; and Triple C and DANC (Disabled artists Network), Caroline O'Neil, Bryony Arnold and Charlie Pheby (Deaf and Disabled people in TV), who all campaign for the rights of disabled talent. These voices for change have played an important role in the industry's shift towards greater engagement around inclusion.

For the small and medium-sized production companies who are responding to the calls for action and targets there are huge challenges. In a sector which is informal and where social networks are powerful, how can we create a more inclusive sector, diverse crews and better on-screen representation?

I believe the key is to embed inclusion across all processes and practice. The next chapter highlights some of the frameworks and solutions in the Pact Inclusion tool, which I designed with industry collaborators to help production businesses to create more effective strategies for change.

Solutions for individual production businesses – Embed inclusion across all processes and practice

1. KNOW YOUR NUMBERS
Cross sectoral data and specific reports in TV and Film give us a good picture of where we have gaps and where groups are underrepresented across the sector. Based on this data we can design interventions to tackle the barriers and gaps. Many production companies now monitor their own workforce data using snap-shot surveys twice a year.

2. ENGAGING LEADERS IS VITAL
Work with leaders to help them to understand how bias can impact on their decision making and ultimately on their business and creative process. Understanding bias is just one part of the process, the training does not eliminate bias but puts individuals on a journey to better understand how they can then take action to counter bias. We worked with Stephen Frost and the *Included* team to roll out their Inclusive leadership training for our members.

3. CREATE A BESPOKE STRATEGY FOR YOUR BUSINESS

Many of our member companies are small, without back-office function and just don't have the resources to work with consultants and experts to help them create strategies for change. We understand that there isn't a one-size-fits-all approach to inclusion for this sector. Different businesses, genres and projects need to take approaches which work for them. Pact, the Producers association for cinema and television, created The Pact Inclusion tool to enable production companies to create their own bespoke strategy with action plans, nudges and frameworks for many areas of the production process.

4. EMBED INCLUSION ACROSS ALL PROCESSES

It is vital that businesses identify the biases in their specific processes in order to create strategies to counter these. The Pact Inclusion tool helps companies to identify bias and suggests practical actionable strategies to ensure that all production processes are inclusive. It is also designed to help companies to create a bespoke diversity and inclusion strategy.

5. INCLUSIVE HIRING

It is widely acknowledged that one of the biggest barriers to greater diversity and inclusion in the TV and Film sectors is the informality of hiring practices. Very often, projects need to be staffed within weeks of receiving the greenlight (go-ahead). This limits how widely roles can be advertised, and formal processes followed. Production businesses still need to remain lean and agile to respond to specific project-focused challenges and needs. A company may in one quarter make an investigative documentary and in the next quarter make a large reality show on location and the two projects may require differing skills sets and experience. So completely formal hiring processes with a sitting staff base like those in a large bank or corporation would just not be workable. We suggest that producers work towards greater formality on a continuum, from the very informal 'meet for a coffee' chat to formal processes of advertising each job, interview panels, and time-limited processes.

- Ensure you understand equality law and positive action measures.
- Network in your down time to create a more diverse talent pool for your organization. This allows you to hire in a hurry while still drawing on a more diverse talent pool – avoiding the 'usual suspects'.

- Set internal diversity targets for talent managers and Heads of Department who bring in their own teams.
- Standardize the interview process, write job descriptions and use the same questions with a scoring system.
- Cast the net wider – advertise openly where possible. Many production companies are now advertising roles on industry networks on social media using databases as well as crew search agencies can help producers to find and hire talent from under-represented backgrounds. A full set of the guidance is available to Pact members on the Inclusion Tool.[8]

6. INCLUSIVE CASTING

- Consider inclusion at all stages of the casting process.
- Ask casting directors to supply mixed short lists.
- Make casting calls accessible to all, consider cost and timings to accommodate those with caring responsibilities and people from low-income backgrounds.
- Ensure accessible venues and allow disabled actors to self-tape so they do not need to attend face to face castings.
- Adopt NEROPA, a system invented by German actress Belinde Ruth Stieve, which is a method to increase the proportion of women on-screen and to sensitize and raise awareness among those involved. NEROPA uses a simple method to ensure that there is a 50:50 split for in the casting process.[9]

7. INCLUSIVE CULTURE

Creating an inclusive culture is a complex process. A good starting point is to tackle bullying and harassment to ensure everyone feels safe and included. Producers are encouraged to implement cross sectoral principles.

The BFI (British Film Institute) together with the British Academy of Film and Television (BAFTA) has created a set of anti-bullying principles and accompanying guidelines that are easy to implement in the highly-pressured, informal work environments within the TV, film and games industries.[10] Developed in partnership with BAFTA, Pact, Directors UK (The Directors union), Equity (the actors union) the Principles are a condition of BFI funding and have been embedded in the BFI's Diversity Standards.

CASE STUDY
Pablo – Paper Owl Films for the BBC

Pablo is a hugely successful television series for children commissioned by the BBC and sold internationally made by a small animation company in Northern Ireland, Paper Owl Films. The animated series is about an autistic boy who uses magic crayons to create imaginary friends who explain the world to him. The show breaks boundaries with its mainstream depiction of autistic characters, but what is remarkable is that all the cast and nearly all the writers on the show are autistic.

Producer and co-owner of Paper Owl Films, Grainne McGuiness, says:

'Nearly 50% of kids on the autism spectrum, report that they're bullied in school. As a society, we need to celebrate all kinds of minds, and encourage adults and children to respect people who think differently.

We decided we would concentrate on hiring writers with autism. Many of the writers had little or no real experience of writing for TV worked closely with experienced head writer Andrew Brenner. Many of the writers have become established writers for children's television in their own right. For the Kids' TV space, it meant new writers, new ways of looking at the world, and it was just amazing.

The cast is also predominantly made up for actors with autism. It was refreshing to be able to look outside of our usual networks, and we were amazed by the breadth of talent we were able to find for the show.

We opened up our production processes to accommodate neuro difference and it has taught us about new ways of working. We are always saying, we need more original stories, we need new ideas, by opening up the way we did things, it has allowed us to be open to new and exciting stories.'

CASE STUDY
Then Barbara Met Alan – Dragonfly TV (Banijay) and One Shoe Films for BBC 2 and Netflix

A factual drama based on the true story of the people behind the campaign of direct-action that lead to the winning of disabled civil rights in Britain.

The film enters the story through the eyes of Barbara Lisicki and Alan Holdsworth, two disabled cabaret performers who re-framed the debate around disability rights with spontaneous pickets that shut down restaurants, stations and the London underground. Their coordinated attempts to handcuff their wheelchairs to buses brought Westminster to a standstill and a change to the law.

The senior writing and producing team for the project, five times BAFTA winning writer and disability campaigner Jack Thorne and co-writer Genevieve Barr, were determined to ensure that disability would be authentically represented on and off screen. Experienced producer Bryony Arnold, who is a wheelchair user, agreed to join the project on one condition – that there would be no 'cripping up' (a term used in the TV and film industry to critique the casting of non-disabled actors in disabled roles and where the actor mimics the physical characteristics of impairments to play disabled characters).

Casting

Producer Bryony Arnold worked hard to ensure that they did everything possible to ensure that the cast and supporting background artists represented the deaf, disabled and neurodivergent communities. 'We put out an open casting call on social media and through DANC (Disabled Artists Networking Community) and Deaf & Disabled People in TV (DDPTV), 226 disabled people applied with self-tapes. We also ensured that our large crowd scenes of disabled protestors were also made up of mainly disabled actors.'

Finding accessible locations – thinking outside the box

Bryony Arnold said, 'The filming took place in Summer 2021, unfortunately there is a severe shortage of accessible studios so we had to think outside the box to find suitable locations. This led us to using a school for disabled children in North London, which was wheelchair accessible and incredibly well equipped to handle the various access requirements we had.'

Hiring disabled crew – opening up networks

'Many disabled people have not been able to progress their careers due a lack of opportunity and accessibility, but we decided to provide opportunities for stepping up. We also spent time and resources to open up our networks. We were thrilled to have over 30 disabled core cast and crew with another 55 disabled supporting artists featuring throughout.'

Setting the tone – breaking down barriers on set

'Some of the crew were nervous about how to navigate the production. There was some anxiety about how they should behave and what they should say, so to help set the tone we gave the cast and crew some guidance by creating a crib sheet with some do's and don'ts.'

Key takeaways

1 Implement a Diversity and Inclusion strategy – To make a real, measurable difference, you need a roadmap with concrete, defined, time specific goals and actions to ensure accountability

2 Identify bias in your unique business structures so that you can take practical action to ensure greater inclusion across the board.

3 Embed inclusion across all organizational and interpersonal processes. The key to creating sustainable and long-term change is to embed inclusion across all processes in your business.

Further reading

GOV.UK (2021) DCMS Economic Estimates 2019 (provisional) Gross Value Added Department for Digital, Culture, Media & Sport www.gov.uk/government/statistics/dcms-economic-estimates-2019-gross-value-added/dcms-economic-estimates-2019-provisional-gross-value-added (archived at https://perma.cc/YP3T-DL7K)

GOV.UK (2021) DCMS National economics estimates 2011 – 2202 stats on creative sector contribution to the economy, Department for Digital, Culture, Media & Sport www.gov.uk/government/statistics/dcms-sector-national-economic-estimates-2011-to-2020/dcms-sector-national-economic-estimates-2011-2020 (archived at https://perma.cc/8QN3-ZDP6)

References

1 Twohey and Kantor (2017), Harvey Weinstein harassment allegations, New York Times www.nytimes.com/2017/10/05/us/harvey-weinstein-harassment-allegations.html (archived at https://perma.cc/6E5Y-FR5H)

2 Emanuel, L (2017) Hollywood producer Harvey Weinstein fired over sex harassment claims The Times. www.thetimes.co.uk/article/hollywood-producer-harvey-weinstein-fired-over-sex-harassment-claims-dd059vpq5 (archived at https://perma.cc/PW3X-2UCE)

3 BFI (2021) New report shows UK tax reliefs power unprecedented boom in UK screen industries. BDI News www.bfi.org.uk/news/screen-business-report (archived at https://perma.cc/XK9Z-SC2B)

4 Ofcom (2021) Ofcom Annual Report on the BBC 2020-21 www.ofcom.org.uk/__data/assets/pdf_file/0029/228548/fourth-bbc-annual-report.pdf (archived at https://perma.cc/S6ZB-HJJ2)

5 Waterson, J (2018) Channel 4 is Britain's poshest broadcaster, diversity study finds www.theguardian.com/global/2018/aug/22/channel-4-britain-poshest-broadcaster-diversity-study-finds-staff-working-class-background (archived at https://perma.cc/Z53K-AKRN)

6 Creative Diversity Network (2021) Project DIAMOND, The Fourth cut Report creativediversitynetwork.com/diamond/diamond-reports/the-fourth-cut/ (archived at https://perma.cc/L5ES-UZ56)

7 BFI (2019) BFI Diversity Standards www.bfi.org.uk/inclusion-film-industry/bfi-diversity-standards (archived at https://perma.cc/V5VW-H5K7)

8 Pact (2021) 5 Highlights from the Pact Inclusion tool www.pact.co.uk/latest-updates/news/detail.html?id=5-highlights-from-the-pact-inclusion-tool (archived at https://perma.cc/9NXX-W5AD)

9 NEROPA (2022) NEROPA. http://neropa.stieve.com/en/ (archived at https://perma.cc/7WGR-LJD2)

10 BFI (2018) Bullying and Harassment principles and guidance www.bfi.org.uk/inclusion-film-industry/bullying-harassment-racism-prevention-screen-industries/set-principles (archived at https://perma.cc/PUD9-TFN7)

16

The key to inclusion
in financial services

YASMINE CHINWALA AND JENNIFER BARROW

To paraphrase Spiderman, with power comes increased responsibility. The Financial Services (FS) sector has the greatest concentration of money, power, influence, reach and visibility of any business sector, including when it comes to Diversity, Equity and Inclusion (DEI).

Like much of the corporate world, FS is dominated by white, straight, middle-class men – for example, women account for just one in five executive committee members across the sector globally,[1] firms owned by women and/or ethnic minorities represent just 1.4 per cent of US assets under management,[2] and nine out of 10 UK senior managers come from higher socio-economic backgrounds.[3]

We have all seen what happens when things go wrong in this sector. The global financial crisis more than a decade ago was a cataclysmic event that has scarred the banking and finance industry and the wider economy. Household names collapsed, and governments worldwide poured billions into stabilizing the financial system. We are all still living with the repercussions of the crisis, including trillions in lost economic growth and the subsequent increase in inequality – a seemingly ever-widening gap between the haves and the have-nots.

The causes of the crisis were undoubtedly complex and multi-layered, but underlying those causes was a culture and regulatory environment that encouraged excessive risk-taking without accountability for, or connection to, the consequences. While different countries have responded in different ways to prevent another financial crisis, a common theme in their redress mechanisms has been a focus on the industry to improve its culture and conduct.

This is where DEI comes into the frame. Governments, financial regulators and companies themselves widely accept the need for cultural change, adequate challenge in decision-making processes, and increased diversity of viewpoints to improve the quality and inclusiveness of those decisions. When Christine Lagarde led the International Monetary Fund she said: 'If it had been Lehman Sisters rather than Lehman Brothers, the world might well look a lot different today'.[4]

It is against this backdrop of recovering from an existential crisis that DEI has moved up the agenda of the FS industry. Indeed, since the financial crisis, the industry has continued to generate scandal, including widespread manipulation of foreign exchange and derivatives markets as well as mis-selling of financial products, and not forgetting sexual harassment.[5]

Pre-pandemic, the industry DEI landscape had already begun to shift significantly. The stakeholder context – be it government, regulators, policy-makers, investors, clients, customers, society – was transforming, with organizations under more pressure than ever before to deliver on DEI as part of retaining their social license to operate. The pandemic and the tragic murder of George Floyd have served to accentuate DEI concerns. Both internally and externally, the discussion has become more public, and it is not going away.

Diversity is a regular agenda item in C-suite discussions, risk frameworks and regulatory conversations. Targets, now an established part of the diversity discussion, and standardized metrics such as gender pay gap data and definitions of leadership teams provide accountability mechanisms.

Yet, although DEI is acknowledged to be important, worthwhile and a *good* thing, real action to achieve a more diverse, equitable and inclusive FS industry remains to be seen.

What is holding the industry back?

In addition to the general barriers to DEI faced across the corporate landscape, the FS industry faces unique challenges:

The business case hasn't landed

The rapidly changing stakeholder context around diversity in FS has brought more people into the discussion than ever before. The more stakeholders that are brought into the diversity conversation, the more the business case needs to be tailored. Newcomers – and indeed the old timers – need to understand why diversity should matter to them.

But all too often, it is not being used effectively. The FS industry has yet to fully understand why DEI is a core strategic driver at individual, organizational and sector level. Research from think tank New Financial looking at investors[6] outlines the five most common reasons why institutional asset owners, one of the most important sources of capital for the industry, act on diversity:

- To improve decision-making
- To attract and retain talent
- To innovate and compete
- To reflect members and communities
- To enhance financial performance

What matters to one firm will be different to what matters to another. For some, the talent imperative is the priority, for another innovation is the driver, especially if the organization is moving into new markets or geographies. If an organization has not taken the time to fully understand its own business case for DEI that is specific to its unique context, improving diversity will remain a side-of-desk activity and easily fall off the priority list when the going gets tough.

The over reliance on some aspects of the business case, and under-use of others, results in firms failing to recognize how powerful it can be to build a high-level mandate, unlock resources and strengthen the governance and accountability framework that is crucial to achieving DEI goals.

THE FINANCIAL PERFORMANCE PARADOX

It is to be expected that the business world – and particularly the FS sector – should focus on DEI as a means to enhance performance. Of the five reasons above, the financial performance argument is the most clearly captured in numbers, which is the language of senior decision-makers across the industry.

The default is still the McKinsey and Credit Suisse research correlating increased diversity with financial performance (the 'diversity premium') – many articles, speeches and blogs mention one or other, usually within the first three paragraphs.[7, 8] And while the research is robust and high quality, relying too heavily on the financial performance argument has its downsides. Have we ever considered the (unintended) consequences of this message that diversity delivers outperformance? Here are three we commonly see:

- *Higher bar for women and individuals of diverse backgrounds*: The business case is focused on arguing diversity delivers improvement, rather than providing evidence that appointing diverse employees does not compromise performance. If firms will only act if they feel they stand to make a gain, the result is a higher bar for diverse hires compared to the mainstream. While the data is presented in aggregate, its findings are interpreted and applied at an individual level, which in turn feeds a mindset that expects outperformance of diverse colleagues. This results in higher expectations of what people from under-represented groups can deliver and a lower tolerance of failure.

- *What goes up can come down*: What would happen if the numbers flatline over a period of time, or even reverse? Should companies then halt attempts to improve diversity across their workforces? Should they fire all women and people of diverse backgrounds to continue to maximize performance? Because that would be a natural consequence of sticking rigidly to the financial performance argument.

- *Anything goes*: The narrow focus on the supremacy of performance contributes to a tolerance (or indeed the promotion) of any behaviours that deliver performance, including bullying, harassment, and excessive risk-taking. Are we really advocating that anything that delivers outperformance is desirable?

Thus far, the business case has remained too high level and not broken down in a way that links to the strategic direction of the organization in which it is being applied or relevant for different audiences and business units. If the business case remains too generic, diversity won't gain traction or result in demonstrable action.

Money money money – culture of financial services

Finance is a sector that is all about the bottom line – performance is paramount (whatever the cost), the client is king, the financial stakes are high, and there is no time for anything else. This approach embeds inertia, defaulting to shortcuts – for example, hiring a friend of a friend to save time – and perpetuates an old-fashioned, narrow view of who can be a successful leader, and the skills and attributes they require.

The huge amounts of money on offer for successful individuals marks out the finance sector from all other areas of business. While financial regulators have acted to control pay, the sheer quantum of rewards on offer for the cadre of leaders (and senior managers) remain exceptionally high.

The biggest differentiator in how those in finance are paid, compared to other sectors, is the payment of bonuses. This is an industry where those who are perceived to be high performers can receive bonuses of double their base pay (if they work in a country subject to European Union bonus cap rules) and potentially multiples more – for example in trading and investment management. And while regulatory changes have impacted pay and improved methodologies for calculating bonus pay, managers are still afforded substantial discretion in awarding bonuses, allowing the potential for individuals' biases to creep in. In the UK, where gender pay gap reporting is mandatory, the mean pay gap for FS was 28 per cent in 2021; however, the mean bonus gap was 51 per cent, compared to a national average of 20 per cent.[9]

Another knock-on effect of the high pay on offer is an inflation of pay across all areas – for example, a head of HR at a bank will be paid far more than someone in a similar role at a manufacturing firm. When so many employees do well from the existing system, there is little incentive to change it.

Lack of governance and accountability

When businesses see a problem, the immediate reaction is to throw (some) money at it. Hiring a new DEI head or beefing up an existing team or expanding someone's job title has been a common response to the increased pressure on FS organizations to make changes. The FS sector has been working towards becoming a more diverse and inclusive for many years – some organizations have had a head of diversity for a decade or even two, yet change has been marginal at best.

But it is no longer enough to delegate responsibility for creating a diverse and inclusive culture to HR, DEI teams, passionate individuals or to employee networks – they are not responsible for the day-to-day decisions that impact employees' experiences at work.

MANAGERS WHO CAN'T MANAGE

Across business, and particularly true of financial services, promotion to management is a reward for subject matter expertise or strong performance, rather than an individual's ability to manage a team. And how those managers are then rewarded is again rarely based on how well they manage their team.

FOCUS ON ACCESS VS PROGRESSION

For far too long, the industry has counted on recruiting its way to hit diversity targets. For example, the UK's HM Treasury Women in Finance Charter initiative to increase female representation at senior levels found that it took five years for a critical mass of Charter signatory firms to shift their attention from recruitment to building their pipeline as they seek to both achieve and sustain their targets for women in management positions.[10]

Much of the discussion in relation to social mobility and race has been focused on access – that is, raising the aspirations of young people and increasing recruitment of those from under-represented groups. While these efforts are valuable and overdue, these sorts of outreach and access schemes are not enough to drive a step change. Unless FS companies tackle culture and how they define merit, people from under-represented groups will continue to struggle to reach the top ranks.

This is clearly shown in 2020 research on socio-economic diversity in FS from Bridge Group, which found employees from lower socio-economic backgrounds took 25 per cent longer to progress through grades.[11] This progression gap increases to 32 per cent for Black people from lower socio-economic backgrounds. This progression gap cannot be explained by performance alone.

In short, ownership of DEI issues must shift from the silo of HR to the matrix of business and there must be consequences for not taking action to promote a diverse and inclusive workforce. It can no longer be a voluntary, side-of-desk activity where people from under-represented groups are expected to do the heavy lifting of making change happen. Sustainable progress will only occur when DEI is baked into the how an organization functions and how individuals within them succeed.

Inadequate data

The FS industry is all about numbers, yet few firms apply even a fraction of the analytical rigour to their people data compared to their product and market data – and this is even more acutely the case when it comes to data on DEI. The diversity data agenda is being driven by an increased appetite not just for more but better data. Pressure is both internal, from boards, excos and business leaders who are themselves being held accountable for improving diversity, as well as external, from clients, shareholders, regulators and government.

Building a robust dataset is a huge project, taking from three to 12 months to complete and requiring significant investment.[12] The systems integration work is complex, legal and compliance fears need to be allayed, and often HR and/or the DEI function need to source the necessary data expertise to execute. But it is worth the effort. Data enables firms to hold their leaders to account. If managers are expected to deliver a diversity-related objective, they need to have access to the data that shows them how they are doing and can help them create customized strategies.

Collecting and analysing data shifts the DEI discussion from anecdotal to evidential – there is nowhere to hide if the numbers state a problem in black and white or expose a lack of rigour in decision-making. The data increases understanding of the current workforce and can then be used to identify where to focus energy and resources for a targeted approach to DEI planning and future recruitment, retention and promotion opportunities. DEI data needs to look beyond demographics – other data sources need to come into play, for example pulse surveys, grievances and exit data.

However, too often in financial services, the pursuit of DEI data is viewed as an end in itself. Organizations find themselves unable to take action until they have the best quality data and the highest level of self-reporting from employees, particularly in diversity strands other than age and female representation. This makes little sense for an industry which is accustomed to dealing with and extrapolating from imperfect data in its everyday business.

An incoherent approach to DEI

Companies consist of people and products, yet the methodical diligence involved with developing, launching and maintaining products and services is rarely applied to people decisions. People decisions (even the most important ones) often boil down to one individual and their gut instinct – highly subjective decision-making based on woefully incomplete information that goes largely unchallenged, particularly in the performance-dominated culture of the FS sector.

Alongside this, DEI has languished in the realm of the HR function, which has not had the permission, resources or power to change decisions made by managers. There are still too many FS firms at the early stages of the DEI maturity curve focusing their DEI work on events, awareness raising, setting up network groups and initiatives that support diverse individuals to conform to a world of work designed by and for a certain type of man.

The FS sector routinely rewards performance above any and all other factors and gives high performers extra room to manoeuvre – including allowing managers to circumnavigate decision-making protocols. This contributes to a culture of exceptionalism, so even when there are policies and processes to systematize DEI in pay, promotion and recruitment practices, exceptions become the rule.

The opportunity: the keys to inclusion

Even an industry with such a patchy track record has the incentive and ability to change. Indeed, while the last global crisis was a financial one of the industry's own making, the sector has shone through the pandemic.

For example, in the UK, one of the main roles that the industry played in response to the COVID crisis was facilitating the huge amount of government-backed emergency lending to companies. Capital markets demonstrated their valuable role in the economy by providing additional flexibility, speed and scale for companies needing to raise money.[13]

The positive impact of the FS industry when it is functioning as it should illustrates how critical it is for the sector to take DEI seriously. Here are five areas that can drive a step change:

Leveraging stakeholder pressure

So much has changed around the stakeholder context of DEI in recent years, heightened by the pandemic. While some organizations may feel this increased interest and oversight is a burden, it is also an opportunity to harness their arguments to convince the unconvinced of the need for change.

REGULATORY DRIVERS

The biggest driver promoting the strategic importance of DEI is intervention from the industry's regulators. In July 2021, the Financial Conduct Authority, the Bank of England and the Prudential Regulation Authority published a joint discussion paper entitled *Diversity and inclusion in the financial sector – working together to drive change*.[14] Quite simply, the regulators said in the 57-page paper: 'We expect to see diversity and inclusion become part of how we regulate and part of how the UK financial sector does business'.

The paper covers a wide range of proposals that would have far-reaching consequences for regulated firms, including diversity data reporting requirements, targets for under-represented groups, and bringing diversity and inclusion criteria into supervisory conversations, senior appointments and pay.

Regulatory intervention hasn't materialized from nowhere. Over the past few years, the FCA has become increasingly vocal and public about the importance of diversity. As the conduct regulator, the FCA's focus is on how culture, diversity and inclusion influence conduct in order to avoid groupthink in decision-making and risk management, as well as fostering an inclusive culture where staff feel safe to speak up, in addition to a consumer protection aspect. The Bank of England has also built its profile around diversity in recent years, and has come to the conclusion that for the Bank and the Prudential Regulation Authority, diversity and inclusion counter groupthink, which it believes presents 'a serious risk to safety and soundness'.[15]

The UK regulators are breaking new ground, but where they set a precedent, other jurisdictions will be watching closely – for example, the Bank of England, the European Central Bank and the Federal Reserve Board ran an annual conference series on gender progression, and the New York Fed ramped up its public dialogue on reforming culture and behaviour with a series of events, webinars and podcasts.

INVESTORS ON THE BRINK

Investors are also increasing their focus on DEI issues at investee companies. Progressive investors are stepping up their advocacy and engagement on DEI – for example, through their voting policies and increasingly bringing diversity criteria into mainstream investment mandates and decision-making processes. Demand for ESG (environmental, social and governance) data, including DEI data, has rocketed since the pandemic started. This is a sign of a future investor landscape with much closer external scrutiny of human capital management – an area that has been woefully under-examined until now.

Investors are also developing their understanding of the risk of not facing up to the challenge of improving DEI. For example, social media can quickly, widely and loudly expose a lack of authenticity, governance and accountability in an organization's approach to DEI that can damage its brand, leading to negative implications for customer and supplier trust externally as well as staff motivation and retention internally.

Just as the material impact of climate change has become more measurable and therefore tangible for investors, in the next few years the price of the risk attached to DEI issues will be clearer as DEI data and its analysis improves. Indeed, over time the UK regulators will be building the richest ever DEI dataset and be in a position to draw insights and illustrate impacts of DEI on risk, conduct and culture that will benefit the industry, the wider corporate world and society as a whole.

Bringing DEI into BAU

The past five years of Women in Finance Charter data in the UK shows that all the low hanging fruit has gone – there is no more tinkering at the edges to drive incremental improvements.[16] Now comes the hard work of pulling DEI into business as usual and to position it as part of everyone's day job.

A common complaint is that colleagues are overloaded with DEI work – including network group leads and senior people from under-represented groups who are relied on for a lot of heavy lifting, as well as leaders and line managers who can really deliver sustainable change. Thus far, their roles have not been altered to accommodate DEI work, so it remains a side of desk, extra-curricular and voluntary activity. This also extends to how colleagues view DEI communications, especially if messages are not incorporated into mainstream business comms.

Developing tactics to lift the perceived fatigue and sense of overwhelm related to DEI activity across the board will be essential to driving sustainable change. Who is responsible, for what, by when, and how are they held to account?

For the sector to truly become inclusive, clear governance and a framework of accountability is crucial. By this we mean:

- there is leadership from the very top of an organization, with progress linked to performance and reward;
- accountability is cascaded to directors and heads of departments and they are explicit in giving permission to their direct reports to spend time on DEI;
- ensuring that line managers understand their role in fostering a sense of belonging in team members and are equipped to do so;
- those who oversee the key levers of change (e.g. those that design and implement HR policies, communication and recruitment campaigns, risk frameworks, client relationship strategies) execute with DEI in mind.

Against a backdrop of increasing scrutiny and expectation, there is recognition that the agenda must be led from the very top. HR, communications, data insights and DEI teams provide essential support and expertise, but ultimately, DEI needs to be positioned as mission critical, owned by the C-Suite with everyone within an organization understanding the part they play in fostering a diverse, equitable and inclusive workplace.

The most progressive firms are recognizing the hitherto unacknowledged work that people from under-represented groups are doing to avoid them shouldering the burden of making change happen. This was particularly pertinent in the wake of George Floyd's murder in May 2020 where so much was expected from the few senior Black colleagues in FS firms to share their experiences and help their organizations think through the action they should take. Often, DEI work is undertaken on a voluntary basis by people from the very groups that firms are trying to attract and retain, without consideration for the extra work they are doing that their counterparts do not have to think about.

Accountability for DEI needs to sit where decisions are taken that impact diversity. This means that accountability needs to be shared throughout the business and across a range of stakeholders. It requires a move from a siloed approach to a matrix framework, and one that requires clarity and consequences for both action and inaction.

Those consequences must be reflected in performance reviews and pay awards. Pay has such a huge impact on culture and behaviour in FS. If the industry wants to see a step change in DEI, it needs to be presented as a strategic imperative with adequate resource available to execute and be structured, monitored, incentivized and rewarded just as any other business priority.

Making evidence-based people decisions

Formalizing and institutionalizing an evidence-based approach to people decisions will make a vital contribution to drive DEI to the next level. An evidence-based approach seeks to inject rigour into the decision-making process, slowing it down, compelling consultation, increasing consistency and asking for a reasoned assessment before a decision is final.[17]

A shift to evidence-based decision making is a radical leap for the FS industry. This kind of approach is often not embedded in business decisions, let alone for people decisions, but there is an opportunity right now – the COVID crisis is forcing a reassessment of traditional methods for evaluating employee performance and promotion prospects. Creating processes and systems that encourage managers to structure and account for key hiring and firing decisions, performance ratings, pay and promotion recommendations would be a good start.

The aim of a decision-making approach based on evidence is not to eliminate manager discretion entirely from all people decisions. Instead, the idea is to provide consistent and transparent parameters within which that individual manager can apply their discretion. Much of the work of evidence-based decision making (as with the work of DEI) is to make the implicit explicit, to expose unwritten rules and codes of conduct, and to change them if they don't make sense or lead to detriment. An evidence-based approach may not deliver the best decision every time, but it will improve more outcomes more of the time.

A FORENSIC APPROACH TO DEI DATA

DEI data is an essential part of the evidence base. Data allows organizations to measure the impact of their interventions, see what does and does not work in a granular way, debunk unhelpful myths and provide a framework for accountability. Firms that have stepped up the rigour of their approach to diversity data are seeing swift results. For example, the Financial Conduct Authority said the very act of measuring had a transformational impact, and at a UK asset management firm, improved data is changing managers' behaviour.[18]

A UK bank tracked working patterns (part time, job sharing, working from home and compressed hours) by gender, and the performance ratings of those individuals. The data showed there was no detriment to ratings by gender but working patterns did have an impact. The data equipped HR to challenge the business before decisions regarding performance ratings were finalized. A year later, the gap disappeared, and the performance management process had become fairer.[19]

Improved workforce data is not the only source to consider – it needs to be viewed in the context of a range of both external and internal data inputs, such as behavioural insights, academic and industry research, peer benchmarking, employee surveys and not forgetting management expertise (including gut instinct). Weighing up a variety of information sources is critical to the evidence-based approach.

SHIFTING THE BURDEN OF PROOF

A big chunk of the diversity headspace of senior management and those responsible for the DEI agenda still gets eaten up on 'show me evidence that diversity delivers improvement' before anything can happen. The default position needs to change from justification mode of why diversity is important, to instead challenging naysayers to prove that the status quo is optimal or that diversity has a long-term negative impact.

For example, critics often assume setting targets and/or linking a portion of pay to targets creates a perverse incentive. Rather than the DEI function having to prove them wrong, it is time for the cynics to provide hard evidence of the detriment caused by hitting those targets. Using the evidence to reverse the challenge forces a shift in mindset.

Collaborating across the industry

While FS firms see their peers as competitors in business and rivals in the battle for talent, they are also often each other clients and counterparties. This complex web of interconnectivity has paved the way for collaboration to drive positive outcomes for the industry as a whole.

Since the global financial crisis, the increased focus from government and regulators on improving culture and diversity have compelled the industry to come together, through both compulsory and voluntary initiatives. The UK government has been particularly active, with government backed reviews into women and ethnic minorities on corporate boards, supported by initiatives setting voluntary targets, and the introduction of mandatory gender pay gap reporting.

HM TREASURY WOMEN IN FINANCE CHARTER

The UK focused specifically on FS with the Empowering Productivity review into women in senior management in 2016, which provided the foundation of the HM Treasury Women in Finance Charter. This voluntary Charter, backed by HM Treasury, now has more than 400 signatories covering 950,000 employees across the sector. Signatories are required to set targets for female representation in senior management, report publicly against their targets, have an executive accountable for the targets, and link executive pay to the targets. Since its inception, female representation on executive committees has risen from 14 per cent to 22 per cent and from 23 per cent to 32 per cent on boards across the UK finance sector.[20]

Although the work of the Charter is far from done, there is clear evidence of the vital contribution it has made to driving permanent, sustainable change. It has also made a huge impact beyond its original remit – 70 per cent of signatories have applied the Charter principles to other diversity areas, and the Charter has been emulated in other sectors, in other countries and across multiple diversity strands.[21] Following a similar framework, in 2020 the UK government launched a taskforce to improve socio-economic diversity at senior levels in financial and professional services across the UK.

A common stumbling block for international firms is the need for a coherent approach in multiple jurisdictions, but the UK is home to one of the world's biggest financial centres, so what happens in the UK finance sector has far-reaching consequences. Global firms have been able to leverage local pressures to launch regional initiatives, or change the emphasis of existing internal global programmes, to prioritize what is considered to be important at local level –for example, gender pay gap legislation and the Women in Finance Charter in the UK.

These sector-wide collaborative initiatives have provided industry-specific information on actions and are driving accountability and ambition to achieve DEI goals. There is no longer any excuse for an organization (or its leadership) that claims not to know where to begin.

Building a positive pandemic legacy

The nature of the COVID health and safety crisis has brought people and human capital management right into the spotlight and emphasized the inequalities that exist between different groups. It has led to the highly visible integration of DEI into the business operating model – never before has it been so important to reflect the concerns and changing perspectives of staff, clients and communities.

The pandemic has provided different and tangible examples of why inclusion is central to business. Who could have foreseen the role diversity and inclusion issues would play in business continuity? Who could have foreseen that the barriers to remote working would tumble within days, or that diversity data dashboards would be expanded to include new data points, or the urgent focus on race and ethnicity?

COVID-19 has also had a significant impact on the DEI data agenda. Enforced remote working forced organization to use DEI data to better understand and measure the impact of the crisis on colleagues. Diversity data dashboards not only expanded but were also being analysed and discussed more frequently; organizations conducted numerous pulse surveys and response rates rose as employees wanted their voices to be heard. Additionally, many firms started to capture new data points to understand impacts of COVID on specific groups – such as those with caring responsibilities and underlying health conditions – to better support remote working and inform plans for returning to the office. And the murder of George Floyd and Black Lives Matter protests prompted many firms to revisit their approach to (or start) capturing data on race and ethnicity.

CHALLENGING LEGACY THINKING

The pandemic has created a sense of urgency and expectation for DEI goals to be met, and met now, across the board. Those close to the DEI agenda are acutely aware of the golden window of opportunity COVID-19 has presented to challenge legacy thinking, not just on remote working but across all barriers to progress on DEI. The next generation of employees entering the industry care about DEI issues, they want fulfilling careers and work/life balance.

As human beings, we struggle with change; our inertia allows us to tolerate a far-from-perfect status quo. The COVID-19 crisis has shown us radical action is not only possible, but desirable and necessary to create a truly diverse and inclusive FS industry. The business case for DEI has never been stronger as understanding grows of DEI's vital contribution to rebuilding a more robust and resilient economy for us all.

Summary

Rather than diminish the importance of diversity, the pandemic has highlighted the inequities across society. Firms that had been over reliant on the financial performance arguments as the basis of the business case for inclusion have been compelled to return to the moral case for including everyone in building and securing the future of organizations and the communities in which they operate. DEI should not be jettisoned in order to focus on resurrecting the economy – indeed, DEI is central to bolstering a healthy economy, which requires diversity of thought and participation by the many for the many, not just the few.

Now is the time for the FS industry to redouble its focus on DEI. The foundation is in place to support activity, whether that be high quality guidance on implementing programmes or growing regulatory pressure. One by one the barriers and excuses for inaction are being eroded. The FS industry has an opportunity to demonstrate its purpose and relevance – DEI should be an integral part of that discussion and consequent actions.

Key takeaways

1 Be clear on why DEI is important to the industry:

- rethink the business case to make DEI relevant for individuals, business lines and organizations;
- understand and leverage the reasons why key stakeholders including regulators and investors are focusing on DEI;
- consider the consequences of not doing enough.

2 Learn from what has worked:

- adopt innovative practices from widely available sources including academic research, toolkits, and initiatives such as the Women in Finance Charter;
- collaborate across the industry to harness peer pressure and learn from others;
- apply business thinking from other areas into the organization's approach to DEI.

3 Ensure DEI is part of everyone's day job:

- the DEI workload must shift both conceptually and systematically so everyone has to do it;
- DEI must be viewed and communicated as a strategic transformation across the business;
- DEI has to share the same mechanisms for success as other strategic areas for business in terms of resources, data-driven accountability, and clear links to performance and reward.

References

1 Oliver Wyman (2020) Women in financial services 2020 www.oliverwyman. com/our-expertise/hubs/gender-diversity-in-financial-services.html (archived at https://perma.cc/9A3N-W7GZ)

2 Knight Foundation (2021) Knight Diversity of Asset Managers Research Series: Industry knightfoundation.org/wp-content/uploads/2021/12/KDAM_ Industry_2021.pdf (archived at https://perma.cc/SP75-56EL)

3,11 Bridge Group (2020) Who gets ahead and how? static1.squarespace.com/ static/5c18e090b40b9d6b43b093d8/t/5fbc317e96e56f63b563d0f2/ 1606168962064/Socio-economic_report-Final.pdf (archived at https://perma. cc/A3AH-BCL3)

4   Lagarde, C (2018) Ten Years After Lehman—Lessons Learned and Challenges Ahead [Blog] IMF Blog. 5 September. Available from: blogs.imf.org/2018/09/05/ten-years-after-lehman-lessons-learned-and-challenges-ahead/

5   Finch, G (2019) The Old Daytime-Drinking, Sexual-Harassing Ways Are Thriving at Lloyd's, Bloomberg, 21 March. www.bloomberg.com/news/features/2019-03-21/the-old-daytime-drinking-sexual-harassing-ways-are-thriving-at-lloyd-s (archived at https://perma.cc/6RZG-GJA4)

6   New Financial (2017) Diversity from an investor's perspective newfinancial.org/wp-content/uploads/2017/10/Diversity_from_investor_perspective_FINAL.pdf (archived at https://perma.cc/SQ57-4Q36)

7   McKinsey (2015) Diversity Matters www.mckinsey.com/~/media/mckinsey/business%20functions/people%20and%20organizational%20performance/our%20insights/why%20diversity%20matters/diversity%20matters.pdf (archived at https://perma.cc/KKW9-VDAK)

8   Credit Suisse (2021) Gender 3000 in 2021 www.credit-suisse.com/about-us-news/en/articles/media-releases/credit-suisse-gender-3000-report-shows-women-hold-almost-a-quart-202109.html (archived at https://perma.cc/FFB2-QBDK)

9   New Financial (2021) Slow progress: Gender pay gap in banking and finance newfinancial.org/wp-content/uploads/2021/12/2021.11-Gender-pay-gap-report.pdf (archived at https://perma.cc/VV4S-59A5)

10, 16, 20, 21   New Financial (2021) HM Treasury Women in Finance Charter: Five Year Review https://assets.publishing.service.gov.uk/government/uploads/system/uploads/attachment_data/file/1004207/2021.07_WIFC_-_Five_year_review_.pdf (archived at https://perma.cc/DP6Y-2U9J)

12, 18, 19   New Financial (2020) Radical actions: A forensic approach to diversity data newfinancial.org/wp-content/uploads/2020/01/A-forensic-approach-to-data.pdf (archived at https://perma.cc/DP6Y-2U9J)

13   New Financial (2021) Covid & capital markets: part of the solution? newfinancial.org/wp-content/uploads/2021/07/2021.07-Covid-capital-markets-part-of-the-solution-NEW-FINANCIAL.pdf (archived at https://perma.cc/9EZ6-8PSB)

14, 15   Bank of England, Financial Conduct Authority, Prudential Regulation Authority (2021) Diversity and inclusion in the financial sector – working together to drive change www.fca.org.uk/publication/discussion/dp21-2.pdf (archived at https://perma.cc/E3PW-NCMB)

17   New Financial (2020) Radical actions thought paper series: Shifting to an evidence-based approach for people decisions newfinancial.org/wp-content/uploads/2020/08/Radical_actions_Evidence_based_decision_making.pdf (archived at https://perma.cc/G5W7-7AR6)

Conclusion

In the introduction, we shared the intent behind this book: beyond the noise, what really works for inclusion? We write this conclusion during the Russian invasion of Ukraine, a reminder that we still have a long way to go – and a reminder of why this work matters.

We hope you find the concrete strategies, tools and examples in this book helpful as you work to solve the seemingly intractable challenges that get in the way of workplace inclusion.

We've taken you on a journey, from yourself, to your team, to your organization and then to the wider world. We have shared stories and case studies with you that resonated across sectors.

In beginning with you, we looked at your cognitive load, your mindset and your cultural intelligence. These are critical areas to self-reflect on, to engage you and to engage others. If we start with empathy, we engage people who are not currently in the conversation, helping them understand what's in it for them. As Irfaan showed us in Chapter 2, it takes conscious effort to really see people, rather than be a 'sleepwalker'. But if we can intentionally see others, the rewards are great.

We shifted focus to your team, and discussed what inclusive management looks like, before considering different models of team organization and adapting to the Industry 4.0 environment. We saw how companies like AstraZeneca, during an extraordinary period that saw them take a lead role in Covid-19 vaccine development, have worked hard to create active listening and open contributive environments through the use of team-wide events. These proactive examples show us that inclusion doesn't just happen. Most people's experience of inclusive work (or not) will be determined by their immediate colleagues, and, above all, by their boss.

We then considered your organization and looked at five mutually exclusive, collectively exhaustive drivers of inclusion: strategy, data, governance, leadership and systems. They are detailed in a suggested order of execution but it doesn't have to be hard and fast. It's essential to consider all elements and appreciate that, collectively, they are more than the sum of the parts. Doing piecemeal work is insufficient to create inclusive organizations. As Raafi showed us in Chapter 8, data underpins effective interventions. This can be projecting diversity into the future to know what your organization looks like under a range of scenarios. Above all, it's about collecting inclusion data, as well as diversity data. Without inclusion, you won't get the positive outcomes you're looking for. And without measuring inclusion, you can't identify the right levers or measure progress.

With a thorough understanding of ourselves, our teams and our organizations, we can then think even bigger. Where is inclusion work going? We looked at the future of work, the impact of inclusion in an unstable and constantly shifting world, and then the crucial sectors of tech, media and finance. Inclusion is a field with a common goal. We saw examples of how public collaboration between historically competing bodies can drive genuine change across sectors, such as joint thinking on topics such as gender equality and culture change by financial regulators like the Bank of England, the Financial Conduct Authority, the European Central Bank and the Federal Reserve. No matter where you work, this section helps to contextualize the contribution you are making, and to inspire you to make the most effective difference you can, knowing you are not alone.

In each chapter, we have tried to distil the key takeaways which, in our collective experience and expertise, are going to be most helpful to you in your professional role.

In the beginning, we also introduced Imani Dunbar, Head of Equity Strategy at LinkedIn, who challenged Steve to write the book as a collective group, rather than alone, in the first place. Returning to Imani now, we asked her to think about inclusion in its broadest sense – community, belonging and our role in shaping its future. In her own words:

> 'There's nothing like being able to identify, observe, and relate to someone – which I think about as representation. The power of representation is unparalleled. I was 22 when I first came across a woman in my profession who was also part of the LGBTQ+ community. I wasn't out at the time and had experienced several microaggressions and discriminatory comments from colleagues at work socials and similar situations. Seeing a woman who was both a successful leader and out was when I first conceptualized that I, too, could be successful and out at work. My first conversation with this leader was a powerful and emotional experience. Over 20 years later, she is still an incredible mentor and friend.

While representation is exceedingly important, it alone is not enough.

In order to realize success, one must also feel a sense of inclusion and belonging. As a female who has played sports (basketball) her whole life, I spent a lot of my younger years playing exclusively with males. I had plenty of experience not quite fitting in. I had to work hard to earn my place of "respect amongst the boys" and eventually found common ground as an athlete. This role allowed me to feel a deeper sense of connection. But, the reality was that there were always limits to how much we could connect.

In college, things got really interesting! I truly felt the intersectionality of my demographics come into play. I attended an Irish Catholic university that was rife with experiences that did not feel inclusive. Perhaps none more so glaring than behaviours specifically aimed at highlighting how I differed from the majority by way of microaggressions, loaded comments, and targeted "jokes." For example, it was a common microaggression that when white students first met students of colour, their initial question would be "what sport do you play?" Rather than inquiring about the student of colour's name, area of study, or dorm – the question was meant to imply that the student of colour's attendance at the university was solely due to receiving an athletic scholarship. This assumes that the student of colour had neither the academic prowess or economic means to attend the university. Unfortunately, there were not a lot of students I could relate to. Fortunately, I was a member of the basketball team (and an Academic All-Star) – my team was full of diverse talent and was the family that helped me thrive. My college basketball career culminated with a National Championship and bonds that I will have for life.

Part of finding yourself and your place at work, school, or in your community is defining your own version of success. Your path may look different to others' and it should, because we are all unique. Along the way, it's critical to own your impact, learn from your experiences, and create space for others. In my current role as Head of Equity Strategy at LinkedIn, it is a priority for me to walk the walk. For me, this involves:

Actively finding the common ground that exists with every person I meet. I don't leave this to chance. Anyone who's met me knows that I will ask them to tell me about themselves first, then try and tell them about myself with as many parallels as possible to what they shared. I aim to create a space where there is common ground and foster a feeling of inclusion.

Bringing openness and vulnerability to my conversations. I try and discuss my experience with fear and failure as much as (if not more) than accomplishments and successes. This may help foster an environment of psychological safety where others feel safe to share.

Pay attention to what has not been said and to who hasn't spoken in a meeting. In a sensitive, informed way I will invite those who haven't spoken to speak and create space for them to do so and be comfortable probing on things that may not have been said.

Asking informed questions at the comfort level of the person I'm talking to, rather than making any assumptions. Right up front, I let people know "I ask a lot of questions – it's not you, it's me".

Showing up. This isn't just at events and big productions, but being present and active in the community, whether at work or outside of work. Mentoring, coaching, civic, volunteering – I feel I always get just as much back as I give in most experiences of showing up.'

Imani's words speak to a range of experiences that may resonate with you as a reader. Inclusion in our communities, and at work, can be complicated. At the start of this book, Steve outlined five challenges that related to the impossible quest for the silver bullet:

- Stress
- Polarization
- Walking on eggshells
- Diverse representation
- Getting work done.

We have addressed these in the pages that followed. So, this book was, and remains, for you. The time-poor, savvy, yet weary professional, who wants to be inclusive but doesn't want to lower standards, engage in trite sound-bites, or waste time.

Work comes in many forms – from manual to office-based, front line to remote – but professional paid employment can be seen as a privilege. And it's an amazing time to be in work. At this moment in history, we really do stand at a crossroads for inclusion. Whichever part of the book has been most help-ful to you, whether it's the strategic or the tactical, the personal or the organization case studies, we really hope it helps you get inclusive work done.

Diversity is a reality. Inclusion is a choice. Any brief analysis of our work-places and our wider world will surely tell that it's a choice we need to make. But rather than be frozen into inaction in the face of seemingly overwhelm-ing difficulty and challenge, we hope that we have shown that it can be done. Not only does the key to inclusion exist, there are a myriad of people around who will gladly share it with you.

If we understand and appreciate future needs, if we work collaboratively within an organization, if we look after our team, and if we increase our own self-awareness and be kind to ourselves, we can have tremendous impact. It comes down to priorities and to choices. Above all, we hope we have helped and inspired you to choose inclusion.

INDEX

Note: Page numbers in *italics* refer to figures or tables

CPSIA information can be obtained
at www.ICGtesting.com
Printed in the USA
JSHW060533141022
31646JS00007B/144